The Language Impact

The Language Impact
Evolution – System – Discourse

Alwin Frank Fill

Published by

Equinox Publishing Ltd.
UK: 1 Chelsea Manor Studios, Flood Street, London SW3 5SR
USA: DBBC, 28 Main Street, Oakville, CT 06779

www.equinoxpub.com

First published 2010

British Library Cataloguing-in-Publication Data
A catalogue record for this book is available from the British Library.
ISBN   978 1 84553 777 7 (hardback)
          978 1 84553 778 4 (paperback)

Library of Congress Cataloging-in-Publication Data
Fill, Alwin.
The language impact : evolution - system - discourse / Alwin Frank Fill.
    p. cm.
  Includes bibliographical references and index.
  ISBN 978-1-84553-777-7 (hb) — ISBN 978-1-84553-778-4 (pb) 1.
  Discourse analysis. 2. Linguistics—History. 3. Language and
  languages—Globalization. I. Title. P302.F519 2010
  306.44—dc22
                          2010008756

Typeset by S.J.I. Services
Printed and bound in Great Britain by Lightning Source UK Ltd, Milton Keynes

Contents

Preface and Acknowledgements

The title I had in mind when I began writing this book was *Beyond the Limits of my Language*. The allusion to Wittgenstein's 'The limits of my language mean the limits of my world' seemed clear to me and fitting for a book which owed so much to the Austro-British philosopher. But in the process of writing about the whole gamut of effects of language on this earth, I found that a more forceful title seemed to be called for, a title doing justice to this all-pervading influence on the three levels of evolution, system and discourse. An asteroid hitting a planet, it seemed, could not produce a stronger impact than did the development of a device for communication, expression and appeal (called language) by one terrestrial species. So *The Language Impact* it had to be, and the resonance from a famous book by Steven Pinker was a welcome side-effect of this choice.

Many colleagues have encouraged me to write this book and have helped me to make it better. My sincere thanks go first and foremost to Richard Alexander (Vienna) and Andrew Goatly (Hong Kong), who read the whole manuscript and provided invaluable suggestions for improving it. Jennifer Coates, Bernhard Kettemann and Georg Marko read and commented on parts of the book. I am also grateful to Norman Fairclough and Peter Mühlhäusler for their encouragement and to Nicholas Scott for correcting the language and style of the book. I would like also to thank Janet Joyce and Valerie Hall for accepting the book into the programme of Equinox and for making the publishing process such a smooth one.

Picture credits:
The images of Plato, Wittgenstein and Wilhelm von Humboldt were provided by ONB/picturedesk.com.

Introduction

A hiking trail in Lower Austria. On the trees, wooden boards with quotations from the work of the Austrian philosopher Ludwig Wittgenstein, who used to walk on this trail when he was a primary school teacher in the villages nearby. The inscriptions in the first part of the trail are from Wittgenstein's early work, the *Tractatus Logico-Philosophicus* (1922). When he wrote this, he still thought of language as a symbolic system which only describes the world, and of sentences as having the same structure as events and facts: we cannot go beyond language in our understanding of the world; the purpose of language is to show and make accessible to us  the structure of the world. As he puts it in *Tractatus* 5.6, 'The limits of my language mean the limits of my world'.

In his later, posthumously published work, the *Philosophical Investigations* (*PI*, 1953/2003), Wittgenstein presents a view of language dramatically different from his early one. He no longer thinks of language as a sign-system which describes the world; he now sees it as a tool-box with which we pursue certain activities, named by Wittgenstein 'language games'. Wittgenstein lists 19 of them, from telling stories to cursing and praying (see the full list in Part I, section 3.3 below), but suggests that their number is almost limitless. An inscription in the last part of the Wittgenstein-trail epitomizes this new understanding of language: 'There are countless different ways of using what we call signs, words, sentences' (*PI*, 23). For the present volume, this is the starting-point for a journey into the realm of the uses and effects of language, into what we call studying the 'impact' of language.

The Scope of Impact Linguistics

Impact is defined in the dictionaries as 'collision', as 'strong effect or influence', but also as 'the force exerted by a new idea, concept, technology, or ideology'.[1] Around a million years ago, a new 'technology of communication', later to be called 'language', began its journey through evolution, in the course of which it developed an ever-increasing number of functions. The force exerted by this technology is the topic of our book, and the branch of linguistics which studies it may be called 'impact linguistics'.

For a long time, the study of language was the study of language change. In the twentieth century it became the study of structures. Systems of *-emes* and their different realizations were established. Rules were set up which showed the 'correct' use of the systemic elements. Finally, the structures were shown to be on several levels, a surface one and underlying ones: Chomsky's 'Generative Transformational Linguistics' was launched. Then linguistics turned 'constructivist' and 'critical'. What was increasingly investigated was and still is how language construes our conception of the world, and how elements of discourse lead to the hidden exertion of power and to the propagation of ideologies. With the development of Pragmatics, linguistics developed into a study of the uses of language and its effects on the world – a development which is sometimes referred to as the 'pragmatic turn' of linguistics. In some ways, this change mirrors the change in Wittgenstein's thinking as described above. In addition, the link between language and the other media has increasingly become the focus of attention. Discourse analysis has gone critical, and semantics has become intermedial.

This book acknowledges all these stages in the development of linguistics. There may even be an evolutionary element in this development, insofar as linguistic approaches and schools of thought on an increasing usefulness for the human species (and beyond) have evolved. If this is the case, the emergence of impact linguistics is part of this evolution. To study and record what language has done for us and to predict what it may do for us in the future certainly means putting linguistics on a new level so far unattained by scholars.

The aim of the book is twofold: (1) to show in what way and to what extent language (as the result of evolution, as system and as discourse) has left its imprint on this earth, and (2) to give a survey of what linguists, philosophers and sociologists have thought, said and written about the impact of our system of communication. The book is meant to lay the ground for further research on the impact of language, but also to show where to look for thinkers who have concerned themselves with this impact and to assess critically what they have written about the effect of language on 'the world', i.e. on individuals, societies and all forms of life.

The Three Levels of Language Impact

The 'impact of language' is the sum of all the effects language has 'on the world': these are effects on individuals, on societies, and on the human community as a whole. Going beyond these, the impact of language also comprises effects on all other life forms and indirectly even on non-living beings.

The impact of language on all these forms of being will be shown at the following three levels, and the book will be divided accordingly into three parts:

1. **The evolutionary level.** The fact that one species is 'articulate' (*homo loquens*) is the result of evolution; the phylogeny of what Saussure called *langage* had an impact which transformed the world. All other impacts are based on this.

2. **The level of the language system**: sounds, grammar, words and all systemic elements of language shape human thought, thus human actions, and thus interaction between humans and their planet – perhaps differently in the different parts of the world, but everywhere profoundly and 'sustainably'.
3. **The level of discourse:** with spoken and written texts we influence others and ourselves in concrete situations. This impact ranges from curing psychic disorders to causing laughter, from persuading and manipulating to making underprivileged groups visible and trying to create more equality among the inhabitants of this earth.

The impact of language, understood as its effects at these three levels, can hardly be underestimated. All technical achievements, all social structures, all cultural manifestations owe their existence to the evolution of 'language', the influence of the 'language system' on human thought and action, and the effect of speaking and writing (= discourse) in concrete situations. Altogether, this influence amounts to an 'impact' comparable to a natural phenomenon on a gigantic scale.

'Language' can also be combined with other media, and the symbolic sign system of language, together with iconic ones (e.g. images) has further effects which will also be considered in this book. The fact that there is not just *one* language on this earth, but between 5000 and 6000 different ones, has consequences which at first sight seem to weaken the impact of 'language' as such, but which may lead to synergetic effects not visible on the surface. Linguistic diversity (societal and global) is the offspring of human creativity, and its consequence, multilingualism (individual, societal and global), may in its turn enhance the creativity of human ideas. Nor should we forget an indirect effect of language which makes itself felt on the meta-level: talking and writing about language, criticizing language, discussing types of discourse, and quite generally, **doing linguistics** and philosophizing about language are also among the functions of language and are thus, in the widest sense, part of the impact of language.

Note

1.   *Webster's Collegiate Dictionary,* New York: Random House 1996, s.v. impact.

PART I

The Impact of Speech on a Planet: A 'Meteorite' Hits the Earth

1. The Evolution of Language

Speech did not really hit our planet like a meteorite. It developed in an evolutionary process in one of millions of species during a period of more than a couple of million years. But its impact can be compared with that of a meteorite.

> Of all mankind's manifold creations, language must take pride of place. Other inventions – the wheel, agriculture, sliced bread – may have transformed our material existence, but the advent of language is what made us human. Compared to language, all other inventions pale in significance, since everything we have ever achieved depends on language and originates from it. Without language, we could never have embarked on our ascent to unparalleled power over all other animals and even over nature itself. (Deutscher 2005: 1)

The view expressed in Deutscher's text is shared by many authors. The evolutionary development of a certain species of primates, the argument goes, was suddenly accelerated by the development of a system of communication: the continuous development of all species together was disrupted by this 'spurt' of change. Because of language, there is no animal human continuum any more. One species (the human one) got a head start with this device usable for at least three macro-purposes: (1) exchanging information; (2) recording achievements (for future generations) and passing them on to other groups; and (3) resolving conflicts. The (assumed) continuum in the animal world was destroyed in a period lasting from 2.5 million years ago to 50,000 years ago, when a kind of 'explosion' in art and technology occurred. Ever since, this one species has been drifting further and further away from the other animals (cf. Deutscher 2005: 12–15).

The first stone tools came into existence 2.5 million years ago (as a result of a climatic change which made it necessary to open hard shells for food and to work with hard fibres). Apes also have tools, but only local populations learn about them and use them. Their knowledge is not handed on to other populations. Language was the medium of a 'cultural revolution', in which refined ways of communication played an important role. There are two indications of a very early use of 'language': the increasing complexity of tools suggests that information was passed on orally.

> Auch wenn Sprache nicht fossilisiert, sind doch zunehmend verfeinerte Werkzeuge ein Hinweis auf eine möglicherweise komplexer werdende Sprache. (Schrenk and Bromage 2002: 199)

> *Even though language does not fossilize, increasingly refined tools are an indication of a language which became more and more complex.*

And the 'humans' (*homo rudolfensis*) living 2.5 million years ago show indications of having had language centres (Broca's and Wernicke's) in their brains. Information transfer at some time became 'non-genetic' (i.e. not through the genes, but through language) and thus much faster and more comprehensive than is the case with non-human animals (Schrenk and Bromage 2002: 207).

Studies on the phylogeny of language have focused on a number of topics. An important one is the nutritional and climatic factors which were responsible for the development of our system of communication. The sort of questions addressed are for example whether more protein-rich food (meat) led to the enlargement of the frontal, temporal (and other) areas of the human brain, making more complex thinking possible (Dominguez-Rodrigo *et al.* 2007); whether climate changes led to hominids having to live in the savannah (instead of in the forest), which in turn produced the necessity to hunt in groups and thus to communicate by sound in some way, and whether vocal communication developed after gestural (Hewes 1973a) or whether they developed together (see the discussion in Corballis 1999: 50 f. and Corballis 2002).

In the past, monocausal theories of language origin (bow-wow, ding-dong, puh-puh, yo-heave-ho and la-la) were established, each of which stressed one factor (imitation of animal sounds, working together, playing and singing together, etc.) as chiefly responsible for 'the invention of language' (see Jespersen's chapter 'The Origin of Speech', 1922: 412–42, and the summaries in Crystal 1997: 298 and Kennedy 1998: 33 f.; see also Aitchison 1996 and the articles in Gessinger and von Rahden 1989).

More recently, the specifically communicational and social factors of language development have been addressed. Among the questions which are asked now are the following: what kind of relation needed to be established between hominids, and for what purpose? Was it most important to share information or rather to induce others to perform certain actions? Was it important to have a medium with which problems could be thought out and solved together (cf. Mercer 2000: 168 f.)? What were the 'social' forces that made communication important (cf. Barnard 2009: 219 f.)?

The focus of this chapter will be on the impact that the development of an extremely sophisticated system of 'communication' had on the (animate and inanimate, living and non-living) world. It will be assumed that – as with so many things – cause and effect cannot be neatly separated; thus, what 'caused' language to come into existence – say, having to enlist a group of people to undertake a task together – in due course turned into one of the effects of possessing language and thus became one of the 'functions' of language. Instead of cause and effect, a **mutual interaction** between needs and feasibilities must be assumed, in such a way that the support language provided for an important and vital task later became a necessity and the medium language turned into a tool indispensable for cooperation.

1.1   Animals and Humans: from Confrontation to Cooperation

> Nothing would work in the absence of communication. Flowers must communicate with bees in order for pollination to be successful. Male songbirds must communicate with females if they are to mate and rear young. Lions on a cooperative hunt must communicate with each other about how they will attack their prey. (Hauser 1996: 1)

Animals and plants, too, communicate. Plants do it 'silently', animals usually by emitting sounds, like humans. For animals, emitting sounds has many functions: groups can stay together, coordinate their movements, 'warn' other members of their species without seeing them, or call out to make others aware of where they are (Dunbar 1996: 46). The 'contact sound' theory of G. Révész assumes the existence of specific sounds made by animals to establish 'intra-specific' contact (cf. Rosenkranz 1971: 66–8). While Aristotle, Descartes and other philosophers denied the existence of animal communication, others argued that it is the fault of humans that they do not understand 'animal speech' (a 'reflection of our ignorance', cf. Dunbar 1996: 48). Michel de Montaigne, in the sixteenth century, asked why we think animals are speechless if we do not take the trouble to learn their language, and the Abbé Guillaume Bougeant argued (around 1740) that if animals speak, then they certainly do not use human language (cf. Kuckenburg 2004: 29). Let us not forget that some humans took the trouble of researching animal 'language', e.g. Karl von Frisch (1950: 209–214) with his famous investigation of the 'language' of bees.

Darwin's view was that human verbal language and body language have forerunners in animal communication (1908: 58f.), and Ernst Haeckel wrote that the expression of emotions and wishes by apes and the sounds of other mammals as well as the singing of birds must be regarded as 'language', so that the age-old divide between speech-possessing humans and speechless animals disappears (cf. Kuckenburg 2004: 30). The conflict between continuity theorists (no rift between humans and animals) and discontinuity theorists (humans are special because they have reason and language) has not ended and is still being carried on among palaeontologists (the design features of animal communication are described in detail by Hauser 1996: chs 4–7; see also the chapters in Hauser and Konishi 1999).

Maturana and Varela (1987: 229) call into question the old dogma that language is exclusively the privilege of humans. Dolphins, apes and other animals have richer capabilities to communicate than previously assumed, and chimpanzees even to a certain extent interact 'linguistically' with humans. Maturana and Varela discuss the well-known but controversial attempts at teaching human sign language to chimps (see also Aitchison 1989: 33–47 about Washoe and other chimps 'that try to talk'), but then conclude that the linguistic scope of chimpanzees is limited since their evolutionary history differs greatly from human history (1987: 235). One factor important for humans was linguistic interaction during love-making, which contributed to the development of our language 'as the result of loving cooperation' (Maturana and Varela 1987: 237). Quite generally, language is thought to have changed human behaviour 'from confrontation to cooperation' (Schrenk and Bromage 2002) – though there are also interpretations of evolution in which co-operation in animal nature plays an important role (see the discussion of this in Goatly 2007: 140–148).

In contrast to animal communication, human language radically modifies human behaviour and makes self-reflexion and thus higher stages of consciousness possible. One feature of language which was responsible for this is that language enables the speaker to carry out a 'description of him/herself and the circumstances of his/her existence – with the help of linguistic distinctions' (Maturana and Varela 1987: 227). Becoming aware of one's language, being able to use meta-language (speaking about one's speaking and acting) and thus creating the 'realm of language' (1987: 226) is what distinguishes humans from 'other animals'. 'Large-scale cooperation does appear to be unique to humans', and one of its sources may have been language (Corballis 2002: 93).

Animals are not, like humans, 'political beings'. Language made possible cooperation as 'political' interaction. Thus Chilton (2004: 16 ff.) speculates about a possible 'co-evolution of language and politics' in the sense that there is 'presumably a strong evolutionary advantage in being able to plan cooperative action to achieve goals detached from immediate stimuli' (2004: 19). Language is a tool for **interaction between individuals and groupings** (cf. 2004: 201). It may have developed from the necessity to act 'politically', and it now makes political activity possible.

1.2 Language: the Result of Double Exaptation

Whatever our opinion about animal-human continuity or discontinuity, we cannot get round the fact that one species of apes developed a form of 'communication' which is superior 'pragmatically' to that of other mammals. This species seems to have specialized (phylogenetically) in improving communication (in the widest sense), perhaps neglecting other talents such as, say, running faster, climbing higher, flying, diving, etc. Language was the result of 'exaptation', i.e. the use of existing body-parts for purposes not originally theirs. Humans did not, in the first place, have an organ which was only there for language: the lungs, the larynx, the wind-pipe and the 'articulatory' organs in the mouth were originally developed for breathing, keeping particles out (by what is now called the 'vocal cords'), tasting, eating and swallowing. In a trade-off between these original functions and the need for 'communication', the original functions were retained but the communicational ones continuously improved, and thus language gained the upper hand.

But exaptation may have been at work on a higher level as well – on the level of the purposes which language fulfils. A hypothesis developed by Robin Dunbar (1996) states that a more complex language developed in our species to make the **bonding** of larger groups possible. Physical grooming was not enough:

> A more efficient mechanism for bonding was needed to allow group size to continue its upward drift. At this point, the vocalizations began to acquire meaning. But the content was largely social: gossip had arrived. (Dunbar 1996: 115)

According to this hypothesis (also called the 'gossip hypothesis', see Power 1998), this 'function of language' was more important than the coordination of the men's hunting activities or explaining how to make tools: 'Hunting is often best done in silence, and tool-making is best done by demonstration rather than instruction' (Dunbar 2003: 320). Consequently it was the women who talked first (and thus 'invented' language). Even today, this phatic and bonding function of language is extremely important (see Schneider 1988 on 'small talk'). Dunbar (1996: 206 f.) illustrates this with the story of a successful production unit which moved into a new building: suddenly everything seemed to fall apart, and it took some time before they discovered what had gone wrong:

> It turned out that, when the architects were designing the new building, they decided that a coffee room where everyone ate their sandwiches at lunchtime was an unnecessary luxury and so dispensed with it. The logic seemed to be that if people were encouraged to eat their sandwiches at their desks, then they were more likely to get on with their work and less likely to idle time away. And with that, they inadvertently destroyed the intimate social networks that empowered the whole organization. What had apparently been happening was that, as people gathered informally over their sandwiches in the coffee room, useful snippets of information were casually being exchanged. Someone had a problem they could not solve, and began to discuss it over lunch with a friend from another section. The friend knew just the person to ask. Or someone overhearing the conversation would have a suggestion or would go away and happen to bump into someone who knew the answer a day or two later.

If the bonding function was primary, it soon turned out that this method of making contact was usable for other functions as well: coordinating work, giving orders, establishing status and storing information. And with these 'exapted' functions, speech began to have an ***impact*** on the planet.

Heeschen (1989: 214 f.) describes small societies where language at first does not seem to serve any purpose. Why do people speak at all? All they utter, it seems, are trivialities – where X has gone, when rain will be coming, etc. But when it gets dark, people begin to tell of adventures, and children turn the experiences of the day into fairy-tales. Language does not help much to describe an unknown face or to tell how to make a certain tool. But it is the perfect instrument for referring to known paths and faces.

> Obwohl Sprechen ein Werkzeug der 'construction of reality' ist, sind Kooperation sowie agonales und synagonales Verhalten, also die soziale Nutzbarmachung des Sprechens, die treibenden Kräfte der Sprachevolution. (Heeschen 1989:234).
>
> *Although speaking is a tool for the 'construction of reality', cooperation, agonal and synagonal behaviour, i.e. making speech socially usable, are the driving forces of linguistic evolution.*

The study of the 'social' use of speaking could be the topic of an '**Etholinguistics**', which has yet to be developed (cf. Heeschen 1989; Fill 1993: 31–56). Etholinguistics would explore the bonding and cooperative function of language, which is manifest in such speech events as joking, telling stories, quarrelling, getting reconciled, gossiping, etc. Why we are at ease communicating with some people but have problems to achieve 'resonance' with others has not yet been a serious topic of linguistics. Language may well have evolved (among other causes) to give humans an 'instrument' to create this resonance. Some modern neurobiologists see 'social resonance', i.e. acceptance by others and cooperation with others as the main motivating factors for human activity (Bauer 2006: 34). Resonance made it possible to work together, change living conditions (admittedly to some extent by exploiting resources) and thus have an impact on this earth which is still becoming greater and greater.

1.3 Language: a Disadvantage?

Jean-Louis Dessalles (2000, 2007) argues that in some situations possessing language may be a disadvantage since one of its main functions is to give information relevant for the well-being of others at one's own expense and for no apparent gain. Similarly, Ulbaek (1998: 28) sets the costs of language for the species against the benefits:

> [S]ome of the costs are: extra brain tissue, reorganization of the brain, changes in the respiratory system, and many more. What are the benefits? The one benefit that we tend to take for granted is that language enables us to co-operate, to speak to and help each other.

From the Darwinian point-of-view, however, helping others by giving away information seems disadvantageous: 'Why should we share information in the first place, if evolution demands that we enhance *our* fitness, not our neighbors'?' (Ulbaek 1998: 38). Perhaps this altruistic function of language is one of the reasons why not many species developed such an elaborate system of communication: 'if it is better to lie than tell the truth, why do all this elaborate coding of thoughts into speech against which an effective strategy is just not to listen?' (Ulbaek 1998: 40). Thus, reciprocal altruism may have been one of the reasons why human language evolved (cf. *ibid.*). This altruism, however, was combined with the status someone obtains in a community by becoming known to be a giver of relevant information.

Knight (1998: 72–79) discusses the view that **deception ('lying')** is one of the main functions of language and was thus a driving force for linguistic evolution. Apes deceive other apes through their behaviour, e.g. by looking into the distance and thus pretending that a predator is approaching or by pretending to be grooming and thus having the benefit of food not discovered by others (Knight 1998: 75; see also Hauser 1996: 586–594). But while deception in apes is individual and usually committed for purely selfish purposes (Knight 1998: 72–75), 'humans by contrast deceive collectively, recurrently establishing group identity in the process' (Knight 1998: 75 f.).

> Told by his Dorze (southern Ethiopian) informants a patently unbelievable 'fact' – that the local leopards were devout Christians, for example – the social anthropologist Dan Sperber [...] suspected 'symbolism'. Sperber found this to be borne out regularly enough to suggest a rule-of-thumb: 'That's symbolic.' 'Why?' 'Because it's false.' (Knight 1998: 76)

'Myths, dramatic performances, art and indeed all expressions of human symbolic culture may in this light be understood as "collusion in deception" [...] – collaboration in the maintenance of fictions which have social support' (Knight 1998: 76; see also Aitchison 1996: 21 about lying). However, it must be added that lying (or, in pragmalinguistic terminology, 'violating the Gricean maxim of quality'), in humans, also has an individual function, viz. protecting the addressee. Doctors and nurses, people wanting to be polite, as well as wives and husbands make use of this function and value it highly as a means for maintaining good relations with addressees and avoiding hurting them.

We have seen that some authors (e.g. Dessalles and Ulbaek) argue that giving relevant information truthfully may be disadvantageous to the speaker and thus unimportant and even counterproductive for linguistic evolution. On the other hand, talk containing valuable information may serve to **enhance one's status in the group**. 'Relevant information is given in exchange for status' (Dessalles 1998: 146). Thus, the advantage of being able to 'choose profitable coalition partners and maximize individual success' (Dessalles 2007) outweighed the disadvantages, and the support of social cohesion as well as the support of thinking were motives powerful enough to bring about the evolution of this system of communication and representation called language.

Bierwisch (2001) speaks of another **paradox of language evolution**: if communicating verbally provided a selective advantage, there must have been a small population with which verbal communication was already possible. 'In other words, explaining the language capacity by adaptive selection presupposes the property it attempts to explain' (2001: 67). This paradox can be resolved, among other possibilities, by acknowledging that evolution is 'the cumulative result of tiny steps' (2001:69). Thus language may have evolved gradually 'from phylogenetic forerunners' (2001: 70). Bierwisch's solution agrees well with our idea of the step-by-step addition of functions to language as shown in the previous paragraphs.

1.4 Neanderthals and *homo sapiens*

That the *homo sapiens sapiens* were more 'successful' on this earth than Neanderthals may also have been the work of language, as Derek Bickerton (2000: 281) speculates:

> One of several possible scenarios would go as follows. A hundred thousand years ago, modern humans and Neanderthals had both crossed the signal-coherence threshold, but both then had to undergo the cascade of consequences that followed this event. A relatively minor delay in say the development of sophisticated phonology among Neanderthals, which could have been due to differences in cranial structure, could have given a decisive edge to modern humans.

The form of communication developed by this species came to its climax around 40,000 years ago. It did service to:

- Make the bonding of groups possible;
- Store knowledge and pass it on to the next generation;
- Name things and describe actions (e.g. the production of tools);
- Arouse emotions;
- Create works of art (songs, poems);
- Solve conflicts in various ways;
- Arouse laughter, create an atmosphere of pleasantness;
- Influence others, persuade and convince; and
- Deceive others, present reality wrongly (an action called lying; see Aitchison 1996: 21 and above).

A species which could do all these things was clearly better equipped to survive a crisis (such as for instance a severe climate change) than a species like the Neanderthals, whose way of communicating did not include these functions. 'Mapping the real world, creating alternative worlds, making things "special", making detours, specifying the tasks of distinct codes, and learning the oratory required for communicating with strangers all had survival value' (Heeschen 2001: 195).

Steven Pinker, in his chapter 'Language as an Adaptation to the Cognitive Niche' (2003), argues that collecting and passing on information (say, on how to fish) was the driving force behind the evolution of language:

> Language multiplies the benefit of knowledge, because a bit of knowledge is useful not only for its practical benefits to oneself but as a trade good with others. Using language, I can exchange knowledge with somebody else at a low cost to myself and

> hope to get something in return. It can also lower the original acquisition cost – I can learn about how to catch a rabbit from someone else's trial and error, without having to go through it myself. (Pinker 2003: 28)

Another cause (and effect) was 'that language evolved to allow us to think rather than communicate' – and to talk to ourselves! (Pinker 2003: 30). **Self-reflection and self-awareness** may indeed be something specifically human, made possible by an increase in the sophistication and complexity of language.

Christiansen and Kirby, in their book, *Language Evolution* (2003), have included contributions by authors with differing opinions about: (1) the causes that led to the evolution of language; (2) the order in which this evolution proceeded (gestures first? Vocalization first?); and (3) the effects that the different stages of language evolution had on the world. In their own article, Christiansen and Kirby (2003: 1) speak of the impact humans have had on their environment, of the structures they have created, which can be seen from space – by humans who have travelled there. Then they write: 'we contend that the feature of humanity that leads to the strange properties listed above is language.' We hold that few authors will dispute this statement about the impact of language.

1.5   Interaction between Cause and Effect: Survey of Evolutionary Factors

One of the hypotheses of the present volume is that causes and effects cannot be separated, since in an evolutionary development so-called 'effects' determine so-called 'causes'. The following discussion of this interaction between causes and effects is based on Sverker Johansson's chapter 'Why did language evolve?' (2005: 193–218). By summarizing Johansson's survey of causes we can draw up a plausible list of the effects of language on humans. The sum total of these effects represents the impact of linguistic evolution on the human species and, from a wider perspective, on the earth.

Hunting and gathering

Like Dunbar, Johansson argues that hunting is not an activity for which much language is needed. Rather, it may have been a range of different ways of communicating – with speech just one technique among others – which were useful for hunters, as Lewis (2009: 255) argues concerning the Mbendjele Pygmies in northern Congo-Brazzaville: 'the Mbendjele demonstrate the advantage of diverse modes of communication to facilitate spear-hunting and herd animals and big game – from faking animal vocalizations to signing and whistling, and using speech to plan and organize hunters working in a group.'

Gathering, however, may be a more plausible cause of language evolution, since it involves the knowledge of thousands of plants 'the communication and discussion of which may be highly advantageous' (Johansson 2005: 196; cf. Pinker and Bloom 1990). An important effect of language is thus the possibility to hand on to subsequent generations information about plants. This may have prevented disease, promoted happiness and led to a longer life.

Tool making, tool-using

Tool making, too, can occur without language, and '[t]eaching it is typically done by demonstration rather than verbal instruction' (Johansson 2005: 199; cf. Dunbar 2003). Johansson also considers the possibility of tool making having evolved in order to provide 'mental tools' for a more nicely structured language (2005: 202). To describe the making of tools may have required a more sophisticated syntax than the naming of plants. With the syntax growing more sophisticated, the tools, too, may have become more complex – a process of positive interaction, which must have pervaded the whole development of language. Hewes (1973b: 103), who believes in the gestural origin of language, writes: 'In brief, I suggest that gestural language and tool-using developed together for a long time – say, for two million years.' With new tools, 'new gestural "words" arose to accompany them', and tool-using also led to using the mouth for communication (Hewes 1973b: 113).

Sexual selection

It is of course possible that 'the better speakers were preferred as mates and thus got more offspring' (Johansson 2005: 202). But animals mate without having our language. 'Sex may be involved with the origin of language – but more likely indirectly' (2005: 217), viz. in connection with mating ceremonies involving singing and dancing. We might compare this with what Maturana and Varela (1987: 236 f.) and Jespersen (1922: 28 f.) have said about the role of love and love-making in the evolution of language.

Child care and teaching

'[I]t cannot be postulated that language evolved so that we could start teaching our kids. Instead, a selection scenario must postulate that teaching became important *first*, creating a selection pressure for better communication which eventually led to language' (Johansson 2005: 208). With life becoming more complicated, 'learning by doing' was no longer sufficient for everything that had to be learnt. Thus a 'need to be taught' evolved on the part of children, with 'teaching' and being taught eventually becoming one of the most important functions of language.

Social relations in groups and tribes

A number of scholars, including Barnard, Dessalles, Dunbar and Johansson, see social relations (in the widest sense) as the main cause of the emergence of language. In the context of our topic of language impact, the development of more complex social relations can be regarded as the effect (and thus also 'cause') of a more and more sophisticated language. Hand in hand with these 'factors' (for want of a neutral word) went 'better' (protein-richer) food, thus larger brain-size, longer life and other physical effects.

There was certainly a correlation between the development of language and social groups becoming much larger than those of apes (cf. Johansson 2005: 208). Johansson mentions a number of factors which determined group size and in which language may have played a role, including predation, *inter*-group competition, *intra*-group competition for resources and mating opportunities, and intra-group aggression and politics. The latter, in which language certainly played a decisive role (e.g. as a buffer area against physical violence) will be discussed in Chapter 20 (ecological linguistics).

Further factors which may have played a role, but whose importance is not supported by mainstream research, are the following.

Children at play

Language makes creative and combinatorial play possible, which may thus have played a role in furthering linguistic evolution. However, play does not need a full-blown syntax or elaborate lexicalization, and animals, too, show behaviour which could be interpreted as 'play' (Johansson 2005: 214; see also Knight 2000: 111).

Music

Johansson (2005: 214 f.) mentions Rousseau, Darwin and Jespersen as thinkers who gave music a decisive role in language evolution. Singing, rhythm and using primitive musical instruments may certainly have had a bonding effect, although an argument against music having anything to do with language evolution is the fact that language is situated in the left, music in the right hemisphere of the brain. The combination of language and music (with ballads, songs and opera) may have been a later development connected with the mnemonic effects of rhythm and melody.

Storytelling

This uniquely human feature may be responsible for refinement processes of grammar and lexis. Johansson (2005: 215) speaks of 'backwards causation in a scenario where storytelling provides the selective pressure for the origin of language'. Storytelling is also given an important position by Heeschen (1998: 214 f., 2001).

Art

The presence of art in a culture is regarded by some researchers as an indication of the possession of language (cf. Johansson 2005: 168–170). The appearance of art about 40,000 years ago is linked with the notion of a cultural revolution after which the existence of language is almost certain. Whether it was language or rather the lack of language which caused people to produce (cave) art is an open question (Johansson 2005: 215).

1.6   Conclusion (Evolution)

Though animals and plants also communicate, of all communication systems it is human language which has had the greatest impact on this earth. The driving forces behind the evolution of language turned into 'things we can do' with language, as described above. A few further purposes of language on the societal level still have to be mentioned: language made it possible to have '**rituals**' – for burials, weddings and anniversaries (birthdays, etc.). Through language it became possible to create ceremonial situations and to place the meeting of people for a short while on a magic level above every-day life. Religious ceremonies are not possible without language, which thus exerts a 'sacred' power over humans.

Last but not least, it is the merit of 'language' (even though there are more than 5000 individual manifestations of it) that humans perceive themselves as one species and have constituted a world-wide community, in which for instance the **days of the week are the same** all over the earth, the **counting of the years** following the Christian tradition is at least known everywhere, important events affecting the whole of humanity are publicized around the 'world', and at least a pretence of efforts to establish peace and 'save the environment' is made in most countries on earth.

The unifying and uniting effect of possessing 'language' should not be underrated. A more complex question is whether possession of *the same* language by everyone would reinforce this effect of unification. This question is answered in contrasting ways by different schools of thought (Chapter 20 below). It should not be overlooked that the uniting effect of language is in a large measure due to the development of writing systems, without which many messages could not be transmitted and knowledge could not be stored (see Chapter 15.1 on the impact of the internet). To write is 'to communicate relatively specific ideas by means of permanent, visible marks' (Geoffrey Sampson in his book *Writing Systems*, 1985: 26). The **impact of writing** would constitute a separate topic within impact linguistics, a topic no less interesting than the impact of language itself. Research on the impact of writing would also (almost by definition) be less speculative than the theories on the evolution of language presented here.

There are cases in which one specific language exerted a stabilizing effect on an area for a longer period of time. Thus it is said that **the Latin language** held large parts of Europe and the Mediterranean areas together for 500 years. This language contributed to the spread of Christianity and many cultural achievements. According to some scholars, today **English** is more and more adopting this role all over the world. Alastair Pennycook's book *The Cultural Politics of English as an International Language* (1994) and particularly David Crystal's *English as a Global Language* (2003) are attempts to show how this dominance of one language may come about and what the consequences might be. The counter-position to favouring 'global English' is taken, among others, by Robert Phillipson (1992), for whom all attempts at making English the lingua franca of the world amount to 'linguistic empirialism'. (Papers from the controversy about 'the global spread of English' are printed in Seidlhofer ed. 2003: 7–75; see Chapter 20.6 below.)

In 2006, David Graddol wrote: 'English is no longer the "only show in town". Other languages now challenge the dominance of English in some regions. Mandarin and Spanish, especially, have become sufficiently important to be influencing national policy priorities in some countries' (2006: 62). Nevertheless, for many people all over the world, English is still the gateway to affluence and well-being. But it will no longer be the English spoken by its traditional native speakers that will present this gateway: 'Traditionally, native speakers of English have been regarded as providing the authoritative standard and the best teachers. Now, they may be seen as presenting an obstacle to the free development of global English' (Graddol 2006: 114).

Whether Standard English, global English or English as a lingua franca, English has certainly played a major role in the development of new forms of global communication, in particular in the comparatively recent rise of the internet. The effect of this development on the world – as yet impossible to assess – is another aspect of the impact that 'language' (in its spoken and written form) has had on this earth (see Chapter 15 below).

The gist of our argumentation in this chapter has been that the main impact of 'language' on the world arises from its very coming into existence. Increasing social needs were fulfilled by a new system of 'communication', which then adopted more and more functions, as it became more sophisticated. All human achievements and activities (including negative ones) are somehow linked to language. Language is thus responsible for culture and art, surviving in spite of illness or natural disaster, but also for war, racism, pollution of the environment and the diminution of other species. The clouds stirred up by this meteorite hitting the earth are still in the process of spreading out, and with the advent of electronic media and the internet, they will reach new altitudes in the near future.

2. Functional Models of Language

As we saw in Chapter 1, the needs to be fulfilled which caused language to emerge developed into the 'functions' of language, i.e. the 'things we do' with language. Functions are 'meanings in and on the world'. 'Function' implies purpose, but also activity and can thus be equated with 'dynamic use'. An example of the dynamic use of language will introduce our discussion of functional models of language.

Helen Keller, the deaf and blind American author, describes the following experience, from her childhood, about language and the world:

> We walked down the path to the well-house, attracted by the fragrance of the honey-suckle with which it was covered. Someone was drawing water and my teacher placed my hand under the spout. As the cool stream gushed over my hand she spelled into the other the word *water*, first slowly, then rapidly. I stood still, my whole attention fixed upon the motion of her fingers. Suddenly I felt a misty consciousness as of something forgotten – a thrill of returning thought; and somehow the mystery of language was revealed to me. I knew then that w-a-t-e-r meant the wonderful cool something that was flowing over my hand. That living word awakened my soul, gave it light, hope, joy, set it free! There were barriers still, it is true, but barriers that in time could be swept away.
>
> I left the well-house eager to learn. Everything had a name, and each name gave birth to a new thought. As we returned to the house every object which I touched seemed to quiver with life. That was because I saw everything with the strange, new sight that had come to me. (Helen Keller, *The Story of My Life,* 1902: 23 f., quoted from Langer 1957: 62 f.)

Helen Keller's story is an excellent illustration of the most frequently-mentioned function of language: the representative one. Language gives names to things, and the names make thinking about things possible. Keller's experience is a remarkable example of language ('words') creating a consciousness of the world, which in her case created light, hope, joy and 'freedom'. For her, the **representative function** was also the **ideational** one which creates ideas (thoughts) about the world and leads to **knowledge of the world**. Just as the human species acquired knowledge of the world by naming it, for the child Helen Keller 'names' were the keys to reality – as they possibly are for all children. Phylogeny and ontogeny are mirrored, and the functions of language developed by the species are also acquired step by step by individuals.

Apart from the representative and the ideational functions, thinkers have distinguished a number of other functions of language, which will be discussed in the following sections.

2.1 Ogden and Richards: Symbolic and Emotive Uses

In their preface to *The Meaning of Meaning*, the authors C. K. Ogden and I. A. Richards, in 1923, named the following distinction as one of their discoveries of greatest value: 'A division of the functions of language into two groups, the symbolic and the emotive' (1969: viii).

> The symbolic use of words is *statement*; the recording, the support, the organization and the communication of references. The emotive use of words is a more simple matter, it is the use of words to express or excite feelings and attitudes. (Ogden and Richards 1969: 149; authors' emphasis)

The authors express the view that confusion between these functions is at the heart of many controversies and that an understanding of these functions of language would help to solve the conflicts between Vitalism and Mechanism, Materialism and Idealism, Religion and Science, and others.

While today we would not be as optimistic as Ogden and Richards concerning the effect of identifying these two functions, we would agree that the power of language to arouse emotions is still underrated. From the impact point of view, we would note that the most important function was not mentioned by Ogden and Richards, viz. having an effect on the world by changing people's views and making people do things. This function was to be included above all in the functional system of Karl Bühler.

2.2 Functions According to Bühler, Jakobson and Halliday

The first system of functions in which 'effect' played a role was established by **Karl Bühler**, who, in 1934, distinguished three functions of language: the representative, the expressive and the appellative. Bühler (1934: 24–29) starts from Plato, who (in his *Kratylos*) says language is an *organon* with which 'someone' can give messages to 'another' 'about things'. Bühler takes the three elements 'someone', 'another' and 'about things' as the foundations of relation ('*Relationsfundamente*') and draws a diagram in which the three bases of relation form a triangle (1934: 25 and 28) where each of the three sides corresponds to a function, or as he says 'Leistung' (*achievement*) [28] or 'Sinnfunktion' (*meaning function*) [32] of language: **Expression, Appeal** and **Representation** (his original terms proposed in an article of 1918 were 'Kundgabe', 'Auslösung' and 'Darstellung', 1934: 28). While Plato only considered the representative function (language represents things), expression (language expresses the intentions and emotions of a sender) and appeal (language is used to influence a receiver), in Bühler's view, are equally important and open up separate areas in the exploration of language (cf. 1934: 32).

With his triangular model of the functions of language, Bühler became one of the precursors of Pragmatics – particularly through his placing of the **appellative function** on the same level as expression and representation. This function, Bühler writes (1934: 31), becomes most easily comprehensible through the behaviour of the receiver. In animal communication (and in human communication with animals) what we notice first (and investigate above all) is the reaction of the receiver. In the investigation of human language, this aspect (thus Bühler 1934: 30 f.) has so far been neglected.

Bühler's model was expanded by members of the Prague school of linguists, who added several more language functions to Bühler's three. In particular, it was **Roman Jakobson** who in 1960 established his own model of functions, in which some of Bühler's are renamed and three new ones added. In an essay with the somewhat unusual title 'Closing statement: Linguistics and Poetics', Jakobson (1960) starts from a model in which six factors are necessary for communication. These are (1) context, (2) sender (addresser), (3) receiver (addressee), (4) channel (contact), (5) code and (6) message. Every communication starts from a message (source factor) and has one of the above six (including message) as its 'target factor'. Jakobson thus arrives at a system of functions which looks something like this (adapted from Hébert 2006):

Source factor	*target factor*	*function*	*roughly corresponding to Bühler's*	
Message	context	**referential**	representation	(*Darstellungsfunktion*)
Message	sender	**emotive**	expression	(*Ausdrucksfunktion*)
Message	receiver	**conative**	appeal	(*Appellfunktion*)
Message	channel	**phatic**	...	
Message	code	**metalinguistic**	...	
Message	message	**poetic**	...	

As the diagram shows, the functions Jakobson added to Bühler's three are the **phatic**, the **metalinguistic** and the **poetic**. The phatic function (the term is taken from Malinowski's 'phatic communion', see below) describes the use of language for community-creating or 'bonding' purposes – it is the only function human language shares with animal communication (cf. Jakobson 1960: 356). The metalinguistic function concerns the use of language to speak about language. Jakobson tells us that 'metalanguage is not only a necessary scientific tool utilized by logicians and linguists; it plays also an important role in our everyday language' (*ibid.*). Any process of language learning cannot do without metalanguage (Jakobson's example: 'What is a sophomore?' 'A sophomore is a second-year student'). Finally, the poetic function centres on the form of the message itself and concerns aesthetic effects of language. In poetry, the poetic function is dominant, 'whereas in all other verbal activities it acts as a subsidiary, accessory constituent' (*ibid.*). Another member of the Prague school of linguists, Jan Mukařovský, had already suggested an aesthetic function of language which has its climax in poetry (see Portis Winner 1977: 412–425). According to Mukařovský, in poetic language, linguistic features are foregrounded: rhyme, rhythm, metaphor, etc. and other forms of deviation from everyday language characterize this language.

In Jakobson's system, the functions do not stand alone but interact, wherewith a 'hierarchy' may be established: one function can be the dominant, another one the secondary function. In phatic talk the poetic function can play an important role; giving information (referential function) can at the same time be conative/appellative/ directive, as when someone says 'the telephone is ringing' – with the intention of 'telling' and at the same time asking the addressee to do something, viz. answer the phone. This hierarchy of functions is reminiscent of Searle's theory of direct and indirect speech acts (1975), where an utterance can express one speech act (say, reporting an experience) and another one 'on top of it' (say, apologizing for being late).

In the same essay, Jakobson speaks of 'two basic modes or arrangements used in verbal behavior, *selection* and *combination*' (author's italics) and establishes the often-quoted formula '*The poetic function projects the principle of equivalence from the axis of selection into the axis of combination*' (1960: 358; author's italics). Many poetic devices, including metaphor, metonymy and iconicity, have been explained using Jakobson's formula.

Forty years after Bühler and thirteen after Jakobson, **Michael Halliday** established a new, systemic functionalism, in which three (macro-)functions of language are distinguished: the **ideational**, the **interpersonal** and the **textual** one. Halliday (1973: 11–21) arrives at his system of functions by identifying seven 'models of language' which a child might construct from his or her experience with language 'at work'.

The simplest of these models is the 'instrumental' one, where the child realizes that with language one can get things done. Where a chimpanzee might have to construct a long stick and reach for and pull down a bunch of bananas, the child experiences that just saying 'I want a banana' achieves the same effect (1973: 11 f.).

Related to this is the 'regulatory' model of language, where the child experiences that language is used to exercise control over him/her (e.g. by her/his mother, who tells her/him 'you mustn't take things that don't belong to you', or 'you'll make Mummy very unhappy if you do that again'). In another paper (1976: 16), Halliday speaks of a special 'regulatory' function of language: 'the use of language to control the behaviour of others – to manipulate the persons and, with or without their help, the objects of the environment'.

Another model is the 'interactional' one where the child experiences that relationships with other people (e.g. the mother) are negotiated through language and that language also defines and consolidates groups as well as status within the group.

The 'personal' model, on the other hand, shows to the child his/her own identity, makes him/her aware of him/herself and creates the concept of the 'self as a speaker' (1973: 14). The child also develops a 'heuristic' model, when he/she learns that language helps to get to know the world by asking questions and getting answers.

Related to this is the 'imaginative' model, which, like the previous one, provides elements of the metalanguage (with words such as *story* or *pretend*) and in which the child encounters the playful use of language and language about invented truths – in poems, rhymes, riddles, stories, dramatic games, etc. (1973: 15 f.).

The final model is the 'representational' one: the child becomes aware that with language one can convey messages (about processes, persons, objects, etc.).

Like Bühler and Jakobson, Halliday (1973: 16) regrets that the representational model is the only model that many adults [including linguists and philosophers, A.F.] have. For the child, this is neither an early model nor the dominant one – which it only becomes at a later stage, under the influence of what people say about language.

Starting from these models that children possess, Halliday then develops a 'functional view' of language. Following Malinowski (who thought that the structures of language are derived from the practical experiences of the child (1969/1923: 330 f.)) and Bernstein (restricted and elaborated codes may show limitations in the development of the above models, cf. Halliday 1973: 18 f.), Halliday speaks of a 'functional reduction' (1973: 36), by which a small set of 'macro-functions' for adults can be abstracted. These are:

1. **The ideational function** (1973: 37–41): This macrofunction corresponds to Bühler's representational function. With adults, an element of this is always present in language use: 'no matter what [the adult] is doing with language, he will find himself exploiting its ideational resources, its potential for expressing a content in terms of the speaker's experience and that of the speech community. [...] This no doubt is why the adult tends to think of language primarily in terms of its capacity to inform' (Halliday 1973: 37). 'Ideational', it seems, serves for Halliday as a kind of umbrella term which includes elements of creating ideas and transmitting messages. While for the child the 'personal-heuristic' element is dominant, for the adult both the interpretational and the informational element belong to this function. This, by the way, is the function language had for Helen Keller in the story printed at the beginning of this chapter.

2. **The interpersonal function** (1973: 41 f.): This function 'embodies all use of language to express social and personal relations, including all forms of the speaker's intrusion into the speech situation and the speech act' (1973: 41). Interacting with other people and controlling their behaviour are part of this

function as well as what Searle would call speech acts, e.g. approving and disapproving, including or excluding someone in/from a social group, asking, answering, achieving intimacy, greeting, chatting up, taking leave (*ibid.*; [some of these activities remind one of Wittgenstein's language games]).

3. **The textual function** (1973: 42): This function 'fills the requirement that language should be operationally relevant – that it should have a texture, in real contexts of situation that distinguishes a living message from a mere entry in a grammar or a dictionary' (*ibid.*). Through this function, language becomes text and without it, 'we should be unable to make any use of language at all' (1973: 44). This is a function which is not in Bühler's scheme, but which has to do with the organization of utterances and can almost be equated with the Functional Sentence Perspective (FSP) of the Prague school of linguists. In a diagram given in Halliday (1976: 29), 'theme' and 'rheme' appear as structural elements representing this textual function.[1]

The functional view of language requires a certain type of description (or grammar) of a language. In his *Introduction to Functional Grammar*, Halliday (1985: xiv) contrasts traditional grammars with functional ones:

In the history of western linguistics, from its beginnings in ancient Greece, this was the direction that was taken: first the forms of words were studied (morphology); then in order to explain the forms of words, grammarians explored the forms of sentences (syntax); and once the forms had been established, the question was then posed: 'What do these forms mean?' In a functional grammar, on the other hand, the direction is reversed. A language is interpreted as a system of meanings, accompanied by forms through which the meanings can be realized. The question is rather: 'how are these meanings expressed?'

The forms of language – on all the different levels – are seen as means to an end, viz. to express components of meaning and to fulfil one or all of the 'metafunctions' of language. Halliday speaks of two 'main kinds of meaning', two 'very general purposes which underlie all uses of language':

(i) to understand the environment (ideational), and (ii) to act on the others in it (interpersonal). Combined with these is a third metafunctional component, the 'textual', which breathes relevance into the other two. (Halliday 1985: xiii)

Note that Halliday's interpersonal function is not there to transmit information from one person to another (as traditional linguistics would have had it), but to act on others. Halliday does not think that the language system first evolved to give messages and was then adapted to act on others, but rather the opposite: it is the language uses (ideational, i.e. reflective, and interpersonal, i.e. effective) 'that, over tens of thousands of generations, have shaped the system' (1985: xiii). Thus the units of language (word, clause, phrase, etc.) have evolved from the two most important needs, viz. to be able to reflect and to influence others.

In a later book (Halliday and Matthiessen 1999: xi), Halliday writes: 'Language evolved, in the human species, in two complementary functions: construing experience, and enacting social processes.' In this book, Halliday and Matthiessen try to show how the metafunctions (particularly the ideational one) contribute to **construing our experience** (1999: 7–9). The construing function of language is one that neither Bühler nor Jakobson were aware of. This function will be dealt with in the context of Constructivism in Chapter 8 below.

2.3   Other Systems of 'Functions'

In contrast to Bühler, Jakobson and Halliday, Brown and Yule (1983: 1–4) distinguish only two functions, the 'transactional', which serves the expression of content (corresponding to Bühler's representative function) and the 'interactional', which establishes and maintains social relations and corresponds to Bühler's expressive function. While an equivalent to Bühler's appellative function is not mentioned, the authors admit that this division is 'an analytic convenience'. All utterances are bifunctional: 'It would be unlikely that, on any occasion, a natural language utterance would be used to fulfill only one function, to the total exclusion of the other' (Brown and Yule 1983: 1).[2] A similar binary model was established by Klaus P. Schneider (1988: 1), who distinguishes between the phatic function, with which social contact is established and maintained, and the 'instrumental' one, which permits the exchange of information and intentions.

Further functions of language (as discourse) which are mentioned in the literature on the subject include **creating tension** (in drama and narrative – as well as in scholarly texts and in newspaper reports, etc., see Fill 2007) and **attracting attention** (see Leech 1966: 27 f.). The latter is particularly important in advertising, where deviation from a norm and the combination of language and image play a decisive role. In Hartmut Stöckl's 'model of persuasion' (1997: 71–77), the first function mentioned is the attention-attracting function (others are memorability, activating imagination, distraction and making something look attractive).

Finally, a function of language which stands in conflict with the 'usual' role of language as code of communication is **group delimitation**: by using certain manifestations of language (different non-standard varieties, youth slang, rhyming slang, etc.), groups of speakers may receive an identity which sets them apart from other groupings (Laycock 2001: 169). According to this theory, differences in speech have the function of distinguishing friends from mere acquaintances as well as enemies. This **delimitatory or identificatory function** is one of the causes of language variation and perhaps even of the linguistic diversity on this earth (cf. Laycock 2001: 170 f.). Concerning non-standard English, for some time the myth of a 'verbal deprivation' of non-standard speakers was popular. It may be important to remember what William Labov (1972: 202) says about this: 'The most useful service which linguists can perform today is to clear away the illusion of verbal deprivation and to provide a more adequate notion of the relations between standard and non-standard dialects.'

A survey of functional theories of language is given by Bublitz (2001: 43–54), who particularly stresses the fact that individual utterances – be they written or spoken – are mostly **multifunctional**. Thus, a sentence in a personal letter, such as 'Their house was feeling like home again' can be, at the lowest level, a statement of fact, a comment, praise, agreement or contradiction etc. On more complex levels, it can be 'introducing a story' or 'expressing relief', or even (on the interpersonal level) an attempt at amusing, impressing, reassuring or flattering the recipient (Bublitz 2001: 53 f.).

Notes

1. In contrast to Halliday's *Explorations in the Functions of Language* (1973), in the papers from *System and Function in Language* (1976) there are references not only to Bühler's writings on functions, but also to the 'Functional Sentence Perspective' by the Prague school, of which a number of names are mentioned (Halliday 1976: 29; see also Vachek 1966).
2. Against this, Goatly (personal communication) gives the examples of swearing and counting 'one/two/three' when testing a microphone.

3. Religion, Philosophy and Language Impact Theories

Linguistics has a long tradition dating back to the Babylonian, the Hebrew and the Arabian cultures of Antiquity. In China, Japan and particularly India (with Panini as the greatest representative), language began to be studied more than 2500 years ago. But the early 'linguists' concerned themselves chiefly with grammar, with the sounds and the words of language, not so much with the effect language may have on the world (see the relevant chapters in Koerner and Asher eds 1995).

3.1   The Christian Religion and Language Impact

That language does not just 'describe the world', but through humans exerts power over the world was, however, from the beginning common knowledge among the founders of religions and among philosophers. Confucius, when asked what measures he would take first if he had power in a state, is said to have answered: 'I would first of all set the concepts right!' (Störig 1987: 95). This is perhaps the first manifestation of a belief in the power of language: changing the language for the better would change things for the better. When asked why he would do this, Confucius is said to have answered:

> Wenn die Begriffe nicht richtig sind, so stimmen die Worte nicht; stimmen die Worte nicht, so kommen die Werke nicht zustande; kommen die Werke nicht zustande, so gedeiht Moral und Kunst nicht; gedeiht Moral und Kunst nicht, so treffen die Strafen nicht; treffen die Strafen nicht, so weiß das Volk nicht, wohin Hand und Fuß setzen. (Heringer 1982: 24)

> *If the concepts are not right, the words too are wrong; if the words are wrong, actions cannot come to pass; if actions cannot come to pass, morals and art will not thrive; if these do not thrive, punishment will not take effect; if punishment does not take effect, the people will have no guidance on how to act.*

Today we would judge Confucius' cause and effect equations as somewhat naïve and perhaps overemphasizing the importance of words. However, the view of the earth-changing power of words is also expressed in another early account of the effect of language on the world – this time a negative effect: the story of the **Tower of Babel**, as told in Genesis (11:1–9), as follows:

> Now the whole earth had one language and the same words. ²And as they migrated from the east, they came upon a plain in the land of Shinar and settled there. ³And they said to one another, 'Come, let us make bricks, and burn them thoroughly.' And they had brick for stone, and bitumen for mortar. ⁴Then they said, 'Come, let us build

ourselves a city, and a tower with its top in the heavens, and let us make a name for ourselves; otherwise we shall be scattered abroad upon the face of the whole earth.' [5]The LORD came down to see the city and the tower, which mortals had built. [6]And the LORD said, 'Look, they are one people, and they have all one language; and this is only the beginning of what they will do; nothing that they propose to do will now be impossible for them. [7]Come, let us go down, and confuse their language there, so that they will not understand one another's speech.' [8]So the LORD scattered them abroad from there over the face of all the earth, and they left off building the city. [9]Therefore it was called Babel, because there the LORD confused the language of all the earth; and from there the LORD scattered them abroad over the face of all the earth. (Source: *oremus Bible Browser* http://www.devotions.net/bible/00bible.htm)

This looks like an early (second millennium BCE) statement about the importance of language for cooperation – and thus a confirmation of evolutionary theories which stress the political component of language development. The story also suggests a God-given cause of linguistic diversity: if humans all spoke the same language, they would be able to 'reach the sky' by working together – and they would stay in one place and not spread around the world. Language diversity, in this account, is shown to: (1) prevent humans from becoming insolent and aspiring to being like God; and (2) lead to the distribution of the human species all over the world. That the modern understanding of language diversity (cf. Mühlhäusler 2001) is somewhat different from this, viz. that diversity is regarded as the result of evolution and as one of the preconditions of creativity, will be shown in Chapter 20 on language ecology.

Stories about the division of one language into many are also known from Ancient Greece, Kenya, South Australia, Alaska and other parts of the world.

At present there are tendencies to reverse the 'confusion' of languages by introducing one dominant language everywhere (perhaps English in the form of 'English as a lingua franca'), so that everyone may understand everyone. The reactions against these efforts, against 'English as a global language' and against anglicisms in, say, French and German could be seen as part of a struggle for maintaining the preconditions of creativity which were given us in the evolution of linguistic diversity.

In the **New Testament**, the importance of language – as speech (or 'discourse') – is stressed, in particular in the Epistles of St Paul. In 1 Corinthians 13:1 ff., St Paul writes about 'speaking in tongues of men or of angels'. The force of the speech-sound, however, becomes only apparent if someone speaks with love, 'by way of revelation or enlightenment, or prophesy, or instruction' (14:6). As is well known, THE WORD plays an important role in the New Testament. 'When all things began, the Word already was. The Word dwelt with God, and what God was, the Word was' is the famous opening passage of *The Gospel according to John* – a sentence which Faust in Goethe's play of the same name struggles with. (Quotations from *The New English Bible.* Popular edition. Oxford: OUP, CUP, 1961.)

3.2   Greek Philosophy and Beyond

In early Greek philosophy and historiography, the topic of the power of language was already addressed by a number of authors. Among the Pre-Socratic philosophers, it was Heraklitos and Parmenides who acknowledged the importance of language. For **Heraklitos**, a 'logos' is the ruling principle of the world; whether this *logos* is to be understood as language or simply as a general force is still a matter of controversy. The first critic of language seems to have been **Parmenides**, who assumed language to have a negative role in our thinking about the nature of the world: in his philosophical poem 'Peri physeos' (*About Nature*), he says that because there are words for developing and disappearing, for being and not-being, for changing places and altering colours, humans think these 'things' really exist and are manifestations of the truth (see the text in Kirk *et al.* 1994: 277 f. and Diels 1934: 238). The first mention of the role of language in Greek philosophy is thus already a critique of language and of what was later to be called word-realism.

The *locus classicus* of a critique of **language decay** is **Thucydides**' account of the civil unrest on the island of Kerkyra (Corfu), where words fell into disorder and adopted new meanings. Thucydides' examples would in modern semantics be called 'ameliorative/pejorative change of meaning' and euphemism ('the use of fair phrases') (cf. Kraus 1987: 186 f.). Here is Thucydides' text, in an English translation (words and phrases with semantic change are in *italics*, A.F.):

> Words had to change their ordinary meaning and to take that which was now given them. *Reckless audacity* came to be considered the courage of a loyal ally; *prudent hesitation*, specious cowardice; *moderation* was held to be a cloak for unmanliness; *ability to see all sides of a question*, inaptness to act on any. *Frantic violence* became the attribute of manliness; *cautious plotting*, a justifiable means of self-defence. The advocate of extreme measures was always *trustworthy*; his opponent a man *to be suspected*. [...] Thus religion was in honour with neither party; but the use of fair phrases to arrive at guilty ends was in high reputation. (Thucydides, *History of the Peloponnesian War*, Book I 3,82; the Internet Classics Archive http://classics.mit.edu/ Thucydides/pelopwar.mb.txt)

The **Stoics** already distinguished between various **functions of language** (or perhaps rather text-types which have a function). Apart from assertion, they noticed the functions of judgement, interrogation, command, oath, prayer, hypothesis and address (Sextus Empiricus, second century CE, in *Against the Logicians* II, 70–73, quoted by Formigari 2004: 24). During the Middle Ages, this knowledge seems to have got lost, but was revived in modern times (see Nerlich and Clarke 1996, Chapters 2–5, for a discussion of 'protopragmatics' from 1780 to 1930).

Plato accorded language an important position in the world, which is documented by the fact that at least two of his dialogues, the *Kratylos* and the *Gorgias*, have (aspects of) language as their topic. While in the *Kratylos*, the origin of language and the relation between word and object (as well as the meaning of speech-sounds) are the topics of the discussion, the *Gorgias* is an appraisal of the power of rhetoric, which is seen in a decidedly critical light. In other dialogues, too, language plays a role. In his *Euthydemos*, Plato shows the absurdities of the sophist or eristic use of language, and in his *Phidias*, he discusses the effect of 'language decay' (probably a topos even in Plato's time). The *Euthydemos* is particularly interesting, because here even the wise Socrates is shown to be deceived and tricked by two brothers  (Euthydemos and Dionysodoros) who know the art of eristics. Their linguistic tricks make him admit, for instance, that he may give away or sell the goddess Athene ('this is *your* goddess [...] what is yours surely you may give away or sell'), that saying an untruth is impossible and that everyone knows everything. (See Schiewe 1998: 28–50 on Plato's critique of language; see also Leiss 2009: 31–46 for more on Plato's *Kratylos*.)

Aristotle, in several of his works, discusses language, but his approach is chiefly analytical and resembles that of linguists before the pragmatic turn. In his *Rhetoric*, however, he writes about modes of persuasion, and in his *Poetics*, Aristotle shows the effect of poetry and the drama (arousal of pity and fear, 'catharsis') and thus indirectly of language. In Leiss (2009: 26), Aristotle is represented as the originator of the semiotic triangle, which obtained great importance in the twentieth century, particularly through Ogden and Richards' *The Meaning of Meaning* (1969/1923).

The Romans are important for our topic since they above all recognized the power of rhetoric. Cicero and Quintilian in particular are authors concerned with 'the power of language' – more precisely, the **power of speech as discourse** through rhetoric (Kennedy 1994, 1998: 191–214; see also Brian Vickers' chapter 'An Outline of Classical Rhetoric', 1988: 1–82).

Following the Greeks (e.g. Aristotle, *Rhetoric,* book 2), the Romans distinguished genres of **rhetoric** and modes of persuasion, viz. through

Ethos   (persuasion derived from the character of the speaker);
Pathos (persuasion derived from the emotion awakened by a speaker in the audience); and
Logic   (persuasion derived from true or probable argument) (cf. Göttert 1994: 85–91).

The Ancient Rhetoricians established 'functions' of speech, the *officia oratoris*, which were *docere, delectare, movere* (teach, entertain, move; cf. Göttert 1994: 22), they distinguished between levels of style (plain, middle and grand – cf. Vickers

1988: 81) and collected rhetorical figures (from 'alliteration' to 'zeugma', see Plett 2000 and Vickers 1988: Appendix). That rhetoric is not merely an achievement of the ancient Greeks and Romans is shown convincingly by George A. Kennedy in his book *Comparative Rhetoric* (1998). The book includes chapters on rhetoric in the Ancient Near East, in Ancient China and India, as well as in cultures without writing (Native Americans, Australian Aboriginal Culture and others).

Among the **Medieval philosophers**, the most interesting one for our topic is William of Ockham (1285–1349), whose nominalism foreshadowed the linguistic pessimism of the empiricists. In a way, Ockham also anticipated some of the ideas of constructivism: linguistic structures do not mirror the structures of the world, they only show the structure of our thinking. Language is thus useless for understanding the world (cf. Leiss 2009: 83) and its impact on our attempts to order the world is a negative one.

A number of other philosophical schools concerned themselves with the impact of language: these, however, will be dealt with in connection with specific topics in the relevant chapters. Among them are **the Empiricists** (Bacon, Locke, Hume, Berkeley), whose occupation with language was mainly a critique of it, and the **Rationalists**, with Descartes as their main representative, who provided the philosophical background for Chomsky and his school of Generative Transformationalism (J.-J. Hodge 1983). For Chomsky, the 'ratio' (reason) humans are born with also includes the faculty for learning language (or rather all languages of the world) and the possession of a universal grammar which we have internalized (see below about Chomsky).

Among the **Idealists**, the name of Kant is conspicuously absent among those concerned with the effect of language. Schopenhauer (with his 32 eristic devices), Schleiermacher and a few others, however, have expressed their views on the effect language may have on others (see Chapter 17.5 below).

Wilhelm von **Humboldt** and his school (see Chapter 4 below), the twentieth-century Neo-Humboldtians (Chapter 4.1), the American Anthropologists (Boas, etc. Chapter 5.3), and the Phenomenologists (Husserl and Heidegger, Chapter 4.2) will be dealt with in separate sections.

The French **Socio-philosophers**, particularly Pierre Bourdieu and Michel Foucault, have emphasized the close relation between language, power and society. Their work contains a critique of traditional approaches to language including those of Saussure, Chomsky and the speech-act theorists (see the section on language and power in Chapter 18.1 below).

3.3 The Pragmatic Turn in Philosophy

Die Grenzen meiner Sprache bedeuten die Grenzen meiner Welt.
The limits of my language mean the limits of my world.

Wittgenstein's famous dictum about the limits of language and the world is in his early book *Tractatus Logico-philosophicus* (1922: 5.6), in which he expresses the idea of a parallelism between language and the world: the sentence is an image of the world; the world is structured like (the sentences of) our language (see Leiss 2009: 138–142).

However, in his later writings, particularly in his *Philosophical Investigations* (hereafter *PI*), he acknowledges grave errors in his first book, so that we can indeed speak of Wittgenstein's 'abandonment of the picture theory' (Bogen 1972: 102–168) and his adoption of a use and effect theory. In *PI*, language no longer has limits in the sense that only certain concrete truths can be expressed meaningfully; rather, language is a 'toolbox' with which the world can be influenced, perhaps even decisively changed. While in the *Tractatus,* Wittgenstein writes about the *limits of his language,* in *Philosophical Investigations* language is limitless, has countless uses and activities which can be performed with it. Wittgenstein speaks of the 'tools' of language and lists 19 of what he calls 'language games' or activities. Here is the complete list (2003: section 23), in Wittgenstein's text prefaced by 'and others' (see also the section on language rules and language games in Kemmerling 1992: 116–120, and Harris 1993 on the 'game metaphor' in Saussure and Wittgenstein):

Ordering, and following orders;
Describing an object from its appearance, or by measuring it;
Producing an object from a description (drawing);
Reporting an event;
Making surmises about the event;
Setting up a hypothesis, testing it;
Presenting the results of an experiment with tables and diagrams;
Inventing a story; reading it;
Play-acting;
Singing catches;
Guessing riddles;
Making a joke – telling it;
Solving an applied example of calculating;
Translating from one language into another;
Requesting, thanking, cursing, greeting, praying.

One may notice that among Wittgenstein's language games are a few which could be equated with Austin's illocutions or Searle's speech acts (such as requesting, thanking and greeting), but also quite a few more complex ones (such as making surmises about an event, reading a story, making a joke); finally, there are a few (such as play-acting, cursing and praying) which one could almost call settings of discourse.

Wittgenstein's new thinking about language also concerns language learning. This, Wittgenstein says (Section 26), is traditionally thought of as learning to name objects, people, forms, colours, pains, moods, numbers, etc. 'As if all we did with language was talking about things!' (Section 27). Wittgenstein gives a list of exclamations (*water! Away! Ouch! Help! Beautiful! Don't*) and then asks the reader: 'Are you still inclined to call these words "names of things"?'.

Wittgenstein's 'Copernican turn' (Rudolf Haller) has led to an operational view of language which is the basis of the present book. Wittgenstein's 'impact' on contemporary thought is dealt with in detail in Leinfellner *et al.* (eds 1978; see also Formigari 2004: 173–177; Ishiguro 1992; Kemmerling 1992 and the articles in Haller ed. 1981).

Critique of Wittgenstein

A prominent critic of Wittgenstein's theory of language and language learning is Noam Chomsky, who thinks it improbable that language learning may be described with the help of Wittgenstein's 'strange examples of paradigmatically introduced "language games"' (1969: 276). Chomsky's critique of Wittgenstein is discussed at length by Grewendorf (1995: 75–111). However, Wittgenstein's 'strange examples' of language games have led to a revolution not only in language learning and language teaching, but also in the position the study of language has in modern society.

What is implied but remains unsaid in Wittgenstein's book (*PI*) is that every '**use**' may have an '**effect**'. Using something (say, language) is not the whole story: the result of this use, its effect on someone or something is the thing that counts – and in the history of linguistic Pragmatics, this was acknowledged before Wittgenstein as well as after him.

In Richard Rorty's book *The Linguistic Turn*, the turn of philosophy towards the analysis of language is also seen as a 'turn in the direction of pragmatism' (Rorty 1967: preface). Particularly the articles in Part III of Rorty's book suggest that the 'linguistic turn' developed into a **pragmatic turn** towards Ordinary Language Philosophy with its emphasis on using words to do things. ('The linguistic turn' in philosophy is discussed at some length in Chapter 6 of Leiss 2009).

If philosophy underwent a linguistic turn, linguistics can be said to have undergone a philosophical turn, which became manifest in two ways: Chomsky's and his school's strong criticism of empiricism and their embracing of Cartesian Rationalism on the one hand, and the rise of Pragmatics in the wake of Wittgenstein and Austin on the other.

3.4   The Philosophical Turn in Linguistics

With **Chomsky**'s *Syntactic Structures* (first published in 1957), linguistics became generative and transformational for a time, but it also turned philosophical. TG linguistics is philosophically grounded in the Rationalism of Descartes and turns against Empiricism in all its manifestations including Behaviorism. Language, for Chomsky, is a set of rules for which our mind (brain?) is already 'preprogrammed' at birth; learning one's native language does not occur by following stimulus response patterns, but rather takes place by building on the structures of a universal grammar which is already there in the brain. This 'Nativist' position (also adopted by Steven Pinker in *The Language Instinct*, 1994) dominated linguistics for some time, but has more recently been severely criticized, for instance by Geoffrey Sampson in *The 'Language Instinct' Debate* (2005).

Unfortunately, Chomsky is not interested in the effect of language: grammar is all important, and syntax is independent of meaning (1957: 13, 17). Chilton (2004: 24) speaks of a (justified) complaint 'that Chomsky's linguistics does nothing to relate language structure to language function'. Thus Chomsky's contribution to our topic comes not so much from his linguistics, but from his critique of the media – as will be shown in Chapter 17.1 ('Strategies on the content level').

The Transformationalists are mainly concerned with the structures of language and rarely talk about use and effect. When Katz (1972: 93 ff.) discusses 'meaning is use' theories, he takes 'use' to mean 'right use', not 'intention to achieve a certain effect'. Katz (1972: 93) writes about Wittgenstein's 'doctrine' that meaning is use:

> The difficulty with this doctrine is that meaning is only *one* factor that contributes to the ways linguistic constructions are used. There are many others, so an explication of meaning in terms of use is bound to falsely represent semantic relations in cases where non-semantic factors contribute to differences in use.

Katz' examples of different uses (*bunny* vs. *rabbit*, *stomach* vs. *tummy*, strictures against 'four-letter words' in polite society, etc.) show that he thoroughly misunderstood Wittgenstein's definition of meaning as use. Language philosophy, for Katz, still relates to linguistic structure and is thus ultimately based on a linguistics of correctness, not of use or impact.

3.5   From Pragmalinguistics to Impact Linguistics

As already mentioned, a philosophical influence more important for our topic is that exerted by Wittgenstein, Austin, Grice and Searle, who heralded the **pragmatic turn** of linguistics. Studying the uses and effects of language (dubbed Pragmatics by Charles Morris) is increasingly becoming one of the central tasks of linguistics (see Chapter 13 about Pragmatics). While Pragmatics studies the uses and effects of language mainly on the discourse level, the present book has a much wider perspective: it looks at the 'impact' of language, i.e. its long-term and short-term effects on the levels of evolution, system and discourse.

Following Harré and Harris (1993: preface), we can make a distinction between the philosophy of language and the philosophy of linguistics. While the philosophy of language is interested among other topics in 'language and thought' and 'language and reality' (cf. Auroux and Kouloughli 1993: 23), the philosophy of linguistics takes an interest in what philosophers and other thinkers *have said* about these topics. In the present book, we will be concerned with both levels, the object level of language and discourse, and the meta-level of thinking and writing about language and discourse.

For other philosophers and philosophical schools concerned with our topic, the reader is referred to **Appendix II**, in which a list of thinkers on language and world, together with short summaries of their views, is given.

Part II

The Impact of Language as a System

The chapters in this part deal with the influence of language on 'the world' – with language now seen as a system of sounds, grammar, and words. In various models of language, the systemic elements, such as the phonemes, the morphemes, the lexemes and the grammatical structures, are shown to shape: (a) human thought; thus (b) human actions; which in their turn shape (c) the interaction between humans and their planet. This interaction may take place in different ways in the different parts of the world, but it is undeniably a central part of the impact of language and has as such been described by many philosophers and linguists, as these chapters will show.

4. Language as *energeia* (Wilhelm von Humboldt)

A close connection between language and thought (or, to be more precise, language and the conceptualization of the world) was discovered by scholars before Humboldt, such as the authors of the Port Royal Grammar, the French philosopher Condillac (see Harris and Taylor 1997: 139–154), and the eighteenth-century German philosopher Hamann, who called language the 'womb of the concepts' (1967: 143; cf. Trabant 1994: 233). However, it was Wilhelm von Humboldt (1767–1835) who in his voluminous work on language (and languages) gave expression to this idea most clearly and most intensely. In the nineteenth century, Humboldt was one of the most widely quoted authors, whose influence still resonated well into the middle of the twentieth century. In particular, Humboldt is frequently quoted as the originator of two revolutionary ideas which he introduced between 1820 and 1835 (cf. Werlen 1989: 43–65):

1. Language (in general) is not a static product (*ergon*), but a dynamic process and activity (*energeia*) which makes (linguistic) sound capable of expressing ideas.[1] (see Werlen 1989: 50)
2. Language structure and the characteristics of thinking of a people are intricately interwoven and derive from each other.[2] (see Werlen 1989: 48)

The first idea is linked to Humboldt's rejection of language as a mere sign system. To see words as mere signs, for Humboldt, was a fundamental error which would prevent the correct evaluation of language (cf. Werlen 1989: 51).

By interpreting language as *energeia*, Humboldt sees in language the 'thought-forming organ' (cf. Werlen 1989: 53). This makes him both a precursor of Sapir and Whorfian linguistic determinism and one of the forerunners of constructivist approaches to language (see Chapters 5 and 8 below).

The second idea occurred to Humboldt as a result of his study of many European and non-European languages, among them the Basque language, with which he came into contact during a journey through Spain and France in 1801. Even more important for the development of this view was Humboldt's contact with scholars who investigated the Kawi language, the old literary language of Java, and with others who studied the Amerindian languages. We may observe an interesting parallel with Boas, Sapir and Whorf, who nearly a century later continued the Humboldtian tradition and conceived of their ideas after getting to know these Amerindian languages in the United States (cf. Trabant 1990: 65).

Humboldt was probably the first scholar to see that language creates 'point of view' by making the explicit or implied use of **pronouns** necessary (1994: 174–182). Speaking usually occurs between a speaker (the 'I') and a hearer (the 'you'); thus it is language which makes us think in terms of *I, you, he/she, we*, etc.

Nerlich and Clarke (1996: 51) detect many 'pragmatic elements' in Humboldt's language philosophy. For Humboldt, words are not only signs of ideas, they are signs which form corresponding thoughts in the act of speaking. '[T]his articulatory *act of speaking* is the hub of Humboldt's philosophy of language, just as the *semiotic act* had been for Locke and the *act of reason* for Kant' (Nerlich and Clarke 1996: 53, authors' original emphasis). For Humboldt, language is not just a system of signs (*ergon*), but 'ever-repeated mental labour' which makes it possible for sound to express thought (Nerlich and Clarke 1996: 53 f.). Language, for Humboldt, is 'the true or the only verifiable *a priori* framework of cognition', as George Steiner puts it in *After Babel* (1975: 81).

Humboldt himself does not talk of 'speech acts' (*Sprechakte*); he uses the term 'Act' [*sic!*] sometimes for the synthesis of a word with its suffix (1998: 325), but more importantly for the creative act by which each language in its own way links sounds with concepts:

> Die Sprache, im einzelnen Wort und in der verbundenen Rede, ist ein Act, eine wahrhaft schöpferische Handlung des Geistes; und dieser Act ist in jeder Sprache ein individueller, in einer von allen Seiten bestimmten Weise verfahrend. Begriff und Laut, auf eine ihrem wahren Wesen gemäße, nur an der Thatsache selbst erkennbare Weise verbunden, werden als Wort und als Rede hinausgestellt, und dadurch zwischen der Außenwelt und dem Geiste etwas von beiden Unterschiedenes geschaffen. (1998: 324)

> *Language, in the individual word and in connected speech, is an Act, a truly creative activity of the mind; and this Act is in every language an individual one, acting in a way determined by different elements. Concept and sound, linked in a way which agrees with their true being and is recognizable only through reality are presented as word and speech, whereby between external world and mind something distinguishable from both is created.*

Humboldt, in several passages, compares language with a tool, but not in Wittgenstein's and Austin's sense of a tool for doing things, but rather a tool for the mind: '[Sprachen] sind Werkzeuge, deren die geistige Thätigkeit bedarf, Bahnen, in welchen sie fortrollt' (1998: 364). (*Languages are tools indispensable for mental activity, roads on which this activity travels.*)

It is thus somewhat problematic to see in Humboldt a forerunner of Pragmatics. He is mainly concerned with language as a vessel of culture and a tool for thinking about the world – not as a means to influence others. Nevertheless, Humboldt's idea of language as energy and 'Act' may have influenced late nineteenth century authors form the German speaking cultural area to link speaking with acting and thus take a dynamic rather than static view of language. Among these are the philosopher **Franz Brentano** (1878–1917) and the Swiss-born philologist **Anton Marty** (1847–1914), who taught in Prague. Brentano wrote in 1885: 'Speaking is often brought into opposition with acting. But speaking is itself an acting. An activity, by means of which one wants to call forth certain psychic phenomena' (quoted from Nerlich and Clark 1996: 189 and Smith 1990: 42). Marty developed a functional theory of language, in which speaking and writing as acting played an important role (see Nerlich and Clark 1996: 190–198).

4.1   The Neo-Humboldtians

In twentieth-century Germany, a number of scholars elaborated on Humboldt's idea of language as a force which shapes thought. They are known as the 'Neo-Humboldtians' (*Neuhumboldtianer*) and were, in a way, the twentieth-century answer to linguistic Positivism. Positivism had manifested itself most conspicuously in the philological school of the Neogrammarians, who were chiefly interested in sound change and in tracing languages back to their origins, particularly to an Indo-European proto-language. While the Neogrammarians saw linguistics as a science on a par with chemistry and physics – where rules (e.g. of sound change) could be established which could be refined so as finally to account for all 'exceptions' – the Neo-Humboldtians were opposed to the integration of linguistics among the natural sciences. 'The rejection of any *science* of language was a common trait of philosophical idealism. It was shared by two philosophers active at the beginning of the 20th century, **Karl Vossler** in Germany and **Benedetto Croce** in Italy. [...] This anti-scientific trend also brought about a final showdown with the Neogrammarian method' (Formigari 2004: 150).

Against the Neogrammarian Positivist interest in the formal side of language, the Neo-Humboldtians set their 'Idealist' emphasis on the 'spirit' and on the 'inner form' of language, an idea first found in Humboldt, then elaborated by Cassirer (1923: 251), Anton Marty (1950) and Walter Porzig (1967); what was meant by 'inner form' were aspects of aesthetic value, of the creation of concepts through language and of the relation between language and the culture of its speakers.

Most prominent among the Neo-Humboldtians were the scholars mentioned above (Karl Vossler, Walter Porzig, Ernst Cassirer), and – as the most radical exponent of this school – **Leo Weisgerber** (1899–1985). Weisgerber, whose 'content-oriented' (*inhaltsbezogene*) idea of grammar achieved a certain prominence after the Second World War, has frequently been compared to Whorf, with whose linguistic determinism his ideas indeed have a certain affinity. A few of Weisgerber's book titles, which show that his approach was not entirely free from ideology, may speak for themselves: *Von den Kräften der deutschen Sprache* [About the forces of the German language], *Die sprachliche Gestaltung der Welt* [The linguistic structuring of the world], *Die sprachliche Erschließung der Welt* [The linguistic unlocking of the world], *Die Muttersprache im Aufbau unserer Kultur* [The native language in the construction of our culture].

For Weisgerber, language creates an 'interworld' (*sprachliche Zwischenwelt*) which mediates between the real world and our psyche. Thus Latin, in this interworld, makes a distinction between 'father's brother' (*patruus*) and 'mother's brother' (*avunculus*), which therefore were differentiated in thinking, while other languages (like German and English) have only one word (*Onkel/uncle*) and thus one concept in the interworld. Nevertheless, speakers of German or English, are, if necessary (!), perfectly capable of distinguishing the two categories in thought and in speech (cf. Werlen 1989: 115). Weisgerber also used the term 'Das Worten der Welt' (*wording the world*) for the power of language to categorize the world for us.[3]

Weisgerber (1963: 16) distinguishes four steps or stages in the investigation of language, of which two are static, and two 'energetic'. Figure 4.1 shows the assignment of these steps to static and dynamic considerations (Weisgerber 1963: 16, my translation). While the form oriented approach considers the signifying side of linguistic signs and comprises the study of sounds, morphemes (inflectional endings, word formation), word classes and syntax without specific reference to meaning, the content oriented approach considers the meaning of linguistic elements in isolation and in combination (e.g. word fields) and corresponds to what is commonly called semasiology and onomasiology.

1. Form oriented	Static research ('grammar')
2. Content oriented	
3. Achievement oriented	Energetic research ('full linguistics')
4. Effect oriented	

Figure 4.1

The energetic stages are those which, for Weisgerber, give to the study of language 'the full title of linguistics' (1963: 92).The first, the achievement oriented (*leistungsbezogene*) stage occupies a central position, since here the power of language to 'grasp' the world for us is investigated (*sprachlicher Zugriff*). It is at this stage that the world-view a language conveys is investigated. The final, effect oriented (*wirkungsbezogene*) stage of the study of language concerns the effects of language on (and in) the life of humans (1963: 93). Studying this includes the investigation of the interrelation (*Wechselwirkung*) of language and culture: language, on the one hand, is a mirror of culture, and on the other hand plays a part in forming the cultural life of a people (cf. 1963: 142).

Weisgerber's achievement oriented approach would in more modern terminology form part of psycholinguistics, while his effect oriented approach has in the meantime been integrated into Pragmatics (or Pragmalinguistics) – branches of linguistics of which Weisgerber was not yet aware.

Though now somewhat outdated, Weisgerber's four approaches to language may still be helpful for students of language since they clarify the nature and range of linguistic research. Particularly the term 'energetic research' with its allusion to Humboldt could be of help since it shows that linguistics goes beyond finding structures and rules in language. Weisgerber's 'achievement oriented' and 'effect oriented approach' is also the approach of Wittgenstein (in his *PI*), of Austin, Searle, Whorf, Fairclough and all scholars (including the author of this book) who are interested in the effect of language and discourse on thought and behaviour as well as their effect on the world.[4]

Ernst Cassirer (1874–1945)

In all Neo-Humboldtian approaches, the **concept-creating power of the language system** (the grammar and the vocabulary) is emphasized, the most comprehensive and philosophical of these approaches being that of Ernst Cassirer. Cassirer goes beyond a mere discussion of the force of language: in his philosophy of 'symbolic forms', following Kant, Cassirer argues that it is the symbolic forms which give humans access to understanding the world. Among these he lists myth, logic, religion and scholarly cognition, and last but not least, language. Taking up Humboldt's idea of language as *energeia*, he writes that the chaos of sensory impressions is structured for us only through '**naming**' (1923: 20). Cassirer speaks of a 'world-view of language' ('Weltansicht der Sprache selbst'), which touches on, but also stands in opposition to, the world-views of scientific cognition, of art and of myth. Every language has its own 'image of the world' ('Weltbild der Sprache', 1923: 252–253), and Cassirer provides a number of examples of how our conceptualization through language progresses from a concrete sensual understanding to a generic and generalizing one (Cassirer's account of Humboldt's theory of language can be found in 1923: 98 ff.).

Using descriptions of native American languages (by Trumbull and Boas) Cassirer tries to show (1923: 257–259) that in these languages – to give an example – the actions of washing, beating, eating and breaking can be designated by a large number of different words depending on the object (e.g. in one language there are 13 different verbs for washing – hands, face, bowls, garments, etc.). Similarly, in some languages different trees, or palms, or parrots, have individual names, while a generic word is lacking. Quoting Hammer-Purgstall, he mentions that there are more than 5700 names for the camel in the Arabian language (at this point one is reminded of the well-known myth of the Inuits' different names for snow – see Pinker 1994: 64).

For Cassirer, language does not simply follow our impressions or ideas, but opposes them 'with independent action' (1923: 273). The world of sensual impressions is penetrated by language with judgement and evaluation (*ibid.*). Cassirer speaks of the spiritual 'articulation' and of the achievement of linguistic imagination ('Sprachphantasie', 1923: 273).

Cassirer spent the last few years of his life in the USA, teaching at Yale University. In 1944, his concise book *An Essay on Man* was published by Yale University Press, a book in which he gives a short summary of his three volume *magnum opus* on the philosophy of symbolic forms. The title was chosen deliberately to echo Alexander Pope's 'Essay on Man' (1744), in which the famous lines occur: 'Know then thyself, presume not God to scan / the proper study of mankind is man.' Cassirer's book contains chapters on 'Myth and Religion', 'Language', 'Art', 'History' and 'Science' – all of them symbolic forms with which humans more or less successfully 'scan' themselves. For Cassirer, all symbolic forms are phases in 'man's progressive self-liberation', another name for which is 'Culture' (cf. 1944: 228).

(For more on Cassirer and the other NeoHumboldtians, the reader is referred to Werlen's chapter 'Neuhumboldtianer' [1989: 103–124] and to Robert L. Miller's book *The Linguistic Relativity Principle and Humboldtian Ethnolinguistics* [1968]).

Hans-Georg Gadamer (1900–2002)

> Gadamer is the last true heir of Humboldt's philosophy, with which he shares (and takes to their ultimate consequence) certain crucial ideas: the belief that language cannot be transcended, that it exists prior to any other possible experience, and that the totality of a language and its associated world-view are contained in every word.
> (Formigari 2004: 150)

Starting from Humboldt, Gadamer poses the question of the relation between language and the world (1990: 442–460), and following Humboldt, he formulates the principle of 'Sprachansicht als Weltansicht' (1990: 446: *view of language as view of the world*). Gadamer starts from the idea of an intimate unity of language and thought (1993: 406). In his essay 'Mensch und Sprache' (1993a), he denies language the status of a 'tool' (thus indirectly criticizing Wittgenstein), since a tool is something we use and then dismiss as soon as it has served its purpose (1993a: 148 f.). The tool analogy is wrong, since we are never without language:

> Sprechen lernen heißt nicht: zur Bezeichnung der uns vertrauten und bekannten Welt in den Gebrauch eines schon vorhandenen Werkzeugs eingeführt werden, sondern es heißt, die Vertrautheit und Erkenntnis der Welt selbst, und wie sie uns begegnet, erwerben. (Gadamer 1993a: 149)

> *Learning to speak does not mean being introduced to the use of an already existing tool, but it means becoming familiar with and knowing about, the world itself and how it faces us.*

All our thinking is preconditioned, even prejudiced by the language with which we grow up:

> Wir sind in allem unserem Denken und Erkennen immer schon voreingenommen durch die sprachliche Weltauslegung, in die hineinwachsen in der Welt *aufwachsen* heißt. (Gadamer 1993a: 150, emphasis by Gadamer)

> *In all our thinking and cognizing we are already prejudiced through the linguistic interpretation of the world, growing into which means* growing up *in the world.*

Gadamer's belief in the predetermining power of language is so strong that he even poses the question whether all events and actions of humans are 'prescribed' by language – in the sense that the initial conditions were created by the (perhaps accidental) way in which language came into existence. In his essay 'Wie weit schreibt Sprache das Denken vor?' (*To what extent does language prescribe thought?*) (1970/1993b) he writes of a 'real suspicion' against language: could it be that the development of language was like fate throwing the dice in such a way that our speaking determines our thinking which will eventually lead to the self-destruction of humanity (cf. Gadamer 1993b: 202)?

His 'suspicion of language' takes Gadamer so far that he even blames on language the technical developments which have led to the human capacity to destroy everything (including humans). What we find here is not just a critique of the 'linguistic seduction of thought' (as with Friedrich Kainz, see below), but a belief in the possibility of a linguistic self-destruction of humans, even the 'global destruction through language'.

In contrast to Habermas, who warns of underestimating extralinguistic experience (and follows Piaget in assuming a pre-linguistic experience of the world), Gadamer holds that all these experiences are continuously translated into the inner dialogue of the soul, i.e. thoughts (cf. 1993b: 204), and are thus shaped by language. Finally, on a more optimistic note, Gadamer refers to Heinrich v. Kleist's argument that thought becomes concretized through speaking:

> Es gibt einen sehr schönen Aufsatz von Heinrich von Kleist mit dem Titel: 'Über die allmähliche Verfertigung der Gedanken beim Reden'. Wenn es nach mir ginge, müsste jeder Professor, der einen Kandidaten zu prüfen hat, vorher einen Revers unterschreiben, dass er diesen Artikel gelesen hat. (Gadamer 1993b:205)

> *There is a beautiful essay by Heinrich von Kleist entitled: 'On the gradual concretization of thought through speaking'. In my view, every professor who has to examine a candidate should previously sign a confirmation that he has read this essay.*[5]

This, according to Gadamer, is the real power of language: not to explain the world through its words, sentences, concepts and opinions ('pre-schematizations'), but to set the dynamic wheel of thoughts (*Schwungrad der Gedanken*, 1993b: 205) in motion. Language is a generative and creative force, which again and again makes all the schematizations flow [*die generative und kreative Kraft, solches Ganzes immer wieder zu verflüssigen*, 1993b: 206].

4.2   The Phenomenologists

Edmund **Husserl** (1859–1938) and Martin **Heidegger** (1889–1976), the chief representatives of phenomenology, oppose the realist view that things simply exist and are given labels by language. For the phenomenologists, consciousness is not static, but a continuous flowing, an unlimited 'river of phenomena' and a sequence of 'acts' constantly growing and being created (cf. Husserl 1965: 37). A key term is the **hermeneutic circle**, which (in contrast to the logical circle) is a spiral which leads to an ever higher understanding of texts, e.g. poems.

Unfortunately, the writings of the phenomenologists are in many places somewhat cryptic, even obscure. In particular, Heidegger's pronouncements on language are frequently based on word-play and cannot really be called contributions to linguistics.

Heidegger's often quoted sentence 'die Sprache ist das Haus des Seins. In ihrer Behausung wohnt der Mensch' (*language is the house of being. In its housing humans live*) was first formulated in a letter of 1947 (published in *Über den Humanismus*, 1947). The sentence was used again in his talk of 1957, 'Das Wesen der Sprache' (*The Nature of Language* in Heidegger 2007: 166), where Heidegger adduces a poem ('Das Wort' *'the word'*) by Stefan George as support for his famous dictum. The last two lines of the poem are as follows:

So lernt' ich traurig den verzicht:
Kein ding sei wo das wort gebricht.

I sadly thus learned to renounce:
No thing be where no word exists.

Heidegger rightly interprets the poem as meaning that the poet sadly acknowledges that it is 'the word' (= language) that creates things and ideas or rather allows them to exist. In an article published in the same volume (2007: 256 f.), Heidegger quotes Humboldt's famous passage (see above) in which language is called an *energeia*, not an *ergon*, and another passage in which Humboldt calls language a 'true world' which the mind has to put between itself and reality. Heidegger expressly extends *Welt* ('world') to *Weltansicht* ('worldview') and writes (2007: 249, his italics): 'Humboldt bringt die Sprache als *eine* Art und Form der in der menschlichen Subjektivität ausgearbeiteten Weltansicht zur Sprache.' (*Humboldt talks about language as* one *type and form of the worldview elaborated in human subjectivity.*)

Heidegger can thus be called a follower of Humboldt in so far as he sees language as an activity which creates a world-view. At the same time – as far as his writings present clear views on language – he expresses opinions which place him in the neighbourhood of linguistic constructivism.

Edmund Husserl, Heidegger's teacher, even uses the term 'Sprechakt' (*speech act*) – but not in the sense of Searle and other speech act theorists. For Husserl, it is the 'speech act', or rather the act of speaking, which creates meaning. Language, for him, has two main functions: conveying facts (*Kundgabe*), and giving expression to the self (*Ausdruck*). An appellative function (as described by Karl Bühler) is not yet part of Husserl's theory.

Alfred Schütz (1899–1959) was another phenomenologist who lectured and wrote extensively on language and 'language sociology' (see Schütz 2003, being Volume 2 of the complete edition of the work). However, his discussion of signs, symbols, language pathology and language sociology starts from an understanding of the linguistic sign as something which chiefly indicates the existence (presence) of an object, event or fact. The effect of language on others does not play an important role in his philosophy.

Phenomenology had a number of followers in France, above all **Marcel Merleau-Ponty** (1908–1961) and **Jean Paul Sartre** (1905–1980). In his *Phenomenology of Perception* (1945/2005), Merleau-Ponty, like Husserl, emphasizes the 'speech-act', but, like Husserl, not in Austin's and Searle's sense of doing things with language, but as the 'act of speaking' which makes sense of the world. Merleau-Ponty's turn from 'structural' phenomenology to 'dialectical' phenomenology is described in James M. Edie's book *Merleau-Ponty's Philosophy of Language: Structuralism and Dialectics* (1987). Sartre's ideas on language are part of his 'Existentialist' philosophy, as expressed for instance in his novel *La nausée* (1938). 'Language appears as a "medium" which "objectifies" the consciousness of the Other and allows it to rest upon me, thereby objectifying me' (quoted from Hawa (n.d.), online, 3).

Notes

1. The exact wording of the passage quoted most frequently is as follows:

    '[Die Sprache] selbst ist kein Werk (*Ergon*), sondern eine Thätigkeit (*Energeia*). Ihre wahre Definition kann daher nur eine genetische sein. Sie ist nämlich die sich ewig wiederholende Arbeit des Geistes, den articulirten Laut zum Ausdruck des Gedankens fähig zu machen' (Humboldt 1998:174).

(Language) itself is not a fact (ergon), but an activity (energeia). Its true definition therefore can only be a genetic one. Language is the ever-repeated mental labour of making the articulated sound capable of expressing thought. (After the translation by Peter Heath, quoted in Harris and Taylor 1998: 175)

2.   One passage in which this is very clearly expressed reads as follows:

'Die Geisteseigenthümlichkeit und die Sprachgestaltung eines Volkes stehen in solcher Innigkeit der Verschmelzung in einander, dass, wenn die eine gegeben wäre, die andere müsste vollständig aus ihr abgeleitet werden können. [...] Die Sprache ist gleichsam die äußerliche Erscheinung des Geistes der Völker; ihre Sprache ist ihr Geist und ihr Geist ist ihre Sprache: man kann sich beide nie identisch genug denken' (Humboldt 1998: 171).

The spiritual character and the linguistic structure of a people are so intimately welded together that if only one were given, the other could be derived completely from it.[...] Language is, so to speak, the outward appearance of the spirit of peoples; their language is their spirit and their spirit is their language: one can never think them as identical as they really are.

3.   The term 'Wording the World' was taken up by Jacob Mey in his *Pragmatics. An Introduction* (2001: 30) and, following Halliday, was used by Richard Alexander as a chapter heading (2009: 65). In Appendix III, the reader may find two more of Weisgerber's examples of different languages 'wording the world' differently.

4.   For a more detailed discussion of Weisgerber, the reader is referred to Werlen (1989: 109–124) and to Miller's chapter 'Weisgerber and the *Weltbild* of Vocabulary' (1968: 52–63).

5.   Kleist's essay can be found at the Kleist-Archiv Sembdner, Heilbronn: www.kleist.org/texte/index.htm

5. Language, Thought, Reality

5.1 General Remarks on Language and Thought

The present volume is not a treatise on the question of whether and to what extent we think with the help of language. Whether or not thought is only possible through words – or totally independent of them – will not be dealt with in detail. But necessarily the relation between language and thought plays a role for the impact of language on human actions. It may thus be useful to present the different theoretical positions concerning this topic as summarized by Friedrich Kainz in his *Handbuch der Psychologie* (1964/II:564 ff.; see also Jaenecke 2002). They are as follows.

Identity theory: thinking and speaking are essentially the same and form a single psychic activity. As a consequence of their being identical, neither a unidirectional nor a mutual influence between the two can be imagined: thinking is quiet speaking, speaking is thinking aloud. Thought is not possible without language, language impossible without thought.

A somewhat milder version of this is the **parallelism theory** (or **mirror theory**), which says that thinking and speaking proceed in a parallel way – in a (Leibnizian) 'prestabilized harmony', or the one as the mirror image of the other. Thought is primary, and speaking is only communication of thought (cf. Plato's *Theaitetos*, in which *logos* is defined as the mirror image of thought (1994, vol. 3, 208 C 5)). Thought uses language, language expresses thought.

A totally different (actually contrary) position is expressed in the **dualist difference theory**. According to this, thought proceeds in total independence of language and follows insights gained in the contemplation of things. Language clothes thought, may sometimes help thought to become clear, but frequently hems in thought by fixing it firmly in one position (cf. Schopenhauer 1987). Vygotsky's (1962: 150) well-known metaphor of thought as clouds and language as rain could be seen as an expression of this theory – though Vygotsky's own theory acknowledges a development from childhood to adulthood: 'Thought and word are not connected by a primary bond. A connection originates, changes, and grows in the course of the evolution of thinking and speech' (Vygotsky 1962: 119).

Kainz's own position can be called the **correlation theory:** thinking and speaking are two different functions which without being parallel act in symbiosis; they develop in conjunction and mutually support each other. Their relation is one of interaction and mutual assistance to reach the level of human-ness. Kainz even found a Latin formula which expresses his mild relativism, or rather probabilism: 'Lingua cogitationem inclinat, non necessitat' (1972: 26): language does not, as the strong hypothesis of Whorf would have it, make it necessary to think in a certain way; it is only more likely that we follow certain categories of our language in thinking about the world.

While older theories of language and thought concerned themselves unidirectionally either with the influence of language on thought or of thought on language, recent theorizing has taken a bidirectional perspective and follows Friedrich Kainz and Theo Herrmann in assuming a mutual influence which can be investigated with theories uniting the psychology of language with the psychology of thought. This presupposes that processes of language production and reception cannot be investigated without looking at processes of thought (Schweizer and Erdfelder 2005: 128). Another recent idea is that language made it possible to 'think aloud together', to do what has been called 'interthinking':

> with the emergence of language, members of our species did not simply become able to share information and co-ordinate individual activity. Rather, they gained a completely new way of using their minds in combination for solving problems, transforming individual experience into shared knowledge and making shared knowledge available to individuals. (Mercer 2000: 168)

This dialogic thinking aloud is certainly something that could still be improved in human interaction – a step yet to be taken in the evolution of language.

5.2 Structuralist Approaches: Saussure, Bally and Baudouin de Courtenay

The idea of a certain influence of language on thought is already expressed in the work of a number of authors belonging to the different structuralist schools. **Ferdinand de Saussure** himself (1857–1913, founder of the Geneva school) expresses this idea in the following way (1968: 253/G 1.9a): 'La pensée, chaotique dans sa nature, est forcée de se préciser en se décomposant. Le bienfait du langage est de forcer la pensée à se décomposer' [*Thinking, chaotic by nature, is forced to become precise by becoming structured. It is the benefit of language to force thought into a structure*] (cf. Werlen 1987: 93). Language creates units in two amorphous masses, sound and thought. In Saussure's drawing (1967: 133, 1968: 252), language forms a ribbon between the shapeless masses of sound and thought. One is reminded of Vygotsky's metaphor mentioned above which compares thought to an amorphous cloud becoming concrete when it dissolves into rain.

A similar interdependence of language and thought was also suggested by Saussure's pupil **Charles Bally** (1865–1947) who, in *Linguistique générale et linguistique française* (first published in 1932) writes about the possible influence of language on the thinking of its speakers: 'Si la pensée agit sur la langue, la langue façonne, elle aussi, la pensée à sa mesure' [*If thought acts on language, language in its turn shapes thought according to its measure*] (Bally 1950: 15, cf. Werlen

1987: 96). By comparing French and German with regard to the fixation of word order, inflexion, word formation (determinant and determinatum), rhythm, and other parameters, Bally arrives at certain tendencies concerning the ways French and German express reality: 'le français tend insensiblement vers le signe simple, l'allemand vers le signe complexe' [*French has a tendency towards simple signs, German towards complex ones*]. As a result, French presents objects and processes 'comme des faits accomplis' [*as finished facts*], while German shows them in their development. French is a static language, German a dynamic one (cf. Bally 1950: 196). French tends to render messages accurately with a minimum of encoding and decoding effort on the part of the speaker and hearer, whereas German is a language of reflexion which offers hearers different ways of interpreting what is communicated.

Bally here moves in the direction of language stereotyping – a tradition which in the twentieth century flourished for a time and was continued by a certain school of Contrastive Linguistics. One representative of this, Mario Wandruszka, takes up Bally's idea with the following formulation (1979: 42): 'Die Vollkommenheit des Französischen besteht darin, einen Gedanken auf die klarste und kürzeste Weise ausdrücken zu können, die des Deutschen darin, ihn in seiner Vielgestaltigkeit hinzustellen' [*The perfection of French consists in expressing a thought in the clearest and shortest way, that of German in presenting it in its diversity*]. A less ideological and more functional stereotyping is present in another approach to Contrastive Linguistics initiated by John Hawkins in the 1980s (*A Comparative Typology of English and German. Unifying the Contrasts*, 1986), whose comparison of different languages stops at the typological level.

Another structuralist who links language with thought is the Danish linguist (and founder of Glossematics) **Louis Hjelmslev** (1899–1965), who takes up the Saussurean idea of the amorphous mass of thought which is structured by language: 'Each language lays down its own boundaries within the amorphous "thought-mass" and stresses different factors in it in different arrangements, puts the centers of gravity in different places and gives them different emphases' (quoted from Werlen 1987: 100). Hjelmslev uses the example of the colour spectrum to show how each language structures the world differently (1969: 53) and 'arbitrarily sets its boundaries' on extralinguistic fact.

In May and June of 1923, the Polish linguist **Jan Baudouin de Courtenay** (1845–1929) gave three lectures in Copenhagen, which were published in 1929 under the title 'Einfluss der Sprache auf Weltanschauung und Stimmung' (*Influence of language on world-view and mood*). The lectures, available in Joachim Mugdan's edition of Baudouin's German essays (Baudouin de Courtenay 1984), address a number of topics on ways in which language (and different languages in their different ways) has an influence on how humans understand the world and behave in it and what kind of creativity they show as a result of linguistic phenomena. Baudouin begins by making language responsible for human *megalomania*, which makes humans think of themselves as the masters of all living beings – a phenomenon which was later called the 'anthropocentrism' of language. Then (1984: 219) he claims that speech – even if pure nonsense – can create in us a certain mood (heroic, pathetic, etc.) and that certain features of the different language systems have an influence on the world-view of their speakers.

Baudouin (1984: 222–226) mentions the following phenomena which may have such an impact:

- forms of address (*tu* vs. *vous* as opposed to just *you*);
- inflexion vs. agglutination: agglutination favours sober and logical thinking, since each ending has only one meaning;
- phenomena of word formation (diminutives and augmentatives, adjective comparison and numerals may contribute to 'quantitative thinking');
- writing systems strengthen national identities (1984: 235);
- grammatical gender (1984: 253–268).

Baudouin's ideas about the influence of grammatical gender on ways of thinking seem particularly speculative (as he himself stresses in several places) but they are not without a certain weird charm: the author (who was 77 when he gave the lectures) speaks of a 'sexualization' of the brain through grammatical gender, which supports the creative power in scholarship, literature and art (1984: 257) – for instance through the poetic personification of 'war', 'sun', 'moon', 'death', etc. which is facilitated through grammatical gender (1984: 262, 266). In Baudouin's view, however, grammatical gender is at the same time a blessing and a curse, since the sexualization of our thinking also leads to a radicalization of attitudes and thus may even be the cause of violence (1984: 268).

5.3   The Anthropological Approach: Franz Boas and Edward Sapir

From the study of native American languages, Humboldt posited the idea of different conceptualizations of reality in different languages. Almost a hundred years after Humboldt, the representatives of American anthropology took the same starting point and arrived at ideas similar to those of Humboldt. In several ways, however, they surpassed Humboldt: they used the results of their own field work, and they also went much further than Humboldt in their radical beliefs and conclusions.

One such figure, who was 'both confirming and denying his filiation to the Humboldtian stream in linguistics' (Leavitt 2006: 57), was **Franz Boas** (1858–1942). In 1883, Boas embarked on a research project about the Inuit and spent a year on Baffin Land to study them (Weiler 1997: 20). In 1886, 1888, 1889 and 1890 Boas took field trips to British Columbia where he collected myths and legends from the native American tribes there, which he published first in a German periodical, later in a book (1895) with the title *Indianische Sagen von der Nord-Pacifischen Küste Amerikas* (now available in an English translation as *Indian Myths and Legends from the North Pacific Coast of America*, Boas 2002). While collecting the legends, Boas came to the conclusion that 'there is no fundamental difference in the ways of thinking of primitive and civilized man' (1938: v, preface; earlier in the same preface, he puts 'primitive' in inverted commas). He also found that each culture is different, has its own principles and should not be evaluated or described in terms of another culture. There are no absolute standards for cultures and no yardsticks by which one culture can be judged as superior to another. Since 'the value which we attribute to our own civilization is due to the fact that we participate in this civilization', anthropological research may serve to teach us more tolerance and a higher evaluation of other cultures than commonly admitted (Boas 1938: 225).

Boas did not fail to note differences in the languages of the various tribes he visited, and even more specifically between these languages on the one hand and Western European ones on the other. Indeed, he described a number of American languages in his *Handbook of American Indian Languages* (1911), but found that many Western ideas could not be expressed in native American languages because there was no need to express them:

> It seems very questionable in how far the restriction of the use of certain grammatical forms can really be conceived as a hindrance to the formulation of generalized ideas. It seems much more likely that the lack of these forms is due to the lack of their need. (Boas 1938: 216)

Boas, who is sometimes thought to be the originator of Whorfian determinism, does not express anywhere that language shapes thought or that culture is dependent on language. He gives several examples of almost the opposite view, viz. that the possibilities of a language are determined by the needs of the culture in which it is used. The most prominent examples of this are abstract terms and numbers:

> As is well known, languages exist in which the numerals do not exceed three or four. It has been inferred from this that the people speaking these languages are not capable of forming the concept of higher numbers. I think this interpretation of the existing conditions is quite erroneous. People like the South American Indians (among whom these defective numeral systems are found), or like the Eskimo (whose old system of numbers probably did not exceed ten), are presumably not in need of higher numerical expressions, because there are not many objects that they have to count. On the other hand, just as soon as these same people find themselves in contact with civilization, and when they acquire standards of value that have to be counted, they adopt with perfect ease higher numerals from other languages, and develop a more or less perfect system of counting [...] In short, there is no proof that the lack of the use of numerals

> is in any way connected with the inability to form the concepts of higher numbers when needed. (Boas 1938: 218–219)

Clearly Boas is of the opinion that cultural requirements determine ways of thought and consequently shape linguistic structures, not the other way round. His 'cultural relativism' is not at the same time a linguistic relativism. Language adapts to culture, not culture to language, as the following seminal sentence shows: 'It does not seem likely, therefore, that there is any direct relation between the culture of a tribe and the language they speak, except insofar as the form of the language will be moulded by the state of culture, but not insofar as a certain state of culture is conditioned by morphological traits of the language' (Boas 1938: 219). This idea of Boas has been called the 'principle of expressibility': every culture is capable of expressing whatever is necessary to be expressed (cf. Werlen 1989: 130).

Boas' *Handbook of American Indian Languages* (1911/2002) has an 80 page introduction about language in general. In this introduction, Boas concedes in a few places the possibility of language influencing culture and even suggests a relation of mutual interdependence, for example in the following passage: 'it is commonly assumed that the linguistic expression is a secondary reflex of the customs of the people; but the question is quite open in how far the one phenomenon is the primary one and the other the secondary one, and whether the customs of the people have not rather developed from the unconsciously developed terminology' (Boas 1911/2002: 73, cf. Werlen 1989: 131; see also Lucy 1992: 11–16).

It is rewarding to follow the thinking about language, thought and culture from Boas to Sapir and finally to Whorf. Boas' idea that language adapts to cultural change almost gradually (!) develops into the view that we all adjust to reality with the help of language. **Edward Sapir** (1884–1939) still follows Boas in denying any necessary connection between language, race and culture. But language gradually rises in stature, and in his book of 1921, *Language: an Introduction to the Study of Speech*, Sapir already writes as follows on the topic of language and thought:

> Language is but a garment! But what if language is not so much a garment as a prepared road or groove? It is, indeed, in the highest degree likely that language is an instrument originally put to uses lower than the conceptual plane and that thought arises as a refined interpretation of its content. The product grows, in other words, with the instrument, and thought may be no more conceivable, in its genesis and daily practice, without speech than is mathematical reasoning practicable without the lever of an appropriate mathematical symbolism. (Sapir 1921: 15)

Sapir's garment metaphor, in his further and later thinking, increasingly gives way to other metaphors, like the road or groove image. In one passage, the word is compared to a key and even a fetter: 'Not until we own the symbol do we feel that we hold a key to the immediate knowledge or understanding of the concept. Would we be so ready to die for "liberty", to struggle for "ideals", if the words themselves were not ringing within us? And the word, as we know, is not only a key; it may also be a fetter' (Sapir 1921: 17).

In an essay of 1929 ('The status of linguistics as a science') Sapir goes even further and speaks of human beings 'at the mercy of a particular language which has become the medium of expression for their society'. Language is not just a medium for communication or reflection, but '[t]he fact of the matter is that the "real world" is to a very large extent built upon the language habits of the group. No two languages are ever sufficiently similar to be considered as representing the same social reality' (Sapir 1929: 162; for a discussion of this, see Leavitt 2006: 62–63 and Lucy 1992: 17–23).

According to Lucy (1996 and 2000), the influence of language on thought can occur in three ways, viz. on the semiotic, the structural, and the functional level:

> The first, or semiotic, level concerns how speaking any natural language at all may influence thinking. The question is whether having a code with a symbolic component (versus one confined to iconic-indexical elements) transforms thinking in certain ways. … The second, or structural level concerns how speaking one or more particular natural languages (e.g. Hopi versus English) may influence thinking. The question is whether quite different morphosyntactic configurations of meaning affect some aspects of thinking about reality [...] This has been the level traditionally associated with the term *linguistic relativity* [...] The third, or functional level concerns whether using language in a particular way (e.g. schooled, scientific) may influence thinking. (Lucy 2000: ix)

Lucy also makes a distinction between the idea that '(1) language embodies *an interpretation* of reality and (2) language can *influence* thought about that reality' (2000: x). Our pattern of thinking may have to do 'with immediate perception and attention, with personal and social-cultural systems and classification, inference, and memory, or with aesthetic judgment and creativity' (2000: x). This distinction will occupy us again in the context of strong and weak claims of the Whorfian hypothesis.

In contrast to Boas and Sapir, Ruth Benedict, a pupil of Sapir's, describes cultures without even mentioning language. In her well-known book *Patterns of Culture* (1959) the word *language* hardly occurs.

5.4 Benjamin Lee Whorf (1897–1941)

The main representative of linguistic determinism and relativism is of course Benjamin Lee Whorf, who from his work as a chemical engineer for the Hartford Insurance Company was inspired to assume a decisive influence of language (more precisely:

of the naming of certain events and phenomena through language) on thought and indirectly on behaviour (cf. Lucy 1992: 25–68).

Whorf first met Sapir at a conference in 1928 and from about 1931 attended Sapir's classes at Yale (cf. P. Lee 1996: 9–11). Though he was accepted into the PhD programme, he never completed the degree; but he remained part of the circle around Sapir and additionally was in touch with America's leading linguists, such as Franz Boas, Leonard Bloomfield, George L. Trager and Charles F. Hockett. Interestingly, he corresponded with Nikolaj Trubetzkoy, who wrote to him to request some of his offprints (cf. Lee 1996: 12). He never had a university post in linguistics (though he briefly taught anthropology at Yale in 1937–1938, cf. Carroll 1956: 16), but worked for the Hartford Insurance Company as a Special Agent (1928) and finally as their Assistant Secretary (1940) until his early death in 1941. Eighty-nine items are listed in Penny Lee's (1996) bibliography of Whorf's writings, many of them, however, letters to other linguists including Boas, Sapir and Trubetzkoy (this letter is dated 17 June 1937). Whorf's most important writings were collected by John B. Carroll and edited in 1956, with the title *Language, Thought, and Reality. Selected Writings by Benjamin Lee Whorf.*

This publication contains 18 articles by Whorf, among them one entitled 'The relations of habitual thought and behaviour to language' (1956: 134–159), in which Whorf most lucidly contrasts the ways of thinking of Western cultures (called SAE by Whorf – for Standard Average European) with the Hopi culture. However, a particularly interesting part of this article is the opening section, in which Whorf shows how his work for a fire insurance company led him to see the connection between language, thought and behaviour.

> I came in touch with an aspect of this problem before I had studied under Dr Sapir, and in a field usually considered remote from linguistics. It was in the course of my professional work for a fire insurance company, in which I undertook the task of analyzing many hundreds of reports of circumstances surrounding the start of fires, and in some cases, of explosions ... in due course it became evident that not only a physical situation *qua* physics, but the meaning of that situation to people, was sometimes a factor, through the behavior of the people, in the start of a fire. And this factor of meaning was clearest when it was a LINGUISTIC MEANING, residing in the name or the linguistic description commonly applied to the situation. (Whorf 1956: 135, emphasis by Whorf)

Whorf then narrates seven events where the description of a situation, in other words, the language used for a fact, was responsible for behavior which led to the breaking out of a fire. The most frequently quoted of these fire stories is the following:

> Thus, around a storage of what are called 'gasoline drums', behavior will tend to a certain type, that is, great care will be exercised; while around a storage of what are called 'empty gasoline drums' it will tend to be different – careless, with little repression

of smoking or of tossing cigarette stubs about. Yet the 'empty' drums are perhaps the more dangerous, since they contain explosive vapor. Physically the situation is hazardous, but the linguistic analysis according to regular analogy must employ the word 'empty', which inevitably suggests lack of hazard. (Whorf 1956: 135)

In another case metal stills were insulated with what was called 'spun limestone', where the linguistic element *-stone* made people think the material was not combustible, which, however, 'to everyone's great surprise burnt vigorously'. In further cases the naming 'pool of water' (a pool which emitted gases) and 'scrap lead' (which however contained paraffin paper) misled workmen to overlook the danger and act carelessly so that fires broke out (cf. Whorf 1956: 136 f.). In all these cases, Whorf concedes, it was individual words and phrases which led to certain ways of thinking and consequently to certain behaviour. However, it is also facts of the *grammar* of a language which are particularly influential on the way we experience the world, and it is here that Whorf's comparison between the Hopi language and what he calls the SAE languages starts.

The best-known points of this comparison are the following (Whorf 1956: 139–159; see also the section 'Languages and World views' in Taylor 1976: 293–306, and Lee 1996: 27–34).

Measuring and experiencing time

The SAE languages count time in the same way as they count concrete objects. 'Ten days' is equally possible as 'ten people'. Consequently, SAE speakers think they can experience ten days as a span of time, although in reality one can only experience one day at a given point in time. 'A "length of time" is envisioned as a row of similar units, as a row of bottles' (Whorf 1956: 140). In the Hopi language, cardinal numbers are only used for concrete objects, and not, for instance, for time. 'They stayed ten days' in Hopi would be 'they stayed until the eleventh day'. Consequently, Hopi people do not experience the span of time, but think only of events which happen later than others.

Nouns expressing quantity

SAE languages have 'uncountable' nouns for substances, e.g. *water, milk, wood, granite, sand, flour, meat.* If distinct quantities are named, constructions like *glass of water, bag of flour, bottle of beer,* etc. have to be used. Hopi does not have 'a formal subclass of mass nouns' (1956: 141). All nouns denoting materials imply a certain amount of the material. 'Water' does not mean 'the substance water', but a certain quantity of water. In the Hopi language, 'a water' could mean 'a glass of water', 'a meat' would mean 'a piece of meat'. Shapeless unmeasurable quantities are not referred to with nouns, but with verbs and other symbols. This is the difference referred to by Halliday (2001: 194) when he criticizes the grammar of SAE languages for its treatment of names for resources: 'Our grammar (though not the grammar of human language as such) construes air and water and soil, and also coal and iron and oil, as "unbounded" – that is as existing without limit. In the horizons of the first farmers, and the first miners, they did. We know that such resources are finite.' (See Chapter 8.2 below.)

Temporal forms of verbs

'The three-tense system of SAE verbs colors all our thinking about time' (1956: 143). We see time as a row with three entities: past, present and future. The Hopi language does not have tenses, but 'validity forms ("assertions"), aspects and clause-linkage forms (modes), that yield even greater precision of speech' (1956: 144). The validity form corresponding to our past or present is the report, that corresponding to our future the expectation. Hopi verb forms do not lead to an 'objectification' of time and thus not to the measuring of time. A Hopi physics would thus be totally different from our Western physics.

Metaphors for duration, intensity, and tendency

SAE languages express duration with the help of metaphors which we hardly recognize as such, e.g. *long, short, great, much, quick, slow.* Thus we think of duration as of a physical body. The same is true of other non-spatial things: 'I "grasp" the "thread" of another's argument, but if its "level" is "over my head" my attention may "wander" and "lose touch" with the "drift" of it' (1956: 146). In Hopi, there is a striking absence of such metaphors. 'Hopi has abundant conjugational and lexical means of expressing duration, intensity and tendency directly as such' (1956: 146), and there is no need for space metaphors. Hopi, with its large number of words denoting only duration, intensity and tendency, may become 'abstract almost beyond our power to follow' (1956: 147).

Synaesthesia (Whorf 1956: 155 f.)

Using expressions for one of the senses to express another is common in SAE languages. 'Thus we speak of "tones" of color, a gray "monotone", a "loud" necktie, a "taste" in dress: all spacial metaphors in reverse. Now European art is distinctive in the way it seeks deliberately to play with synaesthesia.' Music takes ideas from painting and vice versa. 'The European theater and opera seek a synthesis of many arts' (1956: 156). It may be possible that it is synaesthesia which has produced various forms of Western art. Hopi has games, races and dancing, but has not developed the same sophisticated system of art forms.

Quite generally, Whorf claims that language differences do not just affect thinking in individual events, but have a great influence on the 'model of the universe' of a culture (1956: 57–64), on philosophy, art, inventions, 'industry, trade, and scholastic and scientific thought' (1956: 157). Western science and philosophy were greatly influenced by the metaphors (and other language patterns) of Latin (1956: 156 f.).

It has sometimes been claimed that Whorf did not study the Hopi language himself. This is not entirely true. Here is what he himself has to say about this:

> The writer's studies have been made over several years with Mr Ernest Naquayouma, a Hopi of Toreva long resident in New York City, with the aid of funds supplied by the Committee on native American languages [...], checked by a field trip to Toreva and the other dialect regions made with his own funds. He wishes to express his thanks to the Committee, and to Mr Naquayouma, to whose excellence as an informant he is much indebted. (Whorf 1971: 158)

George Lakoff, in *Women, Fire, and Dangerous Things* (1987: 304–337) discusses Whorf at some length and asks the question of the link between thought and action:

> The importance of relativism comes out most clearly in the issue of its effect on action. Presumably, the way we think has a lot to do with the way we act. But exactly what is the connection? Not just any conceptual difference will necessarily affect actions. What kinds of conceptual differences will affect what kinds of actions? Are actions that we take to be natural and normal actually a product of the conceptual system we happened to grow up with? (1987: 325)

Lakoff shows how the notion of languages 'cutting up' the world in different ways is itself a metaphor with which the world is compared to some kind of loose material, and language to a knife or other cutting instrument, a comparison which he also found in Whorf's writings:

> Part of [Whorf's] romance with the Hopi language was that he thought it was superior because he saw it as making fine distinctions that English did not make – distinctions that enabled it to fit the objective world better. Hopi was for Whorf 'a rapier' to the 'blunt instrument' of English. (Lakoff 1987: 325)

That the categories established by our language may help us to understand the world was shown in a number of experiments with speakers of different languages in which different distinctions are made (e.g. concerning the colour spectrum). One of these experiments was carried out by Kay and Kempton (see Lakoff 1987: 332 f.), another one in the 1930s by L. Carmichael *et al.* (see Insup Taylor 1976: 285 f.): a drawing showing two circles linked by a line was shown to a number of informants, who had to reproduce the drawing after a time. Those informants with whom the label 'eyeglasses' had been used showed a decisive tendency to reproduce the drawing with the line as a slight curve and the circles as ovals; while other informants to whom the label 'dumbbells' had been given reproduced the drawing with a straight double line between the circles (see Taylor 1976: 286). The linguistic label determined the recollection of the drawing.

5.5   Critique of Whorf

Whorf's linguistic relativism was criticized as too radical by a number of authors. One of these critics is Einar Haugen, who (1977: 19) speaks of 'the Cult of Relativity' and of 'Whorf's one-sided view of the thought-language relationship', which he does not even see as original, since it can be traced back to Vico, Hamann, Herder, Fichte and von Humboldt (cf. 1977: 19 f.). Haugen suggests testing the hypothesis with bilinguals, 'who can personally testify to the differential effect of the "world view" imposed by different languages, at least if their use of them includes actual intimate experience with monolingual speakers of each language' (1977: 23 f.). The evidence from bilinguals discussed by Haugen (1977: 24–26) is divided: on the one hand there are examples such as the Austrian born anthropologist Robert H. Lowie, who speaks of altering one's personality when speaking another language and the French-born American author Julian Green, who speaks of becoming another person when writing in English; on the other hand, the German-Italian bilingual linguist Theodor W. Elwert and Haugen himself (Norwegian-English) contend that speaking and thinking in another language does not make one a different person: 'But one does adopt a different set of expectations. In formulating some ideas one may feel that one language facilitates the formulation while another hinders it and forces a rather different formulation. Each language has its shortcuts and its circumlocutions. But these have nothing to do with the grammar in the usual sense: phonology, morphology, syntax' (Haugen 1977: 25). As an example Haugen adduces the definite article in Norwegian and English:

> [T]he definite article is not the same in Norwegian as in English, whether phonologically, morphologically, or semantically. But to claim from this that Norwegians 'think' differently with respect to the article is unwarranted [...] For one's 'world view' it has no more significance than has the mortar that joins the bricks in a wall for the thinking of those who live in the house. (1977: 25 f.)

Most authors who write about the influence of language on thought today profess that they adopt only the weak claim of the Whorfian hypothesis (see below).

Other critics of the Sapir-Whorf-hypothesis come from the school of Chomsky. The best-known of them is Steven Pinker, who in his chapter 'Mentalese' from his book *The Language Instinct* (1994: 59–67) writes a sharp and entertaining refutation of Whorf's ideas – a refutation based on the principle that thought is separate from language:

> The idea that thought is the same thing as language is an example of what can be called a conventional absurdity: a statement that goes against all common sense but that everyone believes because they dimly recall having heard it somewhere and because it is so pregnant with implications. (Pinker 1994: 57)

Pinker (1994: 59 f.) quotes the following passage from Whorf's essay 'Science and Linguistics' (1956: 213 f.) and asks the question how Whorf was led to adopt this radical position:

> We dissect nature along lines laid down by our native languages. The categories and types that we isolate from the world of phenomena we do not find there because they stare every observer in the face: on the contrary, the world is presented in a kaleidoscopic flux of impressions which has to be organized by our minds – and this means largely by the linguistic system of our minds. We cut nature up, organize it into concepts, and ascribe significances as we do, largely because we are parties to an agreement to organize it in this way – an agreement that holds throughout our speech community and is codified in the patterns of our language. The agreement is, of course, an implicit and unstated one, *but its terms are absolutely obligatory;* we cannot talk at all except by subscribing to the organization and classification of data which the agreement decrees. (Emphasis by Whorf.)

Pinker then dissects Whorf's story of the workman who caused a fire by thinking that certain gasoline drums were 'empty' (see the first example discussed above) in the following (inimitable) way:

> The hapless worker, his conception of reality molded by his linguistic categories, did not distinguish between the 'drained' and 'inert' senses [of *empty*], hence, flick … boom! But wait. Gasoline vapor is invisible. A drum with nothing but vapor in it looks just like a drum with nothing in it at all. Surely this walking catastrophe was fooled by his eyes, not by the English language. (Pinker 1994: 60)

In the same way, Pinker refutes the claim that the colour words of our language determine the way we 'see' (and divide up) the colour spectrum. Pinker's conclusion: 'the way we see colours determines how we learn words for them, not vice versa' (1994: 63). Similarly, Pinker dismantles Whorf's view that the Hopi – because of their language – had no notion of the transition of time, but rather focused on psychological distinctions between the presently known, the mythical and the conjecturally distant. Pinker writes:

> Perhaps the Hopi are not as oblivious to time as Whorf made them out to be. In his extensive study, the anthropologist Ekkehart Malotki […] also showed that Hopi speech contains tense, metaphors for time, units of time (including days, numbers of days, parts of the day, yesterday and tomorrow, days of the week, weeks, months, lunar phases, seasons, and the year). (1994: 63)

Summing up, Pinker calls Whorf's ideas 'outlandish claims' (*ibid.*) and compares Whorfianism to 'the Great Eskimo Vocabulary Hoax', the much publicized idea that Yupik and Inuit-Inupiaq languages have dozens, even hundreds of word for snow – a myth which originated with Boas and was continued by Whorf (see Pinker 1994: 64 f.).

5.6   Linguistic Relativity and Linguistic Determinism

> An explicitly Einsteinian use of the term 'relativity' in relation to language is first found
> in Sapir. (The phrase 'linguistic relativity' comes into Whorf's currently accessible
> writings only eighteen months before his death.) (Lee 1996: xviii)

The Sapir-Whorf-Hypothesis developed two branches in the 1950s, which became
known as the strong and the weak hypothesis or claim (Slobin 1971: 122). The
strong hypothesis is sometimes called 'linguistic determinism', the weak one 'linguistic
relativity' (though the two pairs are not totally correspondent). The 'weak' version
claims only 'that habitual ways of speaking influence but do not determine thought
or knowing' (McCormack 1977: 5). A key issue in this version is 'ease of codability':
experiments have shown that colours for which a linguistic label is readily at hand
are more easily remembered than 'unworded' colours. What is easy to code is more
readily remembered (Agar 1994: 19–71).

Penn (1972) even speaks of 'two Whorf hypotheses', of which one claims that
'language determines thought', the other, milder one that 'language influences thought'
(Penn 1972: 13). According to Penn (1972: 28 f.), Humboldt and Sapir embraced the
extreme hypothesis which identifies language with thought, while Whorf 'phrased
his hypothesis somewhat less strongly, using qualifying adverbs like "largely" to
soften the assertion' (1972: 29). Empirical evidence seems to support only the weak
claim (Penn 1972: 32–39).

In the last chapter of his book *Sprache, Mensch und Welt*, Werlen (1989)
discusses current approaches to Whorf in which, among others, the following
questions are posed:

- To what extent is Wittgenstein's position one of linguistic relativity? (1989:
  192–200).
- Do speakers of Chinese support Whorfian relativism, particularly with regard
  to logical thinking (cf. Gipper 1972)? Does ideographic writing have an influence
  on thought different from alphabetic writing?
- Does the existence of sexist elements in a language (habitual generic *he*)
  create a tendency to sexist thinking? (Hamilton 1985).

Among the authors whose views on Whorfian relativism are discussed by Werlen
(1989: 183–207) are Dell Hymes, Joshua Fishman, Helmut Gipper, Adam Schaff,
Alfred H. Bloom, Ken Hale and many others.

Sapir's and Whorf's ideas have more recently been interpreted as a kind of
Constructivism. Devitt and Sterelny (1999: 249) see the Kantian idea 'of the known
world being partly created by an act of human imposition' expressed in the writings
of Sapir and Whorf. Increasingly, it seems, Sapir and Whorf are not just understood
on the linguistic level, as having said our language determines our experience of the
world – but rather on the philosophical (meta-)level as having asserted that our

theories about how to see the world are determined by our language (cf. Devitt and Sterelny 1999: 251). We thus arrive at a **meta-relativism**, viz. the view that all scientific thinking, and with this all thinking about the role of language in the world, is relative to our language.

The literature about linguistic determinism and relativism is voluminous and still growing. The debate about Whorf has by no means come to an end. Further critical comments on Whorf's ideas can be found in the works of Joshua Fishman (e.g. 1991, see also the editors' introduction to Cooper and Spolsky eds. 1991) and in many articles such as (to pick two examples) I. M. Schlesinger's 'The wax and wane of Whorfian views' (1991) and John Macnamara's 'Linguistic Relativity Revisited' (1991). A convincing empirical method to obtain more data and plausible results is still a desideratum.

6. The 'Linguistic Seduction' of Thought (Bacon, Locke, Berkeley, Hume; Mauthner, Kainz): the Harmful Impact of Language

Denn eben wo Begriffe fehlen
Da stellt ein Wort zur rechten Zeit sich ein.
Mit Worten lässt sich trefflich streiten,
Mit Worten ein System bereiten,
An Worte lässt sich trefflich glauben,
Von einem Wort lässt sich kein Jota rauben.

Goethe, *Faust*, Schülerszene
(quoted by Mauthner 1921/ I,137)

In some of Whorf's initial examples the topic of language misleading thought and thus resulting in the wrong action is addressed (see Chapter 5.4 above: the workman and the 'empty' gasoline drums). Ever since Antiquity, one group of scholars has approached the topic of the impact of language on thought from the **negative side** with the emphasis on the 'misleading' or in some other way harmful influence of language on our thinking and acting. The 'Sprachverführung des Denkens' [*linguistic seduction of thought*], as it was termed by Friedrich Kainz, has been a recurring theme in philosophy ever since the time of the Ancient Greek philosophers.

Perhaps the first 'critic of language' was the Pre-Socratic philosopher Parmenides (born ca. 513 BCE), who complained that words such as *developing* and *disappearing* make us believe that the processes designated by them exist and 'are true'. Socrates, Plato and Aristotle criticized the language of the Sophists (cf. Kainz 1972: 9). Thucydides, writing around 400 BCE, gives examples of the misleading use of language and the twisting of words during civil unrest on the island of Kerkyra (see Chapter 3.2 above).

The Romans continued this political critique of language: we find critical pronouncements in the works of Cicero, Varro and Quintilianus. The historian Tacitus notes the strategic use of dazzling words such as *freedom* when dominance and the subjugation of others are intended: no one, Tacitus claims, has as yet striven for dominance over others without using the word *freedom* (cf. Kainz 1972: 404).

6.1   British Empiricism

> Nearly everyone who wrote on language during the eighteenth century was concerned with its shortcomings [...] The inadequacies of language were attributed to two causes: human abuse of language which made it more and more inaccurate, and the inherent shortcomings which rendered it incapable of ever reproducing exactly the processes of the mind. (Juliard 1970: 52 f.)

British Empiricism is the ancestor of all modern critique of language. The Empiricists were concerned with exploring the world 'empirically', but they all adopted a critical attitude towards the sign system language which pretends to assist in this empirical investigation. The Empiricists were '**sceptical**' of language and '**pessimistic**' about it. The best-known manifestation of this scepticism is perhaps Francis Bacon's theory of idols (particularly his critique of the *idola fori*), in which the critique of language holds an important position (see below). Apart from Bacon, Kainz (1972: 9 f.) mentions the following philosophers who addressed the topic of the 'linguistic seduction' of thought: John Locke, George Berkeley, David Hume, Bertrand Russell, Alfred J. Ayer, George E. Moore, John L. Austin, Louis Rougier, Moritz Schlick, Rudolf Carnap, Ludwig Wittgenstein and Fritz Mauthner.

Interestingly, the greatest German philosopher is not among the critics of language:

> Der 'alleszermalmende' Kant freilich hat mit seiner Kritik vor der Sprache halt gemacht: ein Versäumnis, das bereits Herder nachdrücklich und mit prinzipiellen Einwänden gerügt hat. (Kainz 1972: 9)

> *Kant's crushing criticism stopped short of language – an omission which was already reprimanded by Herder emphatically and with principal objections.*

Generally, it can be observed that with a few exceptions the critics of language criticize either language in general (Saussure's *langage*) or, without being aware of it, their own specific mother tongue. Very few of these thinkers have considered the **added value** that different languages impart and the wealth of different ways of thinking that the (still existing) **language diversity** on this earth yields. Philosophers (and linguists!) are rarely multilingual, thus the **synergetic effects** for thought provided by the possibilities of languages from different language families have still to be explored by scholars.

Francis Bacon (1561–1626), in his *Advancement of Learning* (written in 1605), establishes a theory of confutations, of which the 'confutations of images, or idols' are the most important, because they are 'the deepest fallacies of the human mind' (1900: 156). These 'idols' are imposed on our understanding in three ways (cf. *ibid.*):

1. by the general nature of mankind = *idola tribus* (idols of the tribe);
2. by the nature of each particular man = *idola specus* (idols of the den);
3. by words, or the nature of communication = *idola fori* (idols of the market).

A fourth type of idol is only mentioned in passing in this work by Bacon, viz. the idols of the theatre, 'being superinduced by false theories, or philosophies, and the perverted laws of demonstration' (Bacon 1900: 156). Later on, Bacon was to elaborate on the idols of the theatre.

As becomes clear, Bacon attributes great significance to the confutations which arise from words and communication (in modern terminology, from language). In *The Advancement of Learning* he even calls words those which 'give the greatest disturbance' (1900: 158). His main point here is that words 'divide things as the common people are capable of: but when a more acute understanding, or a more careful observation, would distinguish things better, words murmur against it' (*ibid.*). As a remedy he suggests a clear definition of words – although this again can be done only through words: 'the seducing incantation of names [...], their doing violence to the understanding' (*ibid.*) remains and would require a new and deeper remedy – which Bacon does not yet provide.

In his later work, the *Novum Organum* (originally 1620), (Book I, 38–62), Bacon returns to the idols and false notions which hinder our understanding, and he forewarns us against them (1900: 319). Among the now four idols (of the Tribe, the Den, the Market and the Theatre), he again attributes the greatest power to those of the market. In Bacon's own words, the confusion created by words arises in the following way:

> The idols of the market are the most troublesome of all, those namely which have entwined themselves round the understanding from the associations of words and names. For men imagine that their reason governs words, whilst, in fact, words react upon their understanding; and this has rendered philosophy and the sciences sophistical and inactive. (1900: 324)

Again Bacon argues that the popular meaning of words often conflicts with their learned one; this causes many solemn disputes to end in controversies about words and names – a problem which can only partly be solved by clearer definition.

In his *Novum Organum*, Bacon is more specific about the nature of the trouble with words (1900: 324 f.). He mentions two kinds of illusions imposed on us by words:

1. Using words for things which do not exist [cf. below about Friedrich Kainz' 'word realism']. As examples Bacon gives *Fortune, primum mobile, the planetary orbits, the element of fire.* These 'fictions which owe their birth to futile and false theories' (1900: 325) should be removed when the theories become obsolete.
2. Using words for existing things, 'but confused, badly defined, and hastily and irregularly abstracted from things' (1900: 325). As an example of this kind of idol, Bacon uses the word *moist*, for which he lists eight meanings (e.g. *that*

> *which yields easily in every direction, that which is easily divided and dispersed, that which easily adheres to and wets another body*). When we now use the word *moist*, it may apply in one sense to flame, in another to powder, in another to glass, etc., 'so that it is quite clear that this notion is hastily abstracted from water only, and common ordinary liquors, without any due verification of it' (*ibid.*).

Related to the idols concerning words are the idols of the theatre which – on a higher level – are based on theories and philosophies 'founded on too narrow a basis of experiment and natural history' (1900: 326).

Bacon ends his discussion of idols with a general plea to do away with them, and he uses a remarkable simile in which people free from these idols are compared to children:

> All [idols] must be abjured and renounced with firm and solemn resolution, and the understanding must be completely freed and cleared of them, so that the access to the kingdom of man, which is founded on the sciences, may resemble that to the kingdom of heaven, where no admission is conceded except to children. (*Novum Organum* I 68; 1900: 331)

Book III ('On Words') of **John Locke's** (1632–1704) *Essay Concerning Human Understanding* (1690) deals with language. The most interesting chapters of this book from our point of view are those on the imperfection of words (ix) and on the abuses of words (x). Since the sounds of words are arbitrary, their meaning is 'doubtful and uncertain' (Locke 1947: 236). This is particularly true of complex ideas which are expressed with uncertainty and obscurity:

> Hence it comes to pass that men's names of very compound ideas, such as for the most part are moral words, have seldom in two different men the same precise signification; since one man's complex idea seldom agrees with another's, and often differs from his own – from that which he had yesterday, or will have to-morrow. (1947: 237)

Even words whose meaning is made up of simple ideas show this 'uncertainty' of meaning, such as the word *gold*:

> For, though in the substance of gold one satisfies himself with colour and weight, yet another thinks solubility in *aqua regia* as necessary to be joined with that colour in his idea of gold, as any one does its fusibility; others put into it ductility of fixedness, etc. Who of all these has established the right signification of the word gold? Or who shall be the judge to determine? (1947: 239)

In his chapter 'Of the abuses of words', Locke produces the first 'catalogue of abuses' (cf. Heringer 1982: 6), of which many were to follow. Locke lists six major '*wilful* faults and neglects which men are guilty of in this way of communication' (1947: 242, italics by Locke). These are the following:

1. Using words without clear and distinct ideas or without anything signified. '*Wisdom glory, grace,* etc. are words frequent enough in every man's mouth; but if a great many of those who use them should be asked what they mean by them, they would be at a stand, and not know what to answer' (1947: 243).
2. Inconstancy in the use of words.
3. Affected obscurity.
4. Taking words for things. 'To this abuse those men are most subject who most confine their thoughts to any one system, and give themselves up into a firm belief of the perfection of any received hypothesis' (1947: 243). Thus, the followers of Peripatetic Philosophy will believe 'the Ten Names under which are ranked the Ten Predicaments to be exactly conformable to the nature of things' (1947: 243 f.). [Taking words for things was also listed by Bacon as one of the idols; we will encounter it again as 'word realism' in the list by Friedrich Kainz.]
5. Using words for things which they do or can by no means signify.
6. Believing one's meaning to be always understood. The word *life* seems to contain no ambiguity or uncertainty; 'And yet if it comes in question whether a plant that lies ready formed in the seed have life; whether the embryo in an egg before incubation or a man in a swoon without sense or motion, be alive or no; it is easy to perceive that a clear, distinct, settled idea does not always accompany the use of so known a word as that of life is' (1947: 245).

In a short chapter (xi), Locke gives 'Remedies of the Foregoing Imperfections and Abuses' (1947: 246–251); among these he mentions using the same word always with the same meaning, using all words for ideas 'as near as may be to such ideas as common use has annexed them to' (1947: 247).

If this advice were adhered to, 'many of the books extant might be spared, many of the controversies in dispute would be at an end; several of those great volumes, swollen with ambiguous words [...] would shrink into a very narrow compass; and many of the philosophers' (to mention no other) as well as poets' works, might be contained in a nutshell' (1947: 251). Locke's discussion of the defects and abuses of words is treated more extensively by Formigari (2004: 107–113) and Harris and Taylor in the introduction to their chapter 'Locke on the imperfection of words' (eds. 1997: 126–138; see also Nerlich and Clarke 1996: 17–24).

George Berkeley's (1685–1753) *A Treatise Concerning the Principles of Human Knowledge* (1710), in its 'Introduction', has a section (XX) entitled 'Some of the ends of language'. In this, Berkeley speaks of four ends of language (n.d.: 107): (1) communicating ideas; (2) the raising of some passion; (3) the exciting to or deterring from an action; and (4) putting the mind in some particular disposition. Berkeley then advises 'Caution in the use of language' (XXI), particularly since 'words came to produce the doctrine of abstract ideas' (XIX). From believing (1) to be the only function of words, people conclude that they stand for abstract notions. The remedy Berkeley suggests is to think – as long as this is possible – without using words. The following passage from section XXI is quoted in full so as to show that Berkeley on the one hand acknowledges the work language does for us (particularly storing knowledge and making knowledge available for individuals), but on the other hand warns of the 'deception of words' (n.d.: 110; wording of the 1710 edition in square brackets):

> It cannot be denied that words are of excellent use; in that, by their means, all that stock of knowledge, which has been purchased by the joint labours of inquisitive men in all ages and nations, may be drawn into the view and made the possession of one single person. But at the same time it must be owned that most parts of knowledge have been strangely perplexed and darkened by the abuse of words, and general ways of speech wherein they are delivered [that it may almost be made a question whether language has contributed more to the hindrance or advancement of the sciences.] Since, therefore, words are so apt to impose on the understanding, [I am resolved in my inquiries to make as little use of them as possibly I can.] Whatever ideas I consider, I shall endeavour to take them bare and naked into my view, keeping out of my thoughts, so far as I am able, those names which long and constant use hath so strictly united with them.

By divesting himself of words, Berkeley hopes to avoid controversies 'purely verbal'; he also expresses his hope not to be caught in the 'fine and subtle net of abstract ideas' and, by thinking only in ideas, to prevent mistakes imposed by words. With the following fine metaphor of the *curtain of words* hiding the *tree of knowledge*, Berkeley concludes his advice concerning the avoidance of words:

> In vain do we extend our view into the heavens, and pry into the entrails of the earth; in vain do we consult the writings of learned men, and trace the dark footsteps of antiquity; we need only draw the curtain of words, to behold the fairest tree of knowledge, whose fruit is excellent and within the reach of our hand. (n.d.: 111)

Berkeley acknowledges, however, that drawing the curtain of words and thus achieving 'entire deliverance from the deception of words' (n.d.: 110) is a difficult task which one can hardly hope to fulfil. Since the 'union' between words and abstract ideas was 'so early begun, and confirmed by so long a habit' (*ibid.*), it will be difficult to dissolve it.

In his utopian novel *Gulliver's Travels*, Jonathan Swift makes fun of this advice to communicate without words. In Chapter 5 of Part III, he describes a 'scheme for entirely abolishing all Words whatsoever'. In the 'grand Academy of Lagado', the most learned and wise express themselves with the help of things only, which they carry around with them:

> I have often beheld two of those sages almost sinking under the weight of their packs, like pedlars among us, who when they met in the streets, would lay down their loads, open their sacks, and hold conversation for an hour together; then put up their implements, help each other to resume their burthens, and take their leave. (*Gulliver's Travels*, ed. by Robert A. Greenberg. New York: W. W. Norton, 1961, p. 158)

Like Locke and Berkeley, **David Hume** (1711–1776) complains that many philosophical controversies are merely about words (1902: 312):

> Nothing is more usual than for philosophers to encroach upon the province of grammarians; and to engage in disputes of words, while they imagine they are handling controversies of the deepest importance and concern.

Using as examples the words *virtues* vs *talents* and *vices* vs *defects*, Hume complains that the boundaries between their meanings are not fixed and that a precise definition cannot be given (1902: 313). (Hume, incidentally, is the only philosopher who speaks of 'English, or any other modern tongue', *ibid.*). However, Hume does not blame this on language alone, but rather on the lack of clarity of our concepts: 'But, secondly, it is no wonder that languages should not be very precise in marking the boundaries between virtues and talents, vices and defects; since there is so little distinction made in our internal estimation of them' (1902: 314). All in all, 'it is of greater consequence to attend to things than to verbal appellations' (1902: 322) – a piece of advice which is less radical than Berkeley's 'drawing the curtain of words', but which nevertheless presupposes the possibility of thinking and reasoning without the use of language.

Hume also criticizes the categories of cause and effect (cf. Kainz 1972: 9). All in all, his advice concerning the avoidance of words is less extreme than that of Berkeley.

A note about the position of the Empiricists versus that of twentieth-century philosophers

Nearly everything eighteenth-century British philosophers wrote on the subject of language was a critique of it. This stands in sharp contrast to the philosophers of the so-called 'linguistic turn' in the first half of the twentieth century, who saw in language a key to certain philosophical problems. Bertrand Russell wrote in his *Principles of Mathematics* (1903: 42) that the study of grammar might throw more light on philosophical questions than is generally supposed by philosophers (cf. Black 1967: 331). Jerrold Katz, too, defends the relevance of language and linguistics to the solution of philosophical problems. His thesis is that 'certain philosophical problems can be represented correctly as questions about the nature of language, and that, so presented, they can be solved on the basis of theoretical constructions that appear in linguistic theory' (Katz 1972: 340). Thus it is not so much *language* to which these philosophers turn as the *study* of language and *linguistic theory*.

6.2 Critique of Language by German Language Authors

Der wohl liebenswerteste Ahnherr eines bewußt sprachkritischen Philosophierens ist im deutschsprachigen Raum Georg Christoph Lichtenberg gewesen. (Heintel 1972: 102)

Arguably the most lovable ancestor of a philosophizing consciously critical of language, in the German speaking area, was Georg Christoph Lichtenberg.

Beginning with **Lichtenberg** (1742–1799), a recurring theme of German '*Sprachkritik*' is that language is not 'logical' and therefore 'unphilosophical', a thought also expressed by Marty, but most radically by Mauthner. One of the tasks of philosophy is to point out the 'errors' contained in language.

Lichtenberg's critique of language, expressed in short witty aphorisms, is chiefly contained in his *Sudelbücher* ('scribbled books'), which he wrote from 1742 to 1799 and which fill several volumes. One of these aphorisms reads: 'Unsere ganze Philosophie ist Berichtigung des Sprachgebrauchs' [*The whole of our philosophy is correction of language use*] (*Sudelbücher* II, 297 – quoted from Heringer 1982: 8). In this and other observations, Lichtenberg was strongly influenced by the Empiricists.

The climax of a German language '*Sprachkritik*', however, came with a Swiss born and two Austrian born thinkers, Marty, Mauthner and Kainz.

Anton Marty (1847–1914) was born in Switzerland, but it was in Würzburg that he became a pupil of Franz Brentano's, one of the forefathers of phenomenology. Later he was professor of philosophy in Prague. Most important for our topic of language impact is a short section in Marty's posthumously published writings, entitled 'Vom Nutzen und Schaden der Sprache für das Denken' [*Of the usefulness and harmfulness of language for thinking*] (1950: 79–85).

Here Marty acknowledges that language is important for thought because of the firm associations which have formed between thought and word (1950: 79). That word and thought intimately belong together is, however, something we believe only out of habit. Marty then lists four important ways how words can help thought (1950: 79–82):

1. Words help our memory (the most important point for Marty).
2. Words can be surrogates of thought. Example: large numbers (e.g. a hundred) which can be thought of only by employing the words for them.
3. Words can serve to recognize differences and similarities between ideas.
4. Words help children to form concepts. They teach children and grown-ups the classifications made by former generations. Without being formally taught, adolescents learn through language acquisition 'die ganze allgemeine Philosophie des Zeitalters' [*the whole general philosophy/culture of the age*] (1950: 82).

Of these four points, the first, described by Marty as the best-known and most beneficial influence, is perhaps the most original, which therefore may deserve comment. According to Marty, for many people word memory is more reliable than thought memory. Words also help us to dominate our thoughts and to grasp them firmly, since otherwise thoughts (particularly abstract ones) would tend to fade from our consciousness. By speaking words, but also by writing them, we can make words stay. Perhaps influenced by Kleist (see end of Chapter 4.1 above), Marty says that we frequently think 'pen in hand'; taking down our thoughts like this can be of great help in fixing and retaining an ordered train of thought (1950: 80).

As concerns the negative effects of language, Marty (1950: 82) calls language 'vielfach unlogisch und unphilosophisch' [*in many ways illogical and unphilosophical*] and lists five points which illustrate this:

1. Language frequently has two or more significations for the same idea (synonymy). This surplus of words can be a danger when we seek different ideas behind the synonyms (1950: 83). As examples Marty adduces *Raum* (space) and *Ort* (place) and certain classifications created by Kant which are only different in their words – thereby creating a great number of useless subtleties.
2. The opposite phenomenon is 'equivocation', where one sign (word or sentence) has different meanings. Language did not evolve according to a plan, thus errors may arise where one meaning of a words is confused with another one (examples: *Stoff* and *Form* – [material/stuff/cloth – form].
3. Words not defined and not understood may come to play an exorbitant role, so that 'ein törichter Wortkampf' (*a foolish fight with words*) may arise.
4. Popular classifications (in the language of the people) may cause confusions, and scholarship should 'emancipate' itself from them (examples: *Seehund* [seal, literally 'sea-dog'], which is not a kind of 'dog', *Walfisch* [whale-fish], which is not a kind of 'fish'). This point is reminiscent of Francis Bacon's complaint that ideas expressed in the vernacular are discussed using the same words in scholarship (one of the *idola fori* – see above, Chapter 6.1).
5. A supposedly essential link between language and thought is an illusion – such as when it is believed that a 'judgement' consists of subject and predicate like any sentence. According to Marty, W. Wundt's psychology of thought succumbs to this error.

As a resumé of his thoughts about language, Marty summarizes that language should not be the lodestar of our reasoning. Repeatedly he says that we have to 'emancipate ourselves' from language; we should be the free dominators of language, not its slaves.

Fritz Mauthner (1849–1923), born near Königgrätz (Bohemia, then part of the Austrian empire), wrote three volumes (amounting to more than 2000 pages, 1901–1902) on a critique of language. The first volume deals with language and psychology, the second one is concerned with linguistics, and the third is about grammar and logic. In his preface to the second edition (1906) he states the main idea of his volumes, viz. 'daß Welterkenntnis durch die Sprache unmöglich sei' [*Cognition of the world through language is impossible*] (1921: xi).

Interestingly, Mauthner, writing many years before Wittgenstein's *Tractatus*), uses the image of the ladder which has to be climbed by the critic of language, only to be destroyed after use (1921/I:1 f.):

Will ich emporklimmen in der Sprachkritik, die das wichtigste Geschäft der denkenden Menschheit ist, so muß ich die Sprache hinter mir und vor mir vernichten von Schritt zu Schritt, so muß ich jede Sprosse der Leiter zertrümmern, indem ich sie betrete.

If I wish to climb up in the critique of language, which is the most important business of thinking humans, I have to destroy language behind me and before me step by step; I have to crush every rung of the ladder by stepping on it.

(cf. Wittgenstein 1963: 6.54: 'er muss sozusagen die Leiter wegwerfen, nachdem er auf ihr hinaufgestiegen ist' [*he as it were has to throw away the ladder after he has climbed up on it*].)

For Mauthner, the 'invention' of language has brought few advantages to humanity. One of them is perhaps that words like *virtue* and *goodness* may induce people to be 'virtuous' and do 'good'. Another one is that language is a socially useful means of communication and a medium of artistic expression. But the disadvantages by far outweigh the advantages. Language is 'impertinent' (*frech*) and 'shamelessly' introduces concepts into our heads, the most impertinent one being Plato's 'idea', which is to blame for our word realism (1921/I:85). Other impertinent words and phrases coined by philosophers are 'category' (Aristotle), 'categorical imperative' (Kant), and 'the best of all possible worlds' (Leibniz).

For Mauthner, the most important error inherent in many philosophical systems is to assume that language in its **grammatical or logical categories** contains a 'congruent', i.e. true picture of reality (1921/II:21). That this is nonsense, according to Mauthner, is evident from the fact that different languages not only use different words and express different concepts, but also have different structures and systems of logic (1921/II:2).

Mauthner condemns word realism, word fetishism and word superstition (*Wortaberglaube*) and treats a number of linguistic phenomena as sources of such erroneous thought. Folk etymology (1921/II: 213–221) is one of them (some of his instances of this are well-known standard examples):

Friedhof < *vrithof* = fenced in yard, now interpreted as *Fried-hof* (peaceful yard);

Sündflut < *sinfluot* = universal flood, now interpreted as *Sünd-flut* (sin-flood);

Place-names like *Berlin*, which is wrongly interpreted as connected with bears.

A long chapter (II: 449-534) is devoted to metaphor whose importance became evident to Mauthner through reading Vico (II: 455 f., 479–485). He acknowledges that languages 'grow' chiefly through metaphor, but following Locke and Kant he criticizes metaphor as 'anthropocentric' [*sic!*]: our thinking (which is not possible without language) never arrives at a point where it can actually perceive reality, i.e. the things themselves, but always stops at images of reality which we believe to be real entities (example: cause and effect) (II: 476; see also Kainz 1972: 107). An even sharper critique of metaphor is expressed by Kainz (see below), together with a critique of negation and similar linguistic phenomena (Kainz 1972: 306–310).

One of Mauthner's points of critique which is not contained in other models of *Sprachkritik* and Scepticism deserves discussion, viz. the insight that **language is always behind the times** and never follows the developments of science and scholarship. Mauthner reminds us:

> daß die Kategorien unserer Sprache nicht mehr mit unserer gegenwärtigen Welterkenntnis zusammenstimmen, daß wir z.B., was die Physik als Bewegungen zu erkennen geglaubt hat, nach wie vor in Adjektiven und in Verben unterscheiden. (1921/I: 79)

> *that the categories of our language do not fit any more with our present knowledge of the world; for instance, what physics has recognized as movements is still distinguished through adjectives and verbs.*

At no time is language 'auf der Höhe der Zeit' [*up to date*] (1921/I: 79). We still speak of 'sunrise' and 'sunset', just as our railway trains still show the narrowness of the old horse-drawn stage coach. The philosopher's main task is to disentangle himself from the network of old categories, like a fisherman whose head has got caught in his own net (1921/I: 79).

In his second volume, Mauthner criticizes language philosophy and linguistics which he believes to be in a crisis (1921/II: 588) because it produces legends rather than facts (concerning the origin and the genealogy of languages). The fact that 'language' exists must be called into question anyway (compare this scepticism with what Vossler and Davidson have to say about the non-existence of 'language', see Appendix II). (It must be remembered, however, that Mauthner's work was written 15 years before Saussure's *Cours de linguistique générale* was published, and thus before dichotomies such as 'synchronic vs diachronic' and 'langue vs parole' were established.)

Mauthner's pessimism of language is best expressed in the following words which he wrote at the end of his first volume (1921/I: 713):

> Die Kritik an der Sprache muß Befreiung von der Sprache als höchstes Ziel der Selbstbefreiung lehren. Die Sprache wird zur Selbstkritik der Philosophie. Diese selbstkritische Philosophie wird durch ihre Resignation nicht geringer als die alten selbstgerechten Philosophien. Denn von der Sprache gilt wie von jedem anderen Märtyrer der Philosophie das tapfere Wort: Qui potest mori, non potest cogi.

> *Language criticism must teach liberation from language as the highest goal of self-liberation. Language turns into self-critique of philosophy. This self-critical philosophy is no less valuable than the old self-righteous philosophies. For about language, as about every martyr of philosophy, the courageous word is valid: He who can die cannot be forced to anything.*

Freeing oneself from language is the highest aim. Criticism of language becomes criticism of philosophy from inside. Language is thus like a martyr who dies but in his death makes his beliefs (= philosophy) live on.

Mauthner's influence on other critics of language was profound. Wittgenstein knew Mauthner's work, which is evident from the following remark in the *Tractatus* (1963: 4.0031): 'Alle Philosophie ist "Sprachkritik". (Aber nicht im Sinne Mauthners)' [*All philosophy is 'critique of language'. (But not in the sense of Mauthner)*]. A comparison between Mauthner's and Wittgenstein's critique of language can be found in Leinfellner's article of 1995 in her essay of 2000 'Fritz Mauthner's Sprachkritik', available online at http://ejournal.thing.at/Essay/leinels.html. The language critical passages in Ogden and Richards' *The Meaning of Meaning* (1923) owe a great deal to Mauthner. The authors even quote some of Mauthner's remarks about Aristotle, among them the following, which smacks of Whorfian ideas: 'If Aristotle had spoken Chinese or Dacotan, he would have had to adopt an entirely different Logic, or at any rate an entirely different theory of Categories' (1923: 35 fn. 1). Ogden and Richards, however, find Mauthner's critique of Aristotle's reverence for words exaggerated, since Aristotle, in *De Interpretatione*, 'insists that words are signs primarily of mental affections, and only secondarily of the things of which these are likenesses' (1923: 35).

Mauthner's scepticism had a strong impact on analytical philosophy (more about this can be found in the articles in Leinfellner and Schleichert eds 1995). Mauthner also influenced the critique of political language – through his friend Gustav Landauer (1870–1919), a political activist, anarchist and pacifist. Criticism of political language later developed into a separate branch of linguistics (see Heringer 1982), which found its modern manifestation in Critical Discourse Analysis (see Chapter 18 below).

6.3   Friedrich Kainz and the 'Linguistic Seduction of Thought'

The most comprehensive presentation of a post-Empiricist critique of language can be found in the work of the Austrian psychologist of language, Friedrich Kainz (1897–1977), particularly in his book *Über die Sprachverführung des Denkens* (1972). Kainz begins with a critique of philosophical language, which apodictically ('im Orakelton' 1972: 8) produces abstract pronouncements about the philosophical inadequacy and vagueness of verbal language, but misses out on providing the forms of this inadequacy, let alone giving satisfactory examples of it (cf. Kainz 1972: 8). Kainz's work is thus important both as a summary of language criticism and as a **critique of language criticism** (see also the 'General remarks on language and thought' in Chapter 5.1 above).

Kainz lists no fewer than 17 specific forms and types of possible seductions of thought through language, which all refer to structural elements which may lead to failures of thinking. Kainz stresses that his criticism of language concerns what Saussure called *langage*, i.e. the human ability to use language, which however manifests itself in specific languages, so that the seduction becomes tangible on the level of *langue*, i.e. in specific communication systems. Kainz does not consider the level of *parole*, i.e. concrete utterances and texts (see Part III of this volume).

Kainz's 17 forms of linguistic seduction can be summarized and condensed to yield the following list of seductions through language (cf. 1972: 20–24, Kainz's own numbering in brackets):

1. Word realism (*Wortrealismus*) – excessive faith in language, whose elements (words) are taken to correspond to entities in the real world, which are 'hypostatized' by the words. (1)
2. Incorrect bracketing of things/ideas in some instances; incorrect separation in others. (2, 3)
3. Synonyms: near-synonyms are taken to have identical meanings. (4)
4. Metaphor: the image is frequently taken to be reality (more on this below). (6)
5. Bacon's 'idola fori': the informational value of everyday expressions (which are frequently used carelessly and uncritically) is overrated, their accidental nature is overlooked in scholarly discourse. (7, 8)
6. Meaningless and contradictory statements clothed in grammatically correct sentences give the impression of making sense and expressing facts. (9, 10)
7. The word classes (particularly noun and verb) suggest forms of being which are not true to reality; the 'agent-action' system of Indo-European languages (subject–predicate) makes us interpret reality in a dualist way (cf. David Bohm's critique, Chapter 20.2 below), as does negation which suggests a polarity between *positive* and *negative*. (11)

8. Believing one's own language system to be the 'valid' one from which all other languages 'deviate'. (13)
9. Seductions through writing systems, through spelling and through associations with the body of the sounds. (12, 14)
10. Emotional associations of slogans (e.g. in proverbs, in advertising etc.); familiar expressions make us overlook contradictions and ambiguities. (15, 17)
11. Euphemism makes us see negative facts in a brighter light. (16)

Several of Kainz's types of seduction repeat the critique expressed earlier by the Empiricists (see above) and will therefore not be discussed in more detail. Only three of his 'seductions' (in our list nos. 4, 7 and 8) will be dealt with more fully in the following commentary.

Metaphor, according to Kainz (1972: 98–160), is seen by many as the main phenomenon deserving of criticism, but Kainz warns of overrating its seductive power. Many metaphors have lost their character as images, have become 'pale' and thus no longer mislead thought. Thus German *Kopf* is no longer associated with a drinking vessel (lat. *Cuppa*), nor is *Messer* with 'meat-sword' (*mat-sahs*). Following Leibniz and Nietzsche, Kainz sees the seductive power of metaphor (1) in the fact that (in contrast to the above examples) the dividing line between image donor and image carrier is not always clear; (2) the comparison (*eo ipso*) rests on similarity, not on sameness; and (3) in our tendency to use metaphors rather than the 'real names', in order to create aesthetic effects and rhetorical brilliance: as a result unwelcome ideas and unsuitable emotions are created which may mislead our judgement.

Following Karl Jaspers, Kainz draws attention to the metaphors used as technical terms in philosophy, which cannot always be avoided but should be used with care and caution. Specifically, he mentions Wittgenstein's term 'Sprachspiele' [*language games*] and Heidegger's metaphor 'Holzwege' [*woodways = wrong tracks*] (1972: 110).

Among the **grammatical categories**, the **word classes** (1972: 208–297) are particularly influential on our ways of thinking. Specifically the noun induces us to think of entities in terms of substances and objects. Thus actions like playing, dancing and changing, and qualities like broad, great, long, lazy[1] when nominalized are 'elevated' to the status of independent phenomena (*breadth, greatness, length, laziness,* but also *play* n., *dance* n., *change* n.). The category noun suggests that the entity expressed with it has being, 'exists' (1972: 210). Following Reiniger and Schlick, Kainz states that the presence of space and time in the category of the noun has led to erroneous speculation about the factuality of space and time.

Another word class which has an impact on thought is the (definite) **article**. Kainz reports conflicting views about the role of the article, which according to some authors has hindered the acquisition of knowledge, according to others has made thinking more precise. Similarly to the article, the **personal pronoun** – not normally expressed in Latin – has, in the modern languages, led to exaggerated subjectivism. Caesar's 'Veni, vidi, vici' suppresses the subject *ego*, although the role of this subject, viz. Caesar, was in reality a very active one. In contrast to this, Descartes, in his *Discours de la méthode*, writes 'je pense, donc je suis', which was translated into Latin (by E. de Courcelles) as 'Ego cogito, ergo sum, sive existo' – thereby violating the Latin language for the sake of expressing a modern subjectivism (cf. 1972: 235). The 'possessive adjectives', too, mislead our thoughts in the direction of assuming a real possessive relation: Thus, 'my wife'/'my husband' still induces many people to assume rights of possession over their spouse, while 'our country' for some people suggests certain rights concerning lost possessions (1972: 233, following G. Patzig).

Auxiliaries are also great seducers of thought, because some of them (*have, be, shall, will*) can also be used as full verbs with their own meaning. Particularly the verb *to be* is confusing because of its wealth of functions. 'Be' is frequently an auxiliary (constituting for instance the progressive form in English), sometimes a full verb ('to be, or not to be') meaning 'to exist', but most frequently the copula between a noun phrase and an adjective or another noun phrase ('Paris is the capital of France'). Confusing these different functions may lead to seduction of thought, for instance when the copula is thought to presuppose the existence of the subject – such as when 'God is merciful' is taken to imply 'God exists' (the 'ontological' proof of God) (cf. 1972: 254 ff.). The same argument is used, incidentally, by Gilbert Ryle, who writes (1967: 87):

> Since Kant, we have, most of us, paid lip service to the doctrine that 'existence is not a quality' and so we have rejected the pseudo-implication of the ontological argument: 'God is perfect, being perfect entails being existent [...]: God exists.'

Other word classes which may seduce thought are *numerals* (the magic and mystique of the numbers 3 and 7, 'round' numbers, i.e. those containing 10) and the *adjective*, which frequently yields tautologies (*dark night*), sometimes contradictions ('unconscious psychic processes'), and misleads thinking in the direction of trivialities (*nice, fine*, etc.). Following Mauthner, Kainz also warns of the dangers of *negation* (1972: 298–325), which is frequently ambiguous (*what* is being negated?), but which also suggests a bipolar (bi-logical, two-valued) world, in which everything is either positive or negative.

Kainz's critique of Heidegger's language

Kainz devotes more than 30 pages to examples from Heidegger's writings which show how the philosopher was misled into a vagueness of thinking by his use of language. For Kainz (1972: 446), Heidegger's philosophy is a collection of the most blatant seductions through language. Kainz (*ibid.*) lists seven types of linguistic seduction which can be found in Heidegger's writings, the most important of these being:

(a) word realism, hypostasis and substantialization through nominalization;
(b) exaggerated etymologizing;
(c) exaggerated use of neologisms;
(d) word-play with homophones, homoiophones and sound allusions.

As examples of the first type, Kainz (1972: 451) adduces Heidegger's coinages 'das Nichts, die Nichtung, das Nichthafte, nichten'; as an example of the fourth he mentions Heidegger's unashamed word-play with 'nichts' (*nothing*) and 'Nichte' (*niece*). Heidegger creates 33 nouns from the verb 'sein' [*to be*] (1972: 450) and divides words by using hyphens (*Ent-schlossenheit, Ge-stell, Un-fug*), thereby pretending to discover new meanings.

Critique of linguistics

Believing the system of **one's own language** to be the **norm** is a frequent source of confusion and seduction. Kainz is one of the few scholars to draw attention to this point: naïve language users think of the structures and processes of their native language as the best, and traces of this tendency can even be found in the work of linguists and other scholars (cf. Kainz 1972: 342).

According to Kainz, it is particularly people who study 'language' who are influenced by the system of their own language or another language they know well. Romance *philology* was influenced by certain properties of the Romance *languages*. As a result of this, linguists writing in French stress the arbitrariness of the linguistic sign, as exemplified in the tenets of Saussure and other French writing structuralists (Kainz 1972: 344; compare Chapter 5.2 above). Saussure's 'trichotomy' *langage, langue* and *parole* has also been traced back to the structure of the French language, in which these three words exist side by side – though, according to others, the terminological distinction was already made in 1848 by Heymann Steinthal, Saussure's teacher in Berlin. On the other hand, many descriptions (grammars) of modern languages were influenced by the grammar of Latin, so that languages which for centuries lacked nominal inflexion were still described in terms of 'Nominative, Genitive, Dative, Accusative and Ablative' (Kainz 1972: 349 quoting Otto Jespersen).

Concerning **English linguistics**, Kainz reports the view of Wilhelm Luther (1970: 178 f.), who surmises that some linguistic schools which arose in English speaking countries owe their theoretical background to the specific qualities of the English language, particularly to its mixed character and the consequent 'dissociation' (i.e. lack of motivation) of its vocabulary. Preferences for investigating *parole* rather than *langue*, particularly the development of contextualism and the taxonomic structuralism of Charles C. Fries, but also the Behaviorism of Leonard Bloomfield, according to Luther, were favoured by the dissociated vocabulary of English and its supposed consequence, the neglect of historical aspects in the study of language (cf. Kainz 1972: 344 f.).

Kainz does not follow Luther's critique of English linguistics. Making a certain language responsible for (scholarly) views held and theories developed by its speakers seems an untenable position which can be compared to the view, in a more radical manifestation, that a specific language is responsible for certain political and ideological developments in the country where it is used (say, the German language for the rise of National Socialism and ultimately for the horrors of the holocaust).

Going beyond Kainz, the following **appeal to language critics** is perhaps in order: do not assume your own language to be the norm; learn other languages, and much of your critique of 'language' will dissolve into thin air. On the other hand, do not believe that a certain language is responsible for ideas developed in it, let alone for actions performed by its native speakers.

6.4   Critique of Language Criticism

If today someone were to ask the question 'Does language restrict thought or make it more easily possible?' the most reasonable answer would be as follows:

> Each language certainly imposes restrictions; but being able to converse (use language in a give and take situation) makes it possible to go beyond these restrictions (cf. Gadamer above), and besides, the knowledge of other languages breaks down many restrictions and synergetically opens up new fields of thought unimaginable to the monolingual speaker.

A thought-provoking critique of language criticism is contained in Max Black's book *The Labyrinth of Language* (1968: 155–190). Black speaks of a general 'distrust of language' and an 'alleged gap between language and reality' (1968: 160). But the critic of language refutes himself by using language to point at the 'barrier between language and reality'. Such a critic stretches the task of language too much. We must be aware that we cannot 'reduplicate reality in words. It is a fundamental mistake to suppose that the task of language is to try to make two worlds out of one' (1968: 165).

The critique of language discussed in this chapter does not include critique concerning correctness or purity, and the kind of conservative critique of language as epitomized in Gustav Wustmann's book *Allerhand Sprachdummheiten* (1891, etc.).

A very instructive volume about the different forms of *Sprachkritik* (and a critique of them) is Heringer's book *Holzfeuer im hölzernen Ofen* (ed. 1982), where the reader may find some interesting contributions to the **political critique of language** in the 1960s, the 1970s and the 1980s. In Germany (then divided into the Federal Republic of Germany, FRG, and the German Democratic Republic, DDR), in the 1960s, a 'Krieg um Worte' (*war about words*) was fought, in which each side (the political Left and the political Right) reproached the other for twisting words, deliberately changing their meaning and using them so as to make them unintelligible to the other side. As a sequel to this, in the 1970s and 1980s, a 'Streit über die Sprachkritik' (*dispute about language criticism*) developed, in which each side, now on the meta-level, accused the other of criticizing in others what they themselves practised (see Heringer's introduction 1982 and the documents in Sternberger *et al.* 1968). Heringer also reports a German politician arguing to the effect that political opposition should start by criticizing the *language* of the other side (Heringer 1982: 31; for more on the topic of power in the 'Sprachkritik' by German authors see Schiewe 1998).

'Language and politics' has since become a research field in its own right, and thus the topic of the critique of political language will not be pursued any further in this chapter. Chapter 17 (on discourse strategies) will focus on the (real and imagined) effect of language in the realm of political discourse; there will also be a section on the critique of political language.

On the level of discourse, **translation** is frequently criticized for being unable to render the fine points of the original – or for even distorting it and causing conflict. The phrase 'traduttore, traditore' (*translator traitor*) is sometimes heard in connection with this critique. Indeed, mistranslation may have serious political consequences, as some examples in the next chapter may show. Examples of **mistranslation**, some with serious, and a few with humorous consequences, can be found in Appendix III.

Note

1.   In this passage, Kainz himself seems to have been misled by the word classes verb and adjective.

7. General Semantics (Korzybski, Hayakawa, Stuart Chase)

Words can start people marching in the streets – and can stir others to stoning the marchers. (Hayakawa in *Language in Thought and Action*, 1974: vii)

General Semantics was a movement in linguistics which is no longer regarded as a serious 'school' by many scholars. For the topic of this book, however, the General Semanticists are important because they believed that:

1. Language has a serious impact on thought and action (cf. Hayakawa's book title).
2. This influence is frequently misleading and induces unnecessary suffering.
3. It is possible to overcome the negative influence of language through awareness of it: everyone should become a semanticist – semantics being understood as 'the study of human interaction through communication' (Hayakawa 1974: ix).

Alfred Korzybski (1879–1950) was a Polish count who went to America, taught at various universities (e.g. Harvard) and in 1938 founded the *Institute of General Semantics* in Lakeville, Connecticut (now in Fort Worth, Texas). His voluminous book *Science and Sanity* (first published in 1933) contains many ideas with which he tried to found a scientific system not based on Aristotelian logic. The book is about a variety of topics including mathematics and Einstein's Relativity Theory, but there is also much on language and linguistics. One metaphor from his chapter 'On Structure' has become famous: the verbal world stands in relation to the 'extensional' world as a map does to the territory it represents. Since this metaphor is frequently referred to in the literature on the subject, Korzybski's text is here given in full (1958: 58; italics by Korzybski, throughout):

> [*Korzybski first gives the example of a map which is wrong, since it puts Paris between Dresden and Warsaw. Then he writes:*]
>
> If, speaking roughly, we should try, in our travels, to orient ourselves by such a map, we should find it misleading. It would lead us astray, and we might waste a great deal of unnecessary effort. In some cases, even, a map of wrong structure would bring actual suffering and disaster, as, for instance, in a war, or in the case of an urgent call for a physician.
>
> Two important characteristics of maps should be noticed. A map is not the territory it represents, but, if correct, it has a *similar structure* to the territory, which accounts for its usefulness. If the map could be ideally correct, it would include, in a reduced scale, the map of the map; the map of the map, of the map; and so on, endlessly, a fact first noticed by Royce.

If we reflect upon our languages, we find that at best they must be considered *only as maps*. A word *is not* the object it represents; and languages exhibit also this peculiar self-reflexiveness, that we can analyse languages by linguistic means. This self-reflexiveness of languages introduces serious complexities, which can only be solved by the theory of multiordinality, given in Part VII. The disregard of these complexities is tragically disastrous in daily life and science.

Korzybski's warning cry 'A map is not the territory it represents' expresses metaphorically what many critics of language have said in their different ways. From Parmenides to Francis Bacon and finally to Friedrich Kainz, all critics are united in one point: the existence of a word symbol should not lead us to believing in the existence of the thing/entity it represents. 'Word realism', 'logocentrism' and other terms have been used for this 'error'. Ogden and Richards' semantic triangle expresses this thought (the relation between word form and thing is only imputed), as does Mauthner's warning of believing the world to be 'congruent' with language – and, in a different medium, René Magritte's picture of a pipe with the words 'Ceci n'est pas une pipe' [*This is not a pipe*] written under it.

But Korzybski adds another facet to this warning (1958: 61):

If words *are not* things, or maps *are not* the actual territory, then, obviously, the only possible link between the objective world and the linguistic world is found in *structure, and structure alone*. The only usefulness of a map or language depends on the *similarity of structure* between the empirical world and the map-languages. If the structure is not similar, then the traveller or speaker is led astray, which, in serious human life-problems, must become always eminently harmful.

Our languages, as inherited from our ancestors, differ in structure from the present structure of the world. Linguistic structures must be adjusted to the structure of the world, and, if necessary, new languages must be 'built' which have a similar structure to the one of our present world (cf. Korzybski 1958: 59).

Korzybski then gives a list of 'structurally and semantically important aspects' of the Aristotelian system, which he rejects (1958: 92 f.). Among these are 'the use of the "is" of identity', the 'uniqueness of subject-predicate representation', two-valued logic (as expressed in the law of the excluded third), the 'postulate of two-valued "cause-effect"' and 'the assumption of the cosmic validity of grammar'.

As may have become clear, Korzybski goes far beyond criticizing word realism: his aim is to create an ideal world based on a non-Aristotelian system of thinking and using a language based on this. Critics agree that with this he was aiming too high and sometimes leaving firm ground, even contradicting himself, such as when he sets 'Un-sanity' [*sic*] against 'Sanity', disregarding his own rejection of a two-valued logic. In linguistics, Korzybski has a certain importance as the founder of 'General Semantics'. Hayakawa acknowledges his indebtedness to Korzybski's 'non-Aristotelian System' (1974: ix), as does Stuart Chase, who writes (1966: 7): 'The first pioneer to help me was Count Alfred Korzybski, a Polish mathematician now living in the United States.' (In Appendix III, the reader may find an anecdote about Korzybski.)

S. I. Hayakawa (1906–1992), a Canadian born American who was for a time President of San Francisco State University and even became US Senator for California (1977–1983), wrote about Korzybski (1974: 202, italics by Hayakawa):

> [Korzybski] was concerned, rather, with how people held their beliefs and convictions: whether with a two-valued orientation ('I am right and everybody else is wrong') or with a multi-valued orientation ('I don't know – let's see'). Korzybski saw the two-valued orientation as an *internalization* of the laws of Aristotelian logic, which say that:
>
> > A is A (law of identity);
> > Everything is either A or not-A (law of the excluded middle);
> > Nothing is both A and not-A (law of non-contradiction).

While these laws seem to be sensible on the surface, they are inconsistent with reality and force us to see reality in a simplified, bipolar way. Adopting the **two-valued orientation** means ignoring the existence of a 'middle ground', seeing the world as a fight between 'right' and 'wrong' or 'good' and 'bad' and thinking that what is 'good' is totally good and good for everyone. Hayakawa gives a great number of examples which show that in everyday language, in proverbs and even seemingly tolerant judgements, this two-valued attitude is expressed. The following examples are adapted from Hayakawa (1974: 192–205):

> 'We must listen to both sides of the problem' (assumption: the problem has two sides, and *only* two sides);
> 'If you are not part of the solution, you are part of the problem' (Black Panther Slogan; assumption: every situation consists of a problem and a solution);
> 'This ruler was a good king/a bad king';
> 'These are un-American ideas';
> 'Whoever is not for us is against us!';
> 'There is no such thing as knowledge for its own sake. Science can only be the soldierly training of our minds for service to the nation' (said by the Rector of Jena University during the NS period; assumption: there is good and bad knowledge).

The General Semanticists advocate a 'multi-valued orientation' which acknowledges the existence of more than two values (and the relativity of all values) and in which statements are not either 'true' or 'false' but have a truth value between 0 and 100 percent (cf. Hayakawa 1974: 211). Our everyday language has scales of judgement and is full of ways of how to express a multi-valued attitude, e.g.: 'sane enough', 'sane on most subjects', 'mildly neurotic' (1974: 207).

Hayakawa distinguishes between reports, inferences and judgements and warns us not to take inferences and judgements for reports of facts. Reports can be verified, but a statement like 'Jack lied to us' or 'the senator was stubborn, defiant, and uncooperative' are judgements which should either be made more precise by the speaker or otherwise be recognized as expressions of subjective opinion (1974: 38 f.). Many words contain a judgement on what is being reported. Negatively connoted expressions such as 'he sneaked in', 'she is a bureaucrat' and 'this dictatorial set-up' could be replaced by 'he entered quietly', 'she is a public official' and 'centralized authority'. As is evident, Hayakawa, with some of his suggestions, forestalls the word replacements by the movement of 'Political Correctness' of the 1990s.

Hayakawa's discussion of 'affective elements' (1974: 102–123) is well-known and was taken up by authors such as Dwight Bolinger, Max Atkinson, and (in part) by the Critical Discourse Analysts. The message is that 'verbal hypnotism' makes us stop being critical. Among the devices Hayakawa discusses as affective elements are lists of three, contrasts, pronouns (*you* and *we*), metaphor, allusion, humour and other elements of literary language.

Hayakawa's distinction between **'snarl-words'** and **'purr-words'** (1974: 40–41) has become famous, but is not always understood in Hayakawa's sense. For Hayakawa, snarl words are denunciations, e.g. 'Reds', 'Wall Street', 'radicals', 'foreign ideologies', while purr-words are, for instance, eulogies about 'our way of life'. Such snarls or purrs should be accompanied by verifiable reports or should be answered with questions such as 'Why do you like (or dislike) the President (or Richard Wagner, or tennis, or Joe Louis)?' – whereupon both parties will be wiser and slightly less one-sided than before (1974: 41). Hayakawa was the first editor of the journal *ETC. Review of General Semantics,* which first came out in August 1943 and is still being published by the Institute for General Semantics. In recent issues of the journal, General Semantics has been linked to Whorf's theory of language determining thought (cf. Kodish 2003).

The following is a list of pieces of advice given by the General Semanticists (collected from Hayakawa 1974 as well as Chase 1954, 1959 and 1966).

1. Abstract nouns high on the 'abstraction ladder' (*'freedom', 'progress'*, etc.): use with inverted commas to show that you are aware of their vagueness.
2. Generalizing statements: 'Find the referent', i.e. find out what fact, process, etc. might be referred to in reality.
3. Descriptions of persons: use *etc.* to show that this is not the only quality or affiliation a person possesses, e.g. 'Mr Smith is a lawyer, etc.' The *etc.* (which has supplied the name for the journal mentioned above) indicates that all other qualities and affiliations of Mr Smith are left unsaid (e.g. New Yorker, Afro-American, tennis-player, etc.). Sometimes it is advisable to use index numbers, such as 'he is a politician[1]' to indicate that there are different kinds of politicians. Dates may indicate your awareness of change, e.g. Smith 1963 is not Smith 1972.

4. Never use 'The Americans', 'The Catholics' or 'politicians', because this suggests that all Americans, etc. are the same. Use quantifiers such as 'some', 'many' or 'most'.
5. Beware of statements which express a two-valued orientation, e.g. 'What you are saying is all wrong'. Assume a certain percentage of truth-value and then say 'tell me more'.
6. Do not simplify reality through language, as is done in the following example (Chase 1966: 380):

> Education implies teaching. Teaching implies knowledge. Knowledge is truth. The truth is everywhere the same. Hence education should be everywhere the same.

With its four abstract nouns (*teaching, knowledge, truth, education*), its assumption of an invariable truth and its strange logic (*is ... is ... should be*), this text, according to Chase, violates a number of 'semantic rules'. By this violation of semantics, a one-valued and levelling declaration ('education should be everywhere the same') is justified.

The General Semanticists were truly convinced of the importance of language for peacefully living together, and their endeavour to make everyone in the world a 'semanticist' in order to prevent misunderstanding and conflict is to be acknowledged. General Semantics, however, has also been criticized sharply, e.g. by members of the Chomsky school, most notably by Pinker (1994), who writes: 'General Semantics lays the blame for human folly on insidious "semantic damage" to thought perpetrated by the structure of language' (1994: 57). After comparing General Semantics to the Sapir-Whorf hypothesis (with its ideas of 'languages that carve the spectrum into color words at different places, the fundamentally different concept of time, the dozens of Eskimo words for snow'), Pinker writes:

> But it is wrong, all wrong. The idea that thought is the same thing as language is an example of what can be called a conventional absurdity: a statement that goes against all common sense but that everyone believes because they dimly recall having heard it somewhere and because it is so pregnant with implications. (1994: 57)

Pinker's arguments against General Semantics are the same as those against linguistic relativity: 'if thoughts depended on words, how could a new word ever be coined? How could a child learn a word to begin with? How could translation from one language to another be possible?' (1994: 58; see the section 'Critique of Whorf' in Chapter 5.5 above).

Pinker disregards the fact that General Semantics does not equate language with thought, but only assumes a strong impact of language on thought. But he is right to warn us of overestimating this impact, when he quotes 'Orwell's caveat': 'at least so far as thought is dependent on words' (Pinker 1994: 56). A defence of General Semantics against Pinker's criticism is given by Kodish (2003).

More on General Semantics can be found in I. J. Lee (1941) and in the issues of the journal *ETC*. To conclude this chapter, here is a story told by Stuart Chase which illustrates that words can change history:

> In July, 1945, the Japanese cabinet and the Japanese Emperor were willing to accept the ultimatum of the Allied Forces to capitulate. They just wanted to have a little more time in order to deliberate about the conditions. A press release was prepared which contained the word *mokusatsu* in the sense of 'suspend decision'. Unfortunately this word has a second meaning, 'ignore', and the statement was translated to mean 'the Cabinet ignores the demand to capitulate'. The atom bombs – Chase tells us – may not have fallen on Hiroshima and Nagasaki, if the word had been translated correctly. 'One single word misinterpreted!' led to disaster. (Adapted from Chase 1955: 16).

8. Linguistic Constructivism

Mirror and *construction yard* are two metaphors which Jonathan Potter (1996: 97) suggests for two contrasting views concerning the relation between language and the world. The **mirror metaphor** makes language into a passive echo of what happens in the world. The world along with everything that 'is the case' (Wittgenstein) moves on, changes and develops, but language merely follows suit and takes account of the occurrences and developments in the world. The **construction yard metaphor**, on the other hand, makes language into an active power which puts things together for us which previously were just fragments (Horace's *disiecta membra*). It is this metaphor which expresses the ideas of linguistic constructivism, a school of thought represented among others by Michael Halliday and Christian Mathiessen, but also by some representatives of feminist linguistics (section 8.3 below; see also the articles in Threadgold *et al.* 1986).

8.1 Constructivism in Philosophy and Art

The term Constructivism (also *Constructionism* with slightly different meaning) has been used in a number of fields, not always in the same sense, but with a general tendency to mean 'not representing and mirroring reality but actively creating it'. For instance, Constructivism is a movement in art which posits that art does not represent any more, but construes reality anew: Piet Mondrian, Kasimir Malewitsch and Paul Klee are representatives of this school.

In architecture, the Bauhaus architects (Walter Gropius, Mies van der Rohe, Lionel Feininger and Oskar Schlemmer) created their works according to the principle of not repeating previous architecture, but 'construing' a new reality with their buildings. Art is sometimes the precursor of philosophical thought, and sometimes the two go together, as was the case with constructivism.

Constructivism, as a philosophical movement, is associated most strongly with Ernst v. Glasersfeld, Heinz v. Foerster, Humberto Maturana, Francisco Varela, Jean Piaget and Paul Watzlawick. Constructionists believe that every individual construes his/her own reality – a reality which is not simply 'there' to be discovered by us, investigated, named, improved and formed. In its most radical form (as suggested by Glasersfeld), constructivism says that there is no reality: what we think is real is simply invented by us. Cognition does not represent *the* world outside, but a continuous creation of *a* world through the process of life itself (Maturana and Varela 1987: 7).

The physicist Werner Heisenberg wrote in 1959 (quoted from Watzlawick 1994a: 97): 'und wir müssen uns daran erinnern, daß das, was wir beobachten, nicht die Natur selbst ist, sondern Natur, die unserer Art der Fragestellung ausgesetzt ist' [*and we have to remember that what we observe is not Nature itself, but Nature exposed to our kind of querying*], and Paul Feyerabend said 'Nicht konservative, sondern antizipatorische Vermutungen lenken die Forschung' [*Not conservative, but anticipatory surmises guide research*] (*ibid.*). In other words, every scholarly investigation carries the virus of construction since it approaches reality from a certain point of view and starts from a certain hypothesis and problematization of what the researcher believes to be real. This idea can also be applied to linguistic research whose data, as some linguists claim, are not collected, but construed. What we find, as Watzlawick says, is determined by our way of looking for it.

Ernst von Glasersfeld, using a phrase first coined by Hilary Putnam, calls most traditional philosophical thinking 'metaphysical Realism'. In spite of Kant's critique, most scholars even today think of themselves as 'discoverers', who investigate the real world and by and by come closer to 'the truth' (cf. Glasersfeld 1994: 18 f.). As opposed to this, 'exploring the truth', for a constructionist, means exploring the order and organization of how we ourselves experience our lives (cf. Glasersfeld 1994: 23). Glasersfeld quotes Piaget, who wrote 'L'intelligence ... organise le monde en s'organisant elle-même'[1] [*Intelligence ... organizes the world by organizing itself*]. Glasersfeld sees in Giambattista Vico an early constructivist, whose dictum *Verum ipsum factum* expresses that 'truth' is *produced* as truth, not discovered. Cognition, for Vico, is to become aware of the operations which produce our experiential world (cf. Glasersfeld 1994: 16 f.).

Both Glasersfeld and Foerster (cf. 1994: 58 f.) admit that radical Constructivism would lead to Solipsism, i.e. the view that only the self exists and the rest of the world is created by the self's imagination. But as soon as cognition is no longer understood as the search for iconic matching with reality but as the search for ways of thinking which might 'fit' reality, the danger of solipsism disappears (Glasersfeld 1994: 37).

8.2   The Role of Language in Construing the World

In their book, *The Social Construction of Reality*, Berger and Luckmann (1966: 39) describe the role of language in creating and 'objectifying' knowledge in our everyday world. Language can make the whole world present in one moment. It can 'make present' people who are absent and meetings of the past. But language also classifies objects and people for us (e.g. in English according to number, and in German according to number and gender; in other languages, further classifications are possible).

Linguistic objectivizations in a certain area of knowledge (e.g. in somebody's professional area) are called by Berger and Luckmann 'semantic fields'. Semantic fields objectivize, preserve and accumulate biographic and historic experience.

Semantic fields decide what elements of individual and social experience are to be 'remembered' and what 'forgotten' (cf. Berger and Luckmann 1966: 43).

While for Berger and Luckmann language objectifies and stores knowledge about the world, for more radical linguistic constructivists it actually creates reality for us. The most notable of these scholars is **Michael Halliday**, whose linguistic constructivism will be dealt with below. But first there will be a few paragraphs about the philosophical background of linguistic constructivism.

In his preface to *Wie wirklich ist die Wirklichkeit* (1983: 7), Paul Watzlawick asserts that what is called 'reality' is the result of communication. In *Pragmatics of Human Communication* (1967), Watzlawick *et al.* show how humans influence each other through communicating and how through this, different realities come into existence (see below, Chapter 14.1). Watzlawick mentions the following philosophers (and scientists) as precursors of or contributors to constructivism (1994: 10): Giambattista Vico, Immanuel Kant, Eduard Zeller, Wilhelm Dilthey, Edmund Husserl, Ludwig Wittgenstein, Jean Piaget, Erwin Schrödinger, Werner Heisenberg, Georg Kelly and Nelson Goodman. The contribution of some of these figures to the topic of 'language and the world' has already been mentioned (see also the list of thinkers in Appendix II). In addition, **Whorfian thought** has elements of linguistic **Constructivism** and is discussed as such by Devitt and Sterelny (1999: 248–251; see also their section 'Scientific Constructivism', 251 ff.)

While Watzlawick focuses on communication between different people (but also between animals and humans and between terrestrial and extraterrestrial beings), other scholars see language itself (i.e. the language system) as a force which construes reality for us. The simplest example which shows how language construes parts of the world for us is colour terminology (used countless times in contrastive studies). The colour spectrum, in 'reality' a continuum, is divided up by the different languages into sections with the colour terms. These colour words 'construe' for us the reality concerning colours: we experience colours as distinct entities and believe, for instance, that a river is either green or blue – while in 'reality' there is simply an impression in our brain produced by the sending out of rays between the frequencies of what we call 'infrared' and 'ultraviolet'. This division of an extralinguistic reality into sections may be quite different in different languages. As a famous study (Berlin and Kay 1969) has shown, conceptually a few 'focal' colours are universal, but colour terminology is very different in different cultures, the number of basic colour terms varying from four to eleven (see also Kövecses 2006: 31–33).

Another example is sexuality which is in most of its forms named from the point of view of the male (e.g. *foreplay, penetration*; see 8.3 below). 'Sexism', in most cases, amounts to construing the world from the male point of view.

Linguistic constructivism is represented above all by M. A. K. Halliday and his school. In his plenary address to the AILA Conference at Saloniki in 1990 (printed and reprinted several times; the edition used here is that of 2001), Halliday distinguishes between three views concerning language and reality:

1. One view is that there is a 'pre-existing reality, or a pre-existing cognitive model of such reality', and our languages are the product of a naming process which took place early in human history (2001: 178 f.).
2. The second view says that language adapts to material and non-material conditions of a culture. Language 'reflects reality through the intermediary of human cultures; hence in the long run the grammar changes in response to the patterns of cultural change, even if the process is a very gradual and indirect one' (2001: 179).
3. The third view is the one that Halliday himself adopts. He names Sapir, Whorf, Hjelmslev and Firth as linguists who, in projection against different intellectual backgrounds, formulated this view. Halliday's description of this view (2001: 179) is here given in full:

   > In this view language does not passively reflect reality; language actively creates reality. It is the grammar – but now in the sense of lexicogrammar, the grammar plus the vocabulary, with no real distinction between the two – that shapes experience and transforms our perceptions into meanings. The categories and concepts of our material existence are not 'given' to us prior to their expression in language. Rather, they are construed by language, at the intersection of the material with the symbolic. Grammar, in the sense of the syntax and vocabulary of a natural language, is thus a theory of human experience.

Halliday then shows how texts (e.g. newspaper articles or industrial reports) construe the world for us to mean 'Growth is good'. This is even the case in environmental reports about a concept totally opposed to growth, viz. 'sustainability'. Halliday's example of this comes from an Australian journal (2001: 195):

> INSECTS may provide the vital factor in making Australia a world leader on sustainable development. (*Australian*, 10 March 1990)

Halliday's comment reads as follows: 'and we are back at leading, being out in front, and so once again to growth' (2001: 196).

But Halliday also shows how the **language system construes** certain **ideologies**, such as speciesism and racism: 'if the linguistic system (that is, our long-term slow motion semiotic praxis) construes us as lords of creation, our shorter-term but no less systematic praxis, the regular exercise of *choice within* the system, construes a fractal pattern whereby some of us are lords over the rest' (2001: 198). In the inner layers of grammar, we find a 'hidden theory of experience' with which we construe reality in 'a way that is no longer good for our health as a species' (2001: 193). Specifically, Halliday mentions the following features (2001: 194 f.; summarized; direct quotations in inverted commas):

1. 'Our grammar (though not the grammar of human language as such) construes *air* and *water* and *soil*, and also *coal* and *iron* and *oil*, as "unbounded" – that is, as existing without limit.' Although our *ratio* tells us that these resources are finite, our thinking, which guides our acting, is still influenced by the grammar, which presents them 'as if the only source of restriction was the way that we ourselves quantify them: a *barrel of oil, a seam of coal, a reservoir of water* and so on – as if they in themselves were inexhaustible.'

2. Pairs of polar adjectives such as *big and small, long and short, fast and slow* show a characteristic asymmetry in such a way that the 'growth-word' is also the neutral word expressing an unspecified grade. We never say '*how small is the house?' or '*How slow is the car' – it's always 'How big?', 'how long?' and 'how fast?'

   > Quality and quantity are always lined up together (as they are also in that expression. The grammar of 'big' is the grammar of 'good', while the grammar of 'small' is the grammar of 'bad'. The motif of 'bigger and better' is engraved into our consciousness by virtue of their line-up in the grammar. (2001: 194)[2]

3. Our grammar normally construes animate beings (particularly humans) as doers, inanimate ones as passive experiencers. 'All the kind of things that forests do' (David Suzuki) sounds ungrammatical to us. 'What's that forest doing (there)' implies that the forest should be removed, instead of making us expect answers such as 'it is stopping flooding, stabilizing the soil', etc. 'The language makes it hard for us to take seriously the notion of inanimate nature as an active participant in events' (2001: 194).

4. The grammar makes a sharp distinction between beings which are conscious and those which are not. Conscious beings are male or female, are *he* or *she*, unconscious ones are *it*. Unconscious phenomena cannot be collocated (except metaphorically) with *say, think, live, die* and other verbs and adjectives reserved for conscious beings, specifically humans. The 'great divide' that our language produces in our thinking is between conscious beings (prototypes humans and farm animals) and unconscious ones (plants, rocks, the planet earth). 'This binary theory of phenomena has obviously been important for our survival, in the stage of history that is now coming to an end; but it imposes a strict discontinuity between ourselves and the rest of creation' (2001: 195).

Halliday is aware that the points he lists apply specifically to English (and some other SAE languages), and he mentions Whorf, who found, for example, that Amerindian languages do not make a distinction between 'countable' and 'uncountable'. His point is that in SAE-languages 'growthism is in the grammar' (2001: 198), resources are construed as unbounded, and humans are unique and not continuous with the other creation. 'These and other features of the language system

construe our experience in such a way that we believe we can expand for ever –
our own numbers, our own power and dominance over other species, our own
consumption and so-called "standard of living"' (2001: 198).

The ideologies of classism and growthism are not just problems for the sociologist,
and the destruction of species: the pollution of air and water are not just problems
for the biologists and physicists: 'They are problems for the applied linguistic
community as well' (2001: 199). Linguists are not powerless onlookers of the
phenomena, but, by making the public aware of the constructedness (and
outdatedness) of many of our beliefs, they can contribute to finding solutions.

In their book *Construing Experience through Meaning* (1999), Halliday and
Mathiessen adopt a semantic perspective concerning construction through language.
For the two authors, cognition is not thinking, but meaning, or even 'just a way of
talking about language' (1999: x).

> Language evolved, in the human species, in two complementary functions: construing
> experience, and enacting social processes. In this book we are concerned with the first
> of these, which we refer to as constructing the 'ideation base'; and we stress that the
> categories and relations of experience are not 'given' to us by nature, to be passively
> reflected in our language, but are actively constructed by language, with the
> lexicogrammar as the driving force. By virtue of its unique properties as a stratified
> semiotic system, language is able to transform experience into meaning. (Halliday and
> Mathiessen 1999: xi)

By using several examples, the authors show how this is done. For instance, through
the text-type 'weather-report', 'the weather has now become *information*; but in
numerical, not yet discursive form' (1999: 354, original emphasis). In their sample
texts, two-thirds of all finite clauses have the operator *will*, another 30% have verbs
expressing probability or expectancy – construing the weather as a thing of the
future (1999: 332 f.), e.g.:

- The chance of showers will end by Sunday night, and winds will shift to the
  north.
- Skies are expected to clear on Wednesday, and afternoon highs will approach.

Similarly, through 'recipes', the culinary world is now 'constrained in terms of the
nature of participants and circumstances' (1999: 370).

In their Chapter 7, the authors show how meaning is construed in Chinese, as
compared with English. They find that English and Chinese are very similar in
organizing the content plane in semantics and grammar, and that on the whole the
similarities are more striking than the differences. In both languages, 'grammatical
metaphor' is possible, i.e. constructing processes as things, for instance through
nominalization (1999: 313). 'But it is in the construction of elements that Chinese
and English differ most' (1999: 305). Thus the process which in English is expressed

by the verb CUT, in Chinese can be expressed by 12 different verbs, depending on the object and the instrument. The different verbs with the following meanings construe a much 'nicer' and more detailed reality (1999: 310) than is possible in English:

> *Cut* meat – *cut* with scissors – *cut* grain (in English also: mow) – *cut* cloth – *cut* skin of fruit (pare) – *cut* nails – *cut* logs (split) – *cut* tree (chop) – *cut* paper (slit) – *cut* skin – *cut* flesh.

On the whole, 'the dichotomy of experience into processes and things is rather more explicitly semanticized in Chinese than in English' (1999: 312). While processes tend to have different names in the whole of China, things are named the same throughout (albeit with different pronunciations).

This example could be called one of '**semantic divergence**', i.e. the fact that language1 cuts up reality more nicely than language2, so that a word in language2 may semantically correspond to two or more words in language1 – which is thus 'semantically divergent'. Semantic divergence plays a role in foreign language learning, where it is frequently a source of error: English 'to know' may be rendered either by German 'wissen' or 'kennen', depending on syntactic, but more specifically semantic distinctions (*Ich kenne diese Stadt* vs. *Ich weiß mir keinen Rat*). No doubt, semantic divergence plays a role in the different construction of reality by children learning different native languages. Thus English *heaven* and *sky* are semantically divergent compared to German where the same word is used for both concepts: *Himmel*. For German children such sentences as 'Gott ist im Himmel' [*God is in heaven*] and 'Die Wolke ist im Himmel' [*the cloud is in the sky*] may produce a different idea of /Deity/ from that of English children. (More on semantic divergence in English and German and vice versa can be found in Leisi 1971 and 1973: 74–91)

Norman Fairclough (2009) makes a useful distinction between 'representing', 'constructing' and 'construing'. '**Represent**' gives an old-fashioned picture of what language does, and does not do justice to claims that language can effect changes. On the other hand, '**construct**' may be misleading in the opposite direction since it claims 'that *everything* we say or write changes the real world'. '**Construe**' suggests grasping the world through language, but not necessarily changing it, thus: 'Construing students as *customers* and *consumers* of a university's *products* does seem to be having constructive effects on Higher Education (HE) in Britain and other countries – it seems to be contributing to change in the nature of HE', because this construal is supported by those in power (Fairclough 2009, original italics).

Language can make the past appear present and make the future seem to exist now. Language is also powerful enough to 'create' certain situations, such as when by using the word 'conflict' an ongoing debate is seen as a conflict, or by using the word 'quarrel', a controversy assumes the status of a quarrel. The German verb *herbeireden* (make something happen by talking about it, 'self-fulfilling prophesy') nicely shows the power of language to create specific situations. Here is an example of this (Jan, 2009, Graz):

> When in a communal election campaign, a politician used language offensive to Islam, an expert was asked: 'Do you think this will have consequences internationally?' His reply was: 'Das möchte ich nicht kommentieren; ich möchte sie nicht *herbeireden*.' [*I do not wish to comment this; I do not want to talk them into existence*.] The mere mentioning of international consequences, it seems, might bring about such consequences! Language (as discourse) can actually make things happen.

8.3   The Construction of Gender and Sexuality through Language

One ontological area in which the construction of reality through language is particularly strong and consequential for certain groups of people is gender and sexuality. It is no wonder that feminist linguists have adopted a constructivist attitude in their treatment of language and gender. In her book *Man Made Language* (1985), Dale Spender has a chapter entitled 'The Politics of Naming', in which the constructivist power of naming the world in the area of the genders is described. Ideally, all members of a society should have the power to name, so that a variety of views and insights are provided.

> Practically, however, difficulty arises when one group holds a monopoly on naming and is able to enforce its own particular bias on everyone, including those who do not share its view of the world. When one group holds a monopoly on naming, its bias is embedded in the names it supplies and these 'new' names help to maintain and strengthen its initial bias. (Spender 1985: 164)

Jennifer Coates (2004: 5–7) distinguishes four approaches to the topic of language and gender. The first three, called by Coates the **deficit** approach, the **dominance** approach and the **difference** approach, embody traditional views of the relation between women and men, which place different emphasis on the issue of power. The fourth and most modern approach, called by Coates **dynamic** or **social constructionist**, sees speakers as '"doing gender" rather than statically "being" a particular gender' (2004: 6). Since Coates' useful distinction of approaches concerns the level of discourse more specifically than the language system, it will be discussed at greater length in Chapter 19.

Adopting the dominance approach amounts to believing that the impact of language is one of the causes of men's power over women. **Dale Spender**, who takes this approach, thinks (1985: 165) that 'it has been males who have named the world'; thus male dominance – as in a vicious circle – has been perpetuated through language. Since 'those who have the power to name the world are in a position to influence reality' (*ibid.*), male supremacy will be maintained until women are given (or take for themselves!) the power to name reality – but also to lay down the rules of how reality is encoded: 'The inferior status of women in society is encoded and perpetuated in language. It has been men who have made the dictionaries of formal and informal usage or slang. Men have been in public positions of power where they could influence usage on a broader scale' (Kramarae and Jenkins 1985: 13).

Perhaps it should be mentioned here that there is a 'feminist debate on whether language reflects or causes women's oppression' (Cameron 1985: 99). In her discussion of the relevance of the Sapir-Whorf hypothesis for feminism, Cameron writes (*ibid.*):

> If language segments the conceptual universe in accordance with non-linguistic cultural norms (e.g. sexual differentiation of an extreme kind, and the devaluing of women), then it is not inculcating a world view but obeying the dictates of one.

As in most ontological areas, we may assume a bidirectional interaction between language and the world: women's oppression is a fact (in some cultures) mirrored in language – which, in its turn, contributes to the continuation of the oppression. Changes usually happen at both ends, language and society – as is the case with the position of women and men at the present time.

Quoting Mary Daly and other feminist theologians, Dale Spender shows how in the **Christian religion** 'the Word', i.e. the Bible, structures reality concerning women and men for us. The following is a list of examples collected from Spender's book (1985: 165–171), which show how the superiority of males is construed by the Bible, a text produced almost exclusively by males.

- God is male (Mary Daly's comment on this is well-known: 'Why […] must *God* be a noun? Why not a verb – the most active and dynamic of all?' 1975: 167). In other religions (and indeed in earlier versions of the Bible) female deities are recognized. In translations into Hebrew, female ('pagan') deities turned into male ones, since the Hebrew language did not have a word for *Goddess* (cf. Spender 1985: 170).
- Religious activities that women were engaged in were called 'pagan cults', in antithesis to real 'religions'. Christians were called upon to destroy pagan idols, most of which had breasts (cf. Spender 1985: 169).
- Adam is created first, and Eve is made from Adam's rib (as if the male were giving birth to the female – Spender 1985: 166).
- Eve is associated with evil; she is responsible for the Fall. Instead of blaming Adam for his weakness, Eve is represented as the temptress and Adam as her victim.
- The ten commandments seem to be directed chiefly at men, the ninth one reading 'Thou shalt not covet thy neighbour's wife'. (The referent of *thou* must be a man!)
- All the 12 apostles are men.

The construction of reality through gender-biased language is particularly blatant in the ontological area of *sexuality* (Spender 1985: 171–182). Sexuality is allocated only to the dominant group with the result that even women themselves were persuaded they did not have 'sexuality' and did not want sex. They were required 'to reconcile the fantasy with the facts' (1985: 173), many of them coming to the conclusion that there was something wrong with them.

In medical textbooks and other texts about sexuality, women have been construed as being incapable of sexual pleasure, while men have been named as having 'an infinite appetite and capacity for intercourse' (quoted by Spender 1985: 174). 'If intercourse is the aim, then it is undoubtedly the male who "sets the pace", but this is not necessarily a pace which the female may find difficult to keep up with, as the medical author implies' (1985: 174).

Again, a list of expressions for male and female sexuality (collected from Spender 1985: 175–182) will show the power of words to construe reality, a construed reality which in many cases is 'against the facts' (Spender):

1. *Foreplay* and *penetration* are particularly male-centred namings. What is described as 'foreplay' could well be the most important part for the woman, while for 'penetration' the term *enclosure* could be substituted to describe the female experience (Spender 1985: 178, quoting Barbara Mehrhof and Susan Brownmiller).
2. Men are *virile* and *potent*, but there is no term for sexual power in women (Dorothy Hage).
3. Women who engage in sexual activity are called derogatorily 'nymphomaniacs' or 'bitches'. If they abstain, they are *frigid*.
4. *Frigidity* suggests coldness; a better word would be *reluctance*, which implies the woman's wish not to participate in intercourse with a man (1985: 177). The lack of parallelism between the corresponding words *frigid* and *impotent* is notable.
5. Nearly all words for sexual intercourse take the male point of view and thus describe the experience of entering and thrusting, e.g. *fuck, screw, root, shag*.
6. The word *rape* is too harmless for what it denotes, particularly since it has been used metaphorically in the sense of spoiling a pleasant sight, as in 'rape of the countryside'.
7. Children born 'out of wedlock' are called 'illegitimate'.
8. Heterosexuality is construed as the normal, homosexuality as the abnormal 'orientation'.
9. Freud's theory of 'penis envy' (suggesting the male to be the norm, the female to be deficient) has become widely accepted; instead, 'vagina gratitude' or 'womb envy' are suggested (Spender 1985: 182) as words to replace Freud's term and present the female as the complete and perfect gender.

Feminist linguists also criticize scholars (including linguists) for using categories which show males as the 'unmarked', females as the 'marked' case (Spender 1985: 19–24). In semantic componential analysis, *woman* has frequently been described as having the features [+human] [+adult] [-male], which again suggests a deficiency of women. The artificial language *Esperanto* was devised by its creator Ludwig Zamenhof so as to show males as 'the paradigms of humanity' (Susan Robbins) and women as the deviation: in Esperanto, all nouns (including nouns denoting people) end in -o, but for feminine designations the infix -*in* has to be used, thus:

English	*Esperanto*	*English*	*Esperanto*
father	– patr-o	mother	– patr-in-o
brother	– fratr-o	sister	– fratr-in-o
boy	– knab-o	girl	– knab-in-o

One notices that the word-stems are all taken from words denoting males in European languages (Lat. *pater, frater,* Germ. *Knabe* [*boy*]).

In many languages, to express 'femaleness' a suffix has to be used, which makes women the 'derived ones' ('*abgeleitet*') – as is the case in German with its suffix-*in*. The 'semantic derogation of women' is a process due to the inferior position of women in society. Spender (1985: 16–19) adduces examples of corresponding pairs such as

Master – mistress	governor – governess
Lord – lady	bachelor – spinster
Courtier – courtesan	professional (man) – professional (woman), a euphemism for *prostitute.*

In each case the feminine designation has undergone a pejorative change of meaning with denotations of lower social status and negative sexual connotations.

The construction of gender in the German language is poignantly discussed by Luise Pusch in her books *Das Deutsche als Männersprache* (1984) and *Alle Menschen werden Schwestern* (1990). The latter title is meant to show how in canonical works of literature a patriarchal society is reflected. In Friedrich Schiller's 'Ode an die Freude' [*Ode to Joy*], we find the lines 'Alle Menschen werden Brüder, wo dein sanfter Flügel weilt' [*all people become brothers where your soft wing dwells*] and 'wer ein holdes Weib errungen stimme in den Jubel ein' [*those who have fought for and won a loving woman may join the joyous song*], lines in which all humans are without question construed as male. The sexism contained in anthems (e.g. 'Heimat bist du großer Söhne' [*home thou art of great sons*] – from the Austrian national anthem) and religious texts (ninth Commandment, Old Testament) has often been commented on.

Different languages treat women and men differently on different linguistic levels (morphology, word semantics, grammar); this is shown in the three volume survey of Hellinger and Bußmann (2001–2003), in which 'the linguistic representation of women and men' is given in 30 languages including English, German and Chinese.

This section is meant to show how most languages construe a world in which men are dominant. However, as the examples have illustrated, this dominance is not just a question of 'construction'. The reality is that language reflects the situation in the world, and if it construes at all, it construes the continuation of an already existing societal system. But the scholarly discussion of 'language and gender' which continues on a high level shows that an awareness of language (with accompanying changes) may change the world! As Luise Pusch observes (1984: 83), those people who say 'change society, not language' are unaware of the power of language: to get out of the vicious circle of 'male dominance in society – therefore sexism in language – consequently male dominance in society, etc.', the 'lever of change' has to be applied somewhere – why not at the language end? Starting at the language end has already borne fruit, as Gisela Klann-Delius (2005: 191) observes concerning German:

> Zu konstatieren ist derzeit, dass die sprachpolitischen Forderungen der Feministinnen eine öffentliche Diskussion provozierten und politische Maßnahmen beförderten, die zu einem markanten Sprachwandel des Deutschen innerhalb nur weniger Jahrzehnte beigetragen haben.

> *We may state at present that the demands of feminists concerning language policy have provoked public discussion and have stimulated political measures which have contributed to a marked change of the German language within only a few decades.*

Hellinger and Bußmann (2003: 165) note concerning German that 'a tremendous number of new personal feminines, derivations [...] as well as compounds with *frau* as second element [...] have contributed to more female visibility in German'. It is to be hoped that this linguistic change and the greater visibility of women in texts will set in motion a 'benign circle' with social change as one of its effects.

Judith Butler's influential book *Gender Trouble* (1999/1991), in which 'the two sexes/genders' and 'heterosexuality' are shown to be the result of social construction, also deals with the role of *language* in this construction. In particular, Butler discusses the work of feminists like Monique Wittig and of structuralists and post-structuralists such as Julia Kristeva, Lévi-Strauss, Lacan and others in the light of the power of language on gender identities. Gender is not static, but something that is 'done' in interaction with others. One chapter of the book is entitled 'Language, Power, and the Strategies of Displacement' (1999: 33–44). Here Butler discusses the role of language in constructing sexual difference and making heterosexuality the norm, and the power of language to subordinate and exclude women. In a later section of the book, Butler gives concrete examples of words which define lesbian and gay identities and destroy the construction of heterosexual norms:

> The terms *queens, butches, femmes, girls,* even the parodic reappropriation of *dyke, queer,* and *fag* redeploy and destabilize the categories of sex and the originally derogatory categories for homosexual identity. (1999: 156)

On the other hand, 'all these terms might be understood as symptomatic of "the straight mind", modes of identifying with the oppressor's version of the identity of the oppressed' (*ibid.*) The influence of Butler's book on how we see gender, but also on how gender is researched is summed up by Coates (2004: 217) as follows:

> In the past, researchers aimed to show how gender correlated with the use of particular linguistic features. Now, the aim is to show how speakers use the linguistic resources available to them to *accomplish* gender. Every time we speak, we have to bring off being a woman or being a man. [original emphasis]

Butler has contributed to the deconstruction of the binary distinction *man-woman.* 'The overthrow of binary thinking has involved the deconstruction of the notion of a single masculinity or femininity. Instead, gender is conceptualised as plural' (Coates 2004: 217). This deconstruction has made possible the rise of a new field of study, **queer linguistics**, in which research on 'the language of gay, lesbian, bisexual and transsexual communities' is carried out (Coates 2004: 218; see more about this in Coates 2004: 218–220).

An interesting aspect is brought in by **Robin Tolmach Lakoff** (1995), who argues that reality can also be constructed through **silence**. Though 'it is easier to perceive what is *there* as meaningful' than perceiving meaning in the absence of something, the specific situation may give meaning to silence. This may be apparent in conversation (through non-response, interruption and topic control, Lakoff 1995: 28), but also in media reports which frequently keep silent about the views of victims and underprivileged persons. Lakoff illustrates this by discussing a number of events involving American women (Hillary Rodham Clinton, the Bobbitt affair, the Nancy Kerrigan–Tonya Harding interaction) and commenting on reports about them in the media (1995: 31 ff.).

Sara Mills (2008) distinguishes between 'overt sexism' (generic *he/him/his, man-made,* etc.) and 'indirect sexism'. For Mills, sexism can be regarded as a 'resource' available within language, so that individuals can construe their own identity (2008: 126). Indirect sexism is expressed, among other ways, through gender stereotypes, which may not even be openly revealed. For instance, interpreting a husband's utterance to his wife 'Is there any ketchup, Vera' as a request for ketchup to be brought (as opposed to a mere request for information) would be in accordance with the stereotype that women's role is to serve men (cf. Mills 2008: 128 after Cameron).

Other stereotypes of femininity expressed in such indirect ways include the nagging woman and the gossip, the over-polite woman and the woman silenced by a dominant male partner (Mills 2008: 128). Stereotypes of masculine language (and behaviour) are aggression, directness, forcefulness, interruption and dominance (2008: 130). 'Macho masculinity' is now under threat 'from changes in the behaviour considered appropriate for women and homosexual males' (2008: 131).

An interesting type of indirectness is the 'ironizing of sexism', which 'both challenges overt sexism and keeps it in play' (Mills 2008: 134). Using sexism ironically (as is done in radio and TV shows, such as *Top Gear,* and in lists of 'women's language translated' and 'men's language translated', 2008: 142 f.), 'does not change the nature of the sexism itself, but rather simply changes the way it can be responded to' (2008: 134). In recent years, the term 'politically correct' (PC) has increasingly been used to mean free from sexism, although its general usage has come to imply paying 'excessive attention to the sensibilities of those who are seen as different from the norm (women, lesbians, gays, disabled people, black people)' (Mills 2008: 100). As a reaction to this, 'politically incorrect' has developed meanings with frequently positive connotations – such as 'daring, against the stream, funny and critical of our society' (for more about 'political incorrectness' see Mills 2008: 108–114).[3]

There will be more on 'language and gender' in Part III on discourse (Chapter 19: 'women, men and discourse'). In particular, the question of the influence of gender-biased (sexist) discourse on thought and action will be discussed in some detail.

In the same way as 'gender', '**race**' can be shown to be merely a construct. Even Darwin is said to have known that individual differences between people are far greater than differences based on so-called 'racial' characteristics. Racism can be said to be a particularly clear example of an ideology based on a linguistic construct.

Notes

1.   Jean Piaget (1937). La construction du réel chez l'enfant. Delachaux et Niestlé. Neuchatel, p. 311.
2.   We will encounter this thought of Halliday's in different clothing again in the chapter on Cognitive Linguistics (Chapter 9 below).
3.   See also the articles in the new journal *Gender and Language* (Equinox Publishing).

9. Cognitive Linguistics: the Impact of Metaphor and Frame

[It can be shown] how the metaphors we think with are realised non-linguistically in many aspects of contemporary life: building tall, levels of obesity, industrialisation, use of time, travelling fast, urbanisation, racial categorisation and exclusion, medical practice, sexual behaviour, militarisation, evaluation of quality by quantity, commodification of nature, treatment of animals, education and the concept of progress.

Andrew Goatly, in his book *Washing the Brain* (2007: 401 f.), lists (in the passage quoted above) a number of ontological areas where the metaphors we think with have an effect on our behaviour. Behind every ideology, there is a complex nexus of metaphors which interact. Goatly thinks that eight metaphors, among them SOCIAL ORGANIZATION is A BODY, RACE is COLOUR, IDEA is DISEASE, DISEASE is INVASION, in their interaction suggest 'that the ideal state is one where the inhabitants are the same colour, and constructs immigrants as invaders, or a disease, or as bearing dangerous ideologies' (2007: 214).

The cognitive theory of metaphor, which is a theory of the **impact of metaphor** on our behaviour, goes back to *Metaphors We Live By*, a book written by George Lakoff and Mark Johnson and first published in 1980. In this book the thesis is postulated that our thinking is pervaded by metaphors and that without noticing, we are led and misled by long-standing metaphorical ideas such as LIFE is A JOURNEY, UP is GOOD and MORE is BETTER, etc. So understood, metaphor is not regarded as an embellishment of a (literary) text or as a poetic device which makes a text have a literal and a figurative meaning; rather, metaphor is seen as an every-day, even hidden phenomenon of thinking, which without our noticing determines the way we think about abstract ideas. Lakoff and Johnson speak of 'conceptual metaphors', not linguistic ones. Metaphor is something characteristic of our thinking; language is only the medium through which this metaphorical thinking is expressed.

This view of metaphor has been linked with prototype semantics, in other words with the idea that categories are not simply collections of entities all on the same level, but have ideal, best, 'prototypical' representatives and less typical ones – an idea first proposed by Eleanor Rosch (1975) and discussed by Aitchison (1994), Kleiber (1993) and Ungerer and Schmid (1996: 1–59). The concept of prototypes is commonly thought to be related to Wittgenstein's idea of 'family resemblances', which also describe categories in a new way: the members of a category do not, as in previous understandings, have one or several features in common, but as we 'wander' through a category, we may find that some features disappear as we go along and new ones arise, to the point where the last member of the category may have nothing in common with the first.

While in the 1980 edition of Lakoff and Johnson's book the authors claimed a certain 'systematicity' for metaphors (e.g. that 'argument' is conceptualized in terms of 'battle' systematically, p. 7), in the edition of 2003 they include an 'Afterword', in which they acknowledge that certain facts or ideas can be expressed with different metaphors, which may have different effects on the world:

> How we think metaphorically matters. It can determine questions of war and peace, economic policy, and legal decisions, as well as the mundane choices of everyday life. Is a military attack a 'rape', 'a threat to our security', or 'the defense of a population against terrorism'? The same attack can be conceptualized in any of these ways with very different military consequences. (Lakoff and Johnson 2003a: 243)

Our private lives, too, are affected by the different ways we conceptualize events and act accordingly:

> Is your marriage a partnership, a journey through life together, a haven from the outside world, a means for growth, or a union of two people into a third entity? The choice among such common ways of conceptualizing marriage can determine what your marriage becomes. Drastic metaphorical differences can result in marital conflict. Take for example the case where one spouse views marriage as a partnership, and the other spouse views it as a haven. The responsibilities of a partnership may well be at odds with the relief from responsibilities characteristic of a haven. (Lakoff and Johnson 2003a: 243 f.)

The main point made by Lakoff and Johnson is that metaphors are not just in language (or even in words), but that they are conceptual by nature – in other words, we do not just speak metaphorically, we *think* metaphorically. The authors adduce a number of types of evidence for this contention, including evidence from semantic change, from discourse analysis and sign language acquisition (2003a: 248 f.). What they claim (2003a: 256) is that as children we are subject to a 'neural learning mechanism', by which we acquire a system of primary metaphors independent of language but persistent in our thinking throughout our lives.

> For example, the metaphor Affection is Warmth (as in 'He's a *warm* person'. Or 'She's a *block of ice*'.) arises from the common experience of a child being held affectionately by a parent; here, affection occurs together with warmth. [...] There is neuronal activation occurring simultaneously in two separate parts of the brain: those devoted to emotions and those devoted to temperature. (2003a: 256)

Because of this neural grounding of metaphor, we cannot help thinking in metaphors and we 'live by them'.

What is somewhat confusing about this theory is that metaphors may be mutually inconsistent, from which we must conclude that our conceptual systems are inconsistent (2003a: 272 f.). Besides, somewhat disconcertingly, Lakoff and Johnson in their 2003 revision of their theory give up some of the most basic tenets of the 1980 book, e.g. the division of metaphors into 'orientational, ontological, and structural', which they now, after having introduced the concept of 'primary metaphor', see as artificial (2003a: 264). One of their most striking examples from 1980, ARGUMENT is WAR, is now said to have been analysed incompletely, since most people learn about argument before they learn about war. Instead, there is a primary metaphor which is learned and later extended in the following way:

> The conflation of physical struggle with associated words in the development of all children is the basis for the primary metaphor Argument Is Struggle. As we grow up, we learn about more extended and violent struggles like battles and wars, and the metaphor is extended via that knowledge. (2003a:265)

In addition, it is not made clear to what extent our metaphors are permanent concepts or whether our conceptualizations can be changed and influenced by political groupings and leading politicians. Lakoff's essay 'Metaphor and War', which was made available on the internet just before the first Gulf War (Lakoff 1991), shows that by means of using words it is possible to conceptualize a situation (in this case the situation in Iraq) in such a way that the public thought war was inevitable. Lakoff's internet article begins as follows (1991):

> Metaphors can kill. The discourse over whether to go to war in the gulf was a panorama of metaphor. Secretary of State Baker saw Saddam Hussein as 'sitting on our economic lifeline'. President Bush portrayed him as having a 'stranglehold' on our economy. General Schwarzkopf characterized the occupation of Kuwait as a 'rape' that was ongoing. The President said that the US was in the gulf to 'protect freedom, protect our future, and protect the innocent', and that we had to 'push Saddam Hussein back'. Saddam Hussein was painted as a Hitler. It is vital, literally vital, to understand just what role metaphorical thought played in bringing us in this war.

In Part I of the article, Lakoff goes on to describe a number of metaphors which we have as concepts and which were used by politicians and by the media to justify the (first) Gulf War of 1991: state as person, war as trade-off between gains and losses, war as medicine (against the cancer of control by the enemy); the most important metaphor, however, was 'The Fairy Tale of the Just War' with the following cast: a villain, a victim and a hero, in which 'the hero is left with no choice but to engage the villain in battle'. The fairy tale metaphor appeared in speeches by President Bush, by the minister of foreign affairs, and again and again in the media, and it contributed to making the war against Iraq appear just. Metaphors 'backed up by bombs can kill'. Lakoff (1991, Part II) has no objections to the use of metaphors, only 'to the failure to look systematically at what our metaphors hide' and to the failure to look for alternative metaphors which might lead to action of a different kind.

In spite of its shortcomings and revisions, Lakoff and Johnson's theory of the pervasive nature of metaphor and of the conceptuality of it has contributed greatly to enabling people to see the impact of language (!) on the world – because in spite of metaphors being conceptual, they are expressed through language, and it is (as Lakoff's 1991/1999 article shows) language which makes conceptual metaphors active in our minds.

In addition, the theory has given rise to a whole school of linguistics, 'Cognitive Linguistics', in which the 'mapping' of language on reality and of reality on language is investigated. Within this framework, the idea of 'conceptual blending' was developed by Gilles Fauconnier and Mark Turner (2002). More recently, Fauconnier and Turner (2008: 53 ff.) have seen mapping or blending as elements of 'integration networks'.

> What we have come to call 'conceptual metaphors', like TIME IS MONEY or TIME IS SPACE, turn out to be mental constructions involving many spaces and many mappings in elaborate integration networks constructed by means of overarching general principles. These integration networks are far richer than the bundles of pairwise bindings considered in recent theories of metaphor. (2008: 53)

Particularly the TIME is SPACE metaphor is shown to be embedded in a complex structure of integration networks (Fauconnier and Turner 2008: 54–60).

Andrew Goatly, in *Washing the Brain* (2007), shows with the help of many examples how clusters of metaphors may contribute to certain ways of thinking, even to certain 'ideologies'. A telling example is the metaphor HUMAN is FOOD, which influences, even determines the way we think of sexual activity and sexual desire (which in this metaphorical frame is appetite, with other humans being the food that satisfies this appetite). Goatly (2007: 90) lists the following words metaphorically used for women (and men) which exemplify this metaphoric scheme:

Crackling, crumpet	sexually attractive woman
Tart	sexually immoral/attractive woman
Mutton dressed as lamb	older woman trying to look young
Lollipop	attractive young girl
Peach	good, attractive person or girl
Arm-candy	attractive companion at social events
Honey	pleasant person
Sugar	person you are fond of
Sweetie	pleasant, kind person
Dish, dishy	sexually attractive person
Beefcake	man […] with muscular body attractive to women
Studmuffin	sexually attractive young man.

As the examples show, the food metaphor is more often used by men to describe women than vice versa. Indeed, one might find a pronounced sexism in the disequilibrium of words for the two genders. As Goatly states (2007: 90):

> Equating sex with eating might suggest that sex is essential for our life, and therefore we are entitled to obtain it by any means, just as a starving man would be entitled to steal food. By applying these metaphors mainly to women, men suggest they are entitled to have sex with them, even by force or illegal means. More obviously, they suggest that the sole purpose of the women is to satisfy the appetites of men, just as food is produced for the sole purpose of eating.

The role of metaphors in the language of desire has been described by Alice Deignan (1997). With the help of metaphor, ideas can be expressed which 'would be unacceptable if stated in non-metaphorical language' (1997: 21). Conceptual metaphors for Desire include DESIRE is AN EXTERNAL FORCE (*a wave of pleasure washed over her, a torrent of passion that sweeps you away*), DESIRE is PAIN (*a stab of pleasure pierced her*), DESIRE is FIRE/ELECTRICITY (*extinguish the flame of passion*) and (cf. Goatly's examples above) DESIRE is APPETITE (*her body hungered for him*) (Deignan 1997: 25–30).

In a similar way, according to this theory, metaphor clusters like the one described determine our way of thinking about other races, social classes, animals and plants, foreigners and many other forms of life. The fact that we view our lives in terms of competition is also constructed through a number of metaphors, among them the following (Goatly 2007: 337, original capitals):

- ACTIVITY IS FIGHTING, HUMANS ARE ARMY, SEX IS VIOLENCE

- ARGUMENT IS WAR, ARGUING/CRITICISING IS FIGHTING, ARGUING/CRITICISING IS ATTACKING – HITTING [...]

- ACTIVITY IS GAME – BALL GAME, CARD GAME, BOARD GAME, GAMBLING GAME.

Metaphors also determine ways of scientific investigation, since a language of scholarship is not possible without metaphors (see the metaphors used above – PROTOTYPES, FAMILY RESEMBLANCES, WANDER through a category, as we GO ALONG). 'The program of research is driven by the metaphor, and different metaphors will highlight or predict certain attributes of the phenomenon under investigation' (Goatly 2007: 161). Thus even when we are writing about language, traditional metaphors may make us see the phenomena in a certain way and blind us to other ways of looking at them (note the metaphors in this sentence).

Here are two examples of metaphors which may lead many people in the wrong direction:

1. Ever since the origin of the Universe was named 'the Big Bang' (*Urknall*), people have been thinking of it as a somewhat noisy event – while in reality the 'Big Bang' (if there ever was one) must have been something sudden but not connected with sound.

2. The source of a river is also called its 'spring' (*Ursprung*) which in both English and German makes us think of water rapidly 'springing' out of the earth or rock – while in reality most 'springs' are muddy areas where water gathers almost imperceptibly, certainly not with a leap and a jump.

Kövesces (2006) develops a view of conceptual metaphor in which the idea of metaphor variation (across time and across cultures) plays an important role. He distinguishes between cross-culture variation and within-culture variation. 'Cross-culturally, metaphors vary because people can use alternative conceptualization for the same target domain. Within-culture variation occurs as a result of such subdimensions as the social dimension, regional dimension, subcultural dimension, individual dimension, and others' (Kövecses 2006: 178).

For cross-cultural variation, Kövecses (2006: 178) gives the example of the English and the Hungarian conception of 'sky'. While 'in English, the "sky" is conceptualized as a three-dimensional entity ("clouds in the sky"), speakers of Hungarian talk about things being "on the sky" (the sky is thus perceived as two-dimensional).' The difference in conceptualization can be shown with the help of two drawings (Kövecses 2006: 352): an English sky can be drawn as a cube in which clouds and aeroplanes fly, while for Hungarians the sky resembles a painting on the ceiling of a hall. In this case, it is clearly the linguistic realization of a metaphor which results in differing conceptualizations.

In their book *Philosophy in the Flesh* (1999), Lakoff and Johnson present three major tenets of cognitive science: 'The mind is inherently embodied. Thought is mostly unconscious. Abstract concepts are largely metaphorical.' The authors ask in what way considering these findings would change philosophy, since 'an empirically responsible philosophy would require our culture to abandon some of its deepest philosophical assumptions' (Lakoff and Johnson 1999: 3; see also Ungerer and Schmid 1996: 114–155). A philosophy based on metaphor would have to consider the existence of different metaphorical models, as Goatly (2007: 332) writes:

> But we have to recognize that truth is relative to purpose. For architects the earth is flat, for astronauts it is, more or less, spherical. If our purpose is the long-term survival of the planet then truth will be whatever promotes that survival, and the metaphorical models will be selected accordingly.

9.1 Metaphor as Tension: the Controversion Theory

The importance of metaphor was first highlighted by Aristotle (in his *Poetics*). By destroying one order and building up another, metaphor (in the Aristotelian sense) is a heuristic force which causes us to see one part of the world in a different light. For example, by calling language 'the house of being', Heidegger made us think of language in a new way. By speaking of 'the company a word keeps', Firth (1957b) made us see words like people who meet more or less frequently – and, conversely, people somewhat like words lined up in a text! That metaphor works both ways (from vehicle to tenor, but also from tenor to vehicle) is the thesis of the controversion or tensional theory of metaphor. Goatly (1997: 118, original emphasis) expresses the main idea behind this in the following way:

> The **tensional** or Controversion Theory of Metaphor [...] stresses that metaphor's main effect is the emotional or logical tension brought about by semantic contradiction.

The theory that metaphor establishes a tension between two areas of life which makes us see *both areas* in a new light was first established by Max Black in his book *Models and Metaphors* (1962), in which he speaks of the 'interaction view of metaphor', which he places in opposition to the Aristotelian 'substitution view' (1962: 38). In his book *la métaphore vive* (English, somewhat misleadingly, *The Rule of Metaphor*, 1978), Ricoeur establishes a theory of metaphor as tension between identity and difference which leads to 'the properly semantic operation consisting in seeing the similar in the dissimilar' (1978: 6).

The Romance philologist Mario Wandruszka (1983) shows how ideas and events are expressed with the help of different metaphors in different languages. Thus, in German 'auf eigene Faust' (literally: 'on one's own fist') is used to express 'independently', 'with no help from others', as in "Wir haben auf eigene Faust Mallorca erkundet" [*We explored Majorca on our own steam*]. For a German native speaker, this metaphor has become pale, while for native speakers of other languages it may be suggestive of an abundance of independence, perhaps even a certain amount of violence (1983: 304). The German native speaker, on the other hand, may be struck by the English equivalent 'on our own steam' or the French one 'de notre propre chef' (cf. *ibid.*). But metaphors which have grown pale can be expanded and thus brought to new life – or 'reduced' to their literal meaning, so that the metaphoricity becomes visible again (cf. Wandruszka 1983: 310).

Metaphor is understood by all these authors as a force by which, through the link between similarity and contradiction, new ways of seeing the world are created. Many ideas, if expressed in non-metaphorical language, would be unacceptable or incomprehensible (cf. Deignan 1997: 21). (For recent research on metaphor and thought, see the chapters in Gibbs ed. 2008.)

9.2 Framing

After the theory of 'conceptual metaphor', more recently the idea of 'framing' has been introduced into Cognitive Linguistics. Framing, in George Lakoff's words, is about having the right words for one's ideology at one's disposal. As in the cognitive study of metaphors, the idea is that a word/name/phrase creates a conceptual frame within which actions and events are seen. Such a frame may determine the policy of a party or of a whole country, but it also may make people see this policy in a certain light. G. Lakoff's book *Don't Think of an Elephant* (2004) begins with the following account of his experience when teaching framing theory:

> When I teach the study of framing at Berkeley, in Cognitive Science 101, the first thing I do is I give my students an exercise. The exercise is: Don't think of an elephant! Whatever you do, do *not* think of an elephant. I've never found a student who is able to do this. Every word, like *elephant*, evokes a frame, which can be an image or other kinds of knowledge: Elephants are large, have floppy ears and a trunk, are associated with circuses, and so on. The word is defined relative to that frame. When we negate a frame, we evoke the frame. Richard Nixon found that out the hard way. While under pressure to resign during the Watergate scandal, Nixon addressed the nation on TV. He stood before the nation and said, 'I am not a crook'. And everybody thought about him as a crook. This gives us a basic principle of framing, for when you are arguing against the other side: Do not use their language. Their language picks out a frame – and it won't be the frame you want.

The concept of 'framing' was originally created by Erving Goffman, who noticed that certain frames (i.e. general concepts about situations) were responsible for specific behaviour in certain situations and contexts. For instance, if the hospital situation is framed as a theatrical 'play', behaviour will be different from framing it as 'prison'. Framing, seen in this way, comes close to the ideas of constructivism, since it assumes that we, on the one hand, behave in accordance with a frame, but on the other create reality to fit within the frame. As G. Lakoff writes (2006, ch. 3):

> 'Framing' is not primarily about politics or political messaging, or communication. It is far more fundamental than that: Frames are the mental structures that allow human beings to understand reality – and sometimes to create what we take to be reality.

The consequences of framing in politics (for example, framing the response to the events of 9/11 as a 'war on terrorism' or as a 'global struggle against extremists') are an important aspect of the role of language in politics (see Chapter 18).

10. Summary (Part II)

In Part II, we have been concerned with language as a system of sounds, words and syntactic structures. We have explored how these systemic elements influence, determine and have an impact on our thoughts, thus our actions and consequently our relation to others and to the phenomena around us. From the Abbé de Condillac to Humboldt, Whorf and finally George Lakoff, we have encountered a considerable number of approaches in which language is seen as a force which shapes, constructs or frames the way we look upon the world and act in it. On the other hand, we have also encountered many thinkers who see in language a system of signs which misleads our thoughts and sends them in the 'wrong' direction.

Recent approaches to the impact of language as a system tend to see in language a 'construing' force which creates reality for us. This view is congruent with feminist ideas about the role of language in construing gender differences and maintaining the dominance of certain social groupings. Representatives of the 'construing force' approach see in language a power strong enough to effect certain changes in our society. The position taken in this book concerning this is that we have to imagine a **bidirectional interaction** between language and society, in which it is impossible to say whether language mirrors social changes or triggers them. The impact of the language system on individuals, societies and the community of living beings is certainly a field worth investigating in more depth and with new empirical resources.

Part III

The Impact of Discourse on the World

Words, so innocent and powerless as they are, as standing in a dictionary, how potent for good and evil they become in the hands of one who knows how to combine them. (Nathaniel Hawthorne)

11. Language as Discourse

The impact of Discourse, or *parole* in Saussure's terminology, is the most immediate of the three types of impact. Speaking and writing can lead to violent action or pacify a crowd, cause pleasant aesthetic effects or make one vomit, confirm ideological and political attitudes or suppress them. Using language in concrete situations can make people buy something, contribute to healing mental disorders, and it can make someone hate you or fall in love with you. With some of these effects, it is not only the 'meaning' expressed in the discourse which produces the effect, but also the formal or 'physical' side of it. Thus to 'make someone fall in love with you' *may* be a question of *what* you say (of 'meaning'), but more frequently of the quality of your voice and the combination of vocal, verbal and non-verbal elements. 'Impact' of this kind may be 'desired', but is frequently unintended.

Discourse has been defined very generally as 'language in action' (Blommaert 2005: 2). There are, however, a number of more specific definitions of 'discourse', which will be presented briefly in the following section.

Fairclough (1992: 3) discusses the following meanings of '**discourse**' in linguistics:

- 'Extended samples of spoken dialogue, in contrast with written "texts".'
- 'Extended samples of either spoken or written language.' 'Discourse', used in this sense 'emphasizes interaction between speaker and addressee or between writer and reader, and therefore processes of producing and interpreting speech and writing, as well as the situational context of language use.'
- 'Different types of language used in different sorts of social situation (e.g. "newspaper discourse", "Advertising discourse", "classroom discourse", "the discourse of medical consultations").'

The use of discourse in the latter (the widest) sense is frequently associated with the French philosopher Michel Foucault, in whose work the term refers to 'different ways of structuring areas of knowledge and social practice' (Fairclough 1992: 3). In Foucault's understanding, discourse is something that 'creates' truth for a society: 'Each society has its régime of truth, its "general politics" of truth: that is, the types of discourse which it accepts and makes function as true' (Foucault 1980: 131; cf. Goatly 2007: 26).

In our book, we will use 'discourse' in all the senses mentioned by Fairclough, viz. **written** and **spoken** manifestations of 'language' which may, but need not be restricted to an individual text. Thus, we might speak of 'political discourse', of 'therapeutic discourse' or of discourse concerning a specific topic, such as the 'discourse about environmental problems'. An individual discourse unit is also called a 'text': the impact of texts will be dealt with in a separate chapter (see 15 below).

In *Approaches to Discourse,* Schiffrin (1994: 20–43) discusses a number of definitions of Discourse, as given by different authors. Among these are 'language above the sentence or above the clause' (Stubbs 1983: 1), 'language in use' (Fasold 1990: 65; Brown and Yule 1983: 1) and language as utterances (not sentences). In the main part of her book, Schiffrin (1994: 45–334) presents six approaches to Discourse, viz. (1) via speech act theory, (2) through interactional sociolinguistics, (3) ethnography of communication, (4) pragmatics, (5) conversation analysis, and (6) variation analysis. While all these approaches are viable and make good sense, the one most important from our impact perspective is the pragmatic approach, which stresses the uses and effects of language and discourse. This approach will therefore be the first to be discussed in this volume.

When, in 1938, Charles Morris postulated (along with syntactics and semantics) a branch of linguistics called **Pragmatics** – to study the origins, the uses and the effects of language – he prepared the ground for a new understanding of language, by which no longer the structures and changes on the different levels of language (sounds, morphemes, lexemes, sentences) were to be studied, but rather the influence of the manifestations of language (texts in the widest sense) on ourselves, on other people and thus on the world (see Morris 1971). The study of this influence, with Morris's threefold distinction, now occupies at least one-third of the research effort of linguists; it has achieved almost equal significance with the study of the units of language (syntactics) and their meaning in the traditional sense (semantics).

When discussing discourse from an effect-oriented point-of-view, we should be aware that language on the discourse level utilizes a number of different sign-systems, not all of them **verbal** or vocal. Indeed, non-vocal communication, consisting of **paralinguistic** elements, 'e.g. gestures, eye-movements, etc. supporting verbal communication' and **gestures** not supporting verbal communication (see the diagram 'Relations between verbal and non-verbal communication' in Hinde 1972: 91), account for much of the effect of spoken discourse. The percentages given in various publications concerning what is communicated non-verbally are quite high but difficult to verify. In this volume, there will be no separation of verbal from non-verbal effects. Let it suffice to say that by 'Discourse' we mean **written** as well as **spoken** discourse and that with spoken discourse the combination between verbal and non-verbal elements (supportive or contradictory) must always be taken into consideration. Following Argyle (1972), John Lyons expresses the 'interpenetration' of the verbal and the non-verbal components of language as follows: "The most we can say, perhaps, is that the verbal component is more closely associated with the 'cognitive' and the non-verbal with the 'attitudinal' or 'social' function of language" (Lyons 1972: 55; see also D. Morris 2002).

12. Precursors of Pragmatics

In their excellent book on the Early History of Pragmatics, *Language, Action and Context,* Nerlich and Clarke (1996) have included chapters on Pragmatics *avant la lettre* in Germany, France and England. For a more detailed discussion of the precursors of Pragmatics in these countries, the reader is thus referred to Nerlich and Clarke's book (particularly pages 177–373). The following chapter is only a short summary of early pragmalinguistic thought with special emphasis on ideas concerning language and its impact on the world.

Among the many thinkers in whose work Nerlich and Clarke find ideas along the lines of twentieth-century pragmatics are the following:

John Locke – his 'semiotic philosophy' influenced, above all, Condillac, Berkeley and Kant; his linguistic scepticism had a decisive influence on German speaking critics of language, above all on Fritz Mauthner (see Chapter 6.2 above). A similar influence was exerted by Berkeley, Burke and Hume (cf. Nerlich and Clarke 1996: 96–100).

Wilhelm v. Humboldt – language as *ergon* and *energeia* (1996: 52; see Chapter 4 above).

Friedrich Schleiermacher (1768–1834) – language system and language use (*Sprachgesetz und Sprachgebrauch*).

Port-Royal Grammar (1660, Antoine Arnaud and Claude Lancelot) – differentiates between propositional content and certain speech act types (e.g. assertion, order, question).

Etienne Bonnot de Condillac (1714–1780) – 'language of action': 'From the outset language is therefore an act before it becomes a means of representation.'

Thomas Hobbes (1588–1679), who makes a distinction between language and speech.

Thomas Reid (1710–1796), for whom an idea is not a 'mental content or object', but a 'mental act'. The following excerpt is from Reid's *Essays on the Intellectual Powers* (1785) and is quoted from Nerlich and Clarke (1996: 103): 'The expression of a question, of a command, or of a promise, is as capable of being analysed as a proposition is; but we do not find that this has been attempted; we have not so much as given them a name different from the operations which they express.' This clearly anticipates the idea of speech-acts, for which Reid even provided a preliminary taxonomy (cf. Nerlich and Clarke 1996: 109).

Michel Bréal (1832–1915), teacher of Meillet and Saussure. Apart from being one of the originators of Semantics (he coined the term 'la sémantique', see Bréal 1899), Bréal also took a 'pragmatic' attitude to language teaching in schools. In 1877 he wrote: 'Language is not only made to say "The sun shines on the countryside", "the rivers flow into the sea". Beyond that language serves mainly to give expression to desires, demands, to be the expression of the will. It is this *subjective* side of language that should be studied more if you want to tempt the pupil to use the instrument that you provide him with' (quoted from Nerlich and Clarke 1996: 246).

Grace De Laguna (1889–1978), who, in her book *Speech: its Function and Development* (1927: 19) wrote: 'Men do not speak simply to reveal feelings or to air their views, but to awaken a response in their fellows and to influence their attitudes and acts' (quoted from Nerlich and Clarke 1996: 140). De Laguna criticizes contemporary linguistics which does not take into consideration this function of language: 'What is lacking so far is the conception of the social *function* of speech. Speech continues to be referred to as the communication of ideas, which are still implicitly regarded as inner processes in individual minds. It would be far more in accord with Durkheim's general theory to regard the *function* of speech equally with the structure of language, as an objective social phenomenon' (1927: 124, note 1; quoted from Nerlich and Clarke 1996: 142). De Laguna's plea to explore the 'function' of speech was soon taken up by Frédéric Paulhan, by Karl Bühler and later by Roman Jakobson and Michael Halliday (see the section on functional models in Chapter 2).

Further precursors of Pragmalinguistics were the representatives of 'Pragmatism', a method of philosophizing aimed at making our ideas clear and thus at facilitating communication. Pragmatism was initiated by C. S. Peirce with an essay 'How to Make Our Ideas Clear' (1878); other representatives are William James (key word: 'usefulness'), John Dewey ('instrumentalism') and George Herbert Mead (1862–1931) one of the teachers of Charles Morris, with his 'Philosophy of the Act'.

In the history of Pragmalinguistics, a special place is to be reserved for **Victoria, Lady Welby** (1837–1912; see Nerlich and Clarke 1996: 294–302). Her circle of friends, which included Frederik van Eeden and George Frederick Stout, called themselves the school of 'significs' (a term used by Welby instead of 'semantics'). However, it is Lady Welby's own work that we are concerned with here. In 1896, she wrote an article 'Sense, Meaning and Interpretation' and another one in 1897, in which she distinguished three types of meaning: sense (word-content), meaning (= intention, volitional, intentional activity) and significance (moral value). In a way, she anticipated Wittgenstein's 1953 definition of **meaning as use**, when she wrote in 1903: 'There is, strictly speaking, no such thing as the Sense of a word, but only the sense in which it is used – the circumstances, state of mind, reference, "universe of discourse" belonging to it. The Meaning of a word is the intent which it is desired to convey – the intention of the user' (Welby 1903: 5–6, quoted from Nerlich and Clarke 1996: 302; cf. W. A. Myers 1995: 14).

Lady Welby did not have any schooling in linguistics but was self-educated. It can be assumed that otherwise she would have concerned herself either with language change or with the structures of language. As it was, she was free of the theoretical background of her contemporaries and developed a theory of language in which the intention of the speaker played the most important role. Her book *What is Meaning? Studies in the Development of Significance* (1903, now available as Welby 1983) was kindly reviewed by one of the founders of semiotics, C. S. Peirce. Her three types of meaning may well have influenced Peirce in the development of his typology of signs (symbol, icon, index), though Peirce himself 'takes pains in one letter to Welby (14 March 1909) to disclaim any influence on him of her triad sense, meaning, significance: "I now find that my division neatly coincides with yours, as it ought to do exactly, if both are correct. I am not in the least conscious of having been at all influenced by your book in settling my trichotomy"' (Myers 1995: 20).

Welby had an eight year correspondence with Peirce; she also corresponded with C. K. Ogden (co-author of *The Meaning of Meaning*), William James and Bertrand Russell (see *Wikipedia*, s.v. Victoria, Lady Welby).

In *The Meaning of Meaning* (Ogden and Richards 1969/1923), Lady Welby is mentioned in the preface among those from whose work 'the writers have derived instruction and occasionally amusement' (1969: ix). In the body of the book, she is referred to several times as one 'who for twenty years eloquently exhorted philosophers and others to concentrate attention on the meaning of meaning' (e.g. 1969: 192 fn.), though her 'insistence on Meaning as human intention' is criticized as vague and lacking the necessary analysis (*ibid.*).

A precursor of pragmatics, who came from the Humboldtian tradition, is **Philipp Wegener**, who saw one of the main functions of language in *Willensbeeinflussung* [influencing other people's wills]. Among the means of influencing others, Wegener lists imperatives, questions, but also threats and promises, acts which frequently have to be surmised [*erschlossen*] (Wegener 1885: 80). Here Wegener clearly talks about levels beyond the sentence and enters into the vicinity of describing illocutions and speech acts. 'For Wegener, it is only in dialogue that the purpose and intention of speech emerge, which is to influence somebody in a certain way. [...] He argues against the common view that the real purpose of uttering a sentence is the communication of thought' (Nerlich and Clarke 1996: 179). Wegener specifically mentions 'the effect of utterances' (1885: 71) and thus, at a time when most philologists studied the laws of sound change, concerned himself with topics which only 100 years later began to be investigated seriously.

In connection with Wegener, the philosophers **Franz Brentano** and **Anton Marty** must be mentioned, with their emphasis on the 'intentionality' of speaking and on speaking as a special kind of acting (cf. Nerlich and Clarke 1996: 189 f.; for Marty, see also above, Chapter 6.2). Intentionality became one of the key concepts of the philosophical school of the Phenomenologists (with Edmund Husserl and Martin Heidegger as its main representatives). Because of this emphasis on intentionality, on acting and the subject-object relation, Phenomenology is sometimes seen as 'practical philosophy', but also as the theoretical background to Pragmalinguistics. However, the Phenomenologists were more interested in meaning being directed towards an object or event than in meaning as effect on the world. Marcel Merleau-Ponty, a follower of this school, was interested in the act of speaking chiefly from the point of view of linguistic creativity, not so much of its effect on thought and action (see above, Chapter 4.2 on the Phenomenologists).

Other precursors of Pragmatics are those linguists who distinguished *several* 'functions' of language, the representative function being just one of them (see above, Chapter 2 on functional models). **Ogden and Richards**, writing in 1923, distinguish between the symbolic and the evocative function and repeatedly stress that language is not just there to convey ideas, a concept which was emphasized even more by **Bronislaw Malinowski** in a supplement to Ogden and Richards's book. Malinowski called speaking 'a mode of action' and (in 1923!) already used the word 'pragmatic': 'language in its primitive function and original form has an essentially *pragmatic* character; that it is a mode of behaviour, and indispensable element of concerted human action' (1969: 316, emphasis added).

Criticism of Ogden and Richards came from **J. R. Firth**, who in his article 'The Technique of Semantics' (1957a, first published in 1935) expressed his view that thinking and acting together make up the whole of the human being:

> I do not therefore follow Ogden and Richards in regarding meaning as relations in a hidden mental process, but chiefly as situational relations in a context of situation and in that kind of language which disturbs the air and other people's ears, as modes of behaviour in relation to the other elements in the context of situation. (Firth 1957a: 19)

In the same article, Firth gives a list of 'linguistic functions' (reminiscent of Wittgenstein's 'language games'), among which he enumerates the language of agreement, encouragement, endorsement, disagreement and condemnation – even of love-making! For Firth, influencing the thoughts, feelings and actions of others were important meanings of language which the linguists of his time had not yet considered sufficiently:

As language is a way of dealing with people and things, a way of behaving and of making others behave, we could add many types of function – wishing, blessing, cursing, boasting, the language of challenge and appeal, or with intent to cold-shoulder, to belittle, to annoy or hurt, even to a declaration of enmity. The use of words to inhibit hostile action, or to delay or modify it, or to conceal one's intention are very interesting and important 'meanings'. Nor must we forget the language of social flattery and love-making, of praise and blame, of propaganda and persuasion. (Firth 1957a: 31)

Firth's view of language is clearly one of 'doing things', not just one of communicating truths or conveying ideas. Firth's proposal to study conversation ('it is here we shall find the key to a better understanding of what language really is and how it works', 1957a: 32) also shows his dynamic understanding of language. Of particular interest is his idea that language can be used to inhibit, delay or modify 'hostile action' – perhaps an early attempt at suggesting a study of 'language, conflict and peace' (see below, Chapter 20.1).

The 'functions of language' (representative, expressive and appellative) were most prominently discussed by Karl Bühler, whose 'appellative function' already implies the idea of language having an effect on others. Jakobson added the phatic, the metalinguistic and the poetic function to the canon, while Halliday developed a system of meta-functions based on language uses experienced by children in the stage of language acquisition (for more on functional models of language see Chapter 2, this volume).

13. Pragmatics

For the development and scope of **Pragmatics** the reader is referred to the many introductions into the field. From the impact perspective, the following are to be recommended specifically: Maas and Wunderlich (eds. 1974), Leech (1983), Thomas (1995), Mey (2001), Bublitz (2001), Grundy (2000), Huang (2007), Cutting (2008) and Lycan (2008: 135–172). Here only a short summary can be given.

Uses and Effects

The study of the **uses and effects** of language began with:

- **Wittgenstein**'s definition of meaning as use, his comparison of language with a tool-box and his list of language games (1953). Here the uses of language were for the first time separated from the sentence types. A statement is rarely used to state something and a question is frequently not a request for information. The 'real meaning' of sentences may be anything – from suggestion, criticism and complaint to apology, boast or declaration of love. (For a critique of Wittgenstein's definition of meaning as use see the chapter on '"Use" theories' in Lycan, 2008: 76–85)

Awareness of uses and effects continued with

- **Austin**'s *How to Do Things with Words* (1962), in which a distinction between constative and performative utterances is made, and the three acts – locutionary, illocutionary (use) and perlocutionary (effect) are distinguished. Austin also makes a preliminary classification of illocutions.
- **Searle** (1969, 1979) introduced the term 'speech-act' for something you do with language. His classes of speech-acts and thus things we do with language are the following (from 'a taxonomy of illocutionary acts', 1979: 1–29):

Assertives	(stating, boasting, predicting, guessing, etc.)
Directives	(ordering, demanding, requesting, inviting, permitting, etc.)
Commissives	(promising, offering, refusing, threatening, etc.)
Expressives	(thanking, congratulating, pardoning, blaming, praising, etc.)
Declarations	(naming, baptizing, declaring open, appointing, etc.).

Searle's notion of the 'indirect speech-act' (1975) is meant to express that one utterance can have more than one use and consequently more than one effect. The two or more speech-acts contained in one utterance can be directed at *one* person, but may also be directed at different addressees (on 'split illocution' see Fill 1986).

If two boys (named, say, John and Kevin) are fighting, the utterance of a third 'I'll help you, John' will be an offer of support to John, but a threat to Kevin (example adapted from Wunderlich 1980: 388). Splitting their illocution is something politicians frequently have to do – when they are speaking to different groupings in their own country, or when on state visits they are addressing their hosts, but everything they say is reported by the media in their home country (examples in Fill 1986).

- **Grice**'s 'Cooperative Principle' (1975) with its four maxims (quantity, quality, relevance and manner) is explained with sufficient clarity in the introductions mentioned above (see specifically Leech 1983: 7 f. and also Newen and Schrenk 2008: 42–48). Breaches of Gricean maxims are perhaps more frequent than their observance, but also more meaningful (and hence interesting). The result of the violation of maxims is meaning on a different level, called by Grice 'implicature'. The following example (from Chilton 2004: 39) shows implicatures resulting from lack of coherence on the truth-conditional level:

  Young girl: Why don't you let a room in your house?

  Old woman: The only people I can get are negroes.

  Young girl: Racial prejudice will get you nowhere in this country.

The old woman's utterance (strictly a violation of relevance) has the implicature: 'One cannot let rooms to negroes', while the young girl's answer (also violating relevance on the surface) implies 'not letting rooms to blacks (and calling them negroes) shows racial prejudice'. The dialogue between the young girl and the old woman thus evolves on the level of implicatures, not on the speech act level.

Grice himself (1975) mentions possible floutings of his maxims, such as metaphor, hyperbole and politeness. For politeness, irony and banter (all violating the maxims of quality or quantity), specific principles doing justice to these phenomena have been postulated (see Leech 1983: 79 ff. about politeness, 1983: 142–145 about irony and banter). Further principles, such as 'Say what is unpredictable, and hence interesting' (Interest Principle, Leech 1983: 146) or the 'Polyanna Principle' ('speak looking on the bright side of life', Leech 1983: 147) may also, for the sake of avoiding dullness, be observed, rather than the original Gricean maxims. Laurence Horn (2001: 194) in a way refined the Gricean maxim of Quantity by postulating a hearer oriented Q-Principle (Quantity): 'make your contribution sufficient: say as much as you can', and a speaker oriented R-Principle (Restriction): 'make your contribution necessary: say no more than you must' (see also Huang 2007: 37–40 about 'the Hornian system').

14. Further Topic Areas in Pragmatics

Austin's, Searle's and Grice's framework has given rise to a number of sub-fields of Pragmatics. The speech-act types 'directives', 'requests' and 'giving advice' have been bracketed together and identified as 'control acts' (Ervin-Tripp *et al.* 1990: 308), giving rise to the study of **control** in language (e.g. Penz 1996 on TV talk shows, Vine 2004 on workplace interaction). Following Leech (1983), the study of politeness was introduced as a topic in its own right (P. Brown and Levinson 1987; Schulze 1985; Holmes 1995; Watts 2003). Topics concerning the subject of politeness are now dealt with in a journal devoted just to that topic area (*Journal of Politeness Research*, published by Mouton de Gruyter), while researchers such as Jonathan Culpeper (Lancaster) and Manfred Kienpointner (Innsbruck) are beginning to investigate rudeness, the opposite of politeness. Grice's maxim of relevance has given rise to '**Relevance Theory**', in which relevance is assumed to embrace all other maxims (Sperber and Wilson 1986; Wilson and Sperber 2004). Wilson and Sperber make a distinction between decoding (a message is encoded by the sender and decoded by the receiver) and inferencing (the meaning of a message is 'inferred', i.e. understood from the available evidence). All messages carry their own 'promise' of relevance to the receiver, relevance being defined in the following way:

> Intuitively, an input (a sight, a sound, an utterance, a memory) is relevant to an individual when it connects with background information he has available to yield conclusions that matter to him: say by answering a question he had in mind, improving his knowledge on a certain topic, settling a doubt, confirming a suspicion, or correcting a mistaken impression. According to relevance theory, an input is relevant to an individual when its processing in a context of available assumptions yields a POSITIVE COGNITIVE EFFECT. A positive cognitive effect is a worthwhile difference to the individual's representation of the world: a true conclusion, for example. (Wilson and Sperber 2004: 608, their emphasis; see also Yus 2006)

Relevance is thought by some researchers to have been one of the decisive factors in the evolution of language: it was of advantage to an individual to be known as a giver of relevant information. The pros and cons of this thesis are discussed in Chapter 1.3 above.

A distinction between **transactional** and **interactional** macro-functions is made by G. Brown and Yule (1983: 1–4) and explained further by Cutting (2008: 21). While the transactional function refers to the communication of information, the interactional one concerns the *phatic* use of language 'to establish and maintain social relationships' (Brown and Yule 1983: 3). Brown and Yule see their distinction in correspondence with Bühler's 'representative' vs. 'expressive' functions, Jakobson's 'referential' and 'emotive', Halliday's 'ideational' vs. 'interpersonal' and Lyons' 'descriptive' vs. 'social-expressive' functions. Somewhat surprisingly only two functions are distinguished, with no equivalent to Bühler's 'appellative' function being presented. (See the section on functional models above, Chapter 2.)

Inferential Pragmatics

For language to have an effect ('perlocution'), the hearer/reader must somehow establish from the literal meaning of what is written (or said) what the writer (speaker) intended to convey. Thus the **inferences** the receiver has to make offer a specific field of study which is addressed by Inferential Pragmatics (Brown and Yule 1983: 256, see also Komlosi 1997 and Carston 2005).

Conversation Analysis

Conversation analysis (CA) is a specific area of Pragmatics in which formal and content elements of conversation are studied. Topics of CA are, among others: the negotiation of topics, the speech acts used, and the turn-taking mechanisms which come into play (see, for instance, Sacks *et al.* 1974; Coulthard 1977: 52–92; Schiffrin 1994: 232–281; Hutchby and Wooffitt 1998; Mey 2001: 134–179).

Deixis

Most introductions to Pragmatics contain chapters on 'Deixis', the study of reference to person, place and time. This field, however, which lies between semantics and pragmatics, is of little importance for our topic of language impact and will therefore be omitted from our discussion (for Deixis, see, for instance, Bublitz 2001: 203–236, where politeness is understood as 'social deixis', and Huang 2007: 132–177).

14.1 Interactional Patterns, Pathologies, and Language in Therapy

The title of this section refers to the subtitle of a well-known book, *Pragmatics of Human Communication* by Paul **Watzlawick**, Janet Beavin **Bavelas** and Don D. **Jackson**. The Pragmatics of Watzlawick *et al.* (1967) is influenced by Gregory Bateson, thus somewhat different from the Pragmatics of Austin and Searle, but nevertheless relevant for language impact. Watzlawick *et al.* concern themselves with pathological and paradoxical communication as well as with certain topics relevant for psychotherapists.

In linguistics, Watzlawick's 'tentative axioms of communication' introduced in Chapter 2 of his book have become famous. These are (1967: 48–71):

1. It is impossible not to communicate (all behaviour is communication).

2. Communication has a content level and a relational level.
3. The participants in a communication frequently have a different 'punctuation of the sequence of events', i.e. they may have different conceptions of cause and effect in their interaction.
4. Communication can be digital (verbal) or analogic (non-verbal, behavioural).
5. Interaction can be symmetrical or complementary.

Particularly axioms (1) and (2) are frequently quoted in work on linguistic interaction. Axiom (1) says that if words have meaning, the absence of words, too, has meaning: even not taking notice of others has meaning.

> The man at a crowded lunch counter who looks straight ahead, or the airplane passenger who sits with his eyes closed, are both communicating that they do not want to speak to anybody or be spoken to, and their neighbors usually 'get the message' and respond appropriately by leaving them alone. (Watzlawick *et al.* 1967: 49)

Axiom (2) says that a communication not only conveys information, but also defines the relationship between the communicants. Communication usually has a 'report part' and a 'command part', where the command part consists of meta-communication about how the report part is to be taken. '"This is an order" or "I am only joking" are verbal examples of such communication about communication. The relationship can also be expressed non-verbally by shouting or smiling or in a number of other ways' (Watzlawick *et al.* 1967: 53). This axiom was extended by Schulz von Thun (1981: 30), who assumed not two, but four aspects of every utterance. These can be represented on the four sides of a rectangle, as follows:

<table>
<tr><td colspan="2" align="center">Factual content (the information I give)</td></tr>
<tr><td>Expression of self
(what I reveal about myself)</td><td>Appeal
(what I want the hearer to do)</td></tr>
<tr><td colspan="2" align="center">Relation (what I think of the hearer)</td></tr>
</table>

In exchanges (say, between husband and wife) the speaker may only have the factual content or the appeal in mind, while the hearer concentrates exclusively on the relational aspect, which s/he may construe as conveying 'You are inferior to me'.

Watzlawick was a psychologist and psychotherapist. He gives many examples of the use of language in psychotherapy, marriage counselling and similar situations. This use of language, which is becoming more and more important, can only be briefly mentioned here, not discussed in any depth. Using the expressive function of language and 'interthinking' has for some time helped many people to get rid of their psychic problems – in individual and group therapy.

In her chapter 'The Talking Cure', Robin Tolmach Lakoff writes (1990: 59): 'Of all forms of communication, psychotherapy takes language the most seriously.' The use of language to bring about a change in another person's psyche and even to be successful in curing psychic problems has, ever since Sigmund Freud, been one of the most striking effects of language as discourse. The effect of language, in this area, is one on the speaker him/herself as well as on the listener. In the ideal case, the effect of curing a disorder is achieved through the giving and taking of turns in dialogue or group talk (see Labov and Fanshel 1977; Flader ed. 1979; Wodak 1981). William Labov's and David Fanshel's study of therapeutic conversation stresses particularly that 'the interview is simultaneously a diagnostic device and the method of therapy' (Labov and Fanshel 1977: 1). In their book, the case of a 19-year-old Jewish young woman from New York suffering from anorexia nervosa is analysed in detail. In her case, the therapy through conversation was successful.

14.2 Language as a Source of Fun (Humorous Effects)

'Your mother so black she sweat chocolate.'

'Your mother so thin she ice-skate on a razor-blade.'

'Your mother sent her picture to the lonely hearts' club; but they sent it right back saying "we aren't that lonely".'

An effect of language (as discourse) sometimes overlooked is that it can make people laugh. Telling prepared jokes and spontaneous joking (in conversation) are the best-known manifestations of this effect. How language (e.g. Black English Vernacular) is used ritually to produce humorous effects and how this is done even in a competitive way is described by William Labov in 'Rules for Ritual Insults' (1972: 297–353); the examples above (with mock-insults of the addressee's mother) are taken from this essay. This activity is also called 'sounding', 'signifying' or 'playing the dozens'. As is well-known, the power of language to make people laugh is used in humour therapy (an internet bibliography concerning this topic is provided by the 'International Society for Humor Studies' ISHS).

Geoffrey N. Leech, in his *Principles of Pragmatics* (1983) postulates a specific 'banter principle', which overrules the 'Cooperative Principle' established by Grice. The 'comic power' of language on its different levels has been described by many authors (e.g. Nash 1985; Raskin 1985; Attardo 1994; Alexander 1997; Ross 1998) and is further investigated in many articles published in the journal *Humor: International Journal of Humor Research,* edited by the ISHS.

The different theories of humour (incongruity theory, superiority theory, psychic release theory, etc.) are discussed in Raskin (1985) and Attardo (1994: 47–59). The theories are explained with the help of examples in Ross (1998). We have to distinguish between prepared jokes ('canned' jokes) and spontaneous context-bound conversational joking (cf. Alexander 1997: 11; Fill 2007: 115–123), though the two types may overlap, as when a canned joke is contextualized in conversation. But whatever the cause of the humour and whether it is prepared or spontaneous, what interests us in the context of our topic is the **effects** of humorous language on hearers and readers (see also Attardo 1994: 322–329 on the social functions of humour). A number of different groups of effect can be distinguished:

- **Bonding effects**: humour/comic effects leading to laughter create a feeling of sociability and link people together. In this context it may be of interest to point out that not all scholars see laughter and smiling as a 'continuum of intergrading signals' (Van Hooff 1972: 235) with smiling representing a kind of 'diminutive of laughter' (1972: 211; cf. German *lachen* [laugh] and *lächeln* [smile]). For some authors, laughing and smiling have different phylogenetic origins (after all, smiling involves baring the teeth), are reactions to different stimuli and have different functions. An overview of the different views is given by Van Hooff (1972).

- **Conflict solving effects**: humour may be a means to avoid a quarrel, solve a conflict or play down disagreement. It may make leave-taking easier and help to overcome awkward situations (e.g. unintentional offence, social gaffes, etc.). In some cultures (in Africa, Asia, Oceania), there are 'joking relationships', i.e. relationships in which communication occurs exclusively in jest. Thus, a man may talk to his mother-in-law only in jest, the purpose being to avoid situations in which a conflict might escalate verbally. Non-serious insults are exchanged, and through 'sham-conflicts' real conflicts are avoided (cf. Radcliffe-Brown 1952: 90 ff.; see 20.1 below). The 'ritual insults' described by Labov (see the examples above) may also be used 'to manage challenges within the peer group' (Labov 1972: 353). Cases in which joking leads to the escalation of a conflict or even to a quarrel are rare, but cannot be excluded.

- **Aesthetic effects**: humour may give pleasure and create an effect similar to that of a work of art. The effect of several genres of literature (comedy, parody, satire, etc.) is based on humour, which is mostly verbal humour.

- **Ideational/attitudinal effects**: these effects come into play particularly with jokes about certain groups (social, regional; race, gender, professions, habits); jokes may perpetuate (but rarely create) clichés and stereotypes about certain groups; on the other hand, they may lead to the rejection of stereotypes. Ross (1998: 55) writes the following concerning stereotypes in Irish jokes and jokes about mothers-in-law:

> Some people claim that language simply *reflects* existing attitudes, that sexism and racism exist 'in the real world' and that words do not change anything. Others maintain that language is a powerful weapon, and that making conscious decisions about the use of language can help to *form or change* attitudes. The latter position leads to a deliberate rejection of humour that relies on a portrayal

> of mothers-in-law as nagging and the Irish as thick, on the grounds that it tends
> to perpetuate harmful social divisions.

Ross notes a decline in Irish jokes and mother-in-law jokes but leaves it open whether this has occurred because of changes in attitudes or external control over language and joking. The movement of Political Correctness has led to the avoidance of jokes about groups and of what Freud called 'tendentious jokes' (Attardo 1994: 55). The view that verbal humour played a greater role in the past than it does now is held by many people. Investigations into this would be welcome, although it will be difficult to prove or disprove this view empirically.

14.3 Language and the Law: Forensic Linguistics

> P: What can you tell me about the house that you burgled last night?
>
> P: How come you told us earlier that you burgled the house?
>
> P: Do you remember burgling the house?

Discourse can send people to prison or acquit them. The example above shows three questions with which a police officer might try to get a confession out of a suspect. A forensic linguist would show the 'coercive' nature of these questions and might suggest a less coercive way of questioning the suspect, e.g. by asking 'Do you remember the events of the 18th of January?' (example from Gibbons 2003: 103–107, adapted).

Reports – even confessions – made by an accused are frequently not genuine but linguistically altered by the police so that the alleged 'guilt' of the arrested person becomes apparent. The forensic linguist's task, in this case, is to find out what the arrested person really said. The reports should be 'verbatim', but frequently they are written in police language, also called 'policese' (Gregory 2000: 19) or 'policespeak' (Hall 2008).

'Discourse in the justice system' has a direct impact on the lives of people and thus represents a particularly interesting topic for linguists. According to Gibbons (2003: 12), the *AILA Scientific Commission on Forensic Linguistics*[1] defines the field as 'the study of the link between language and the law in all of its forms'. In more detail, the following areas, in which this link becomes apparent, are listed:

1. The study of the language of the law, including the language of legal documents and the language of the courts.
2. The study, the provision and the improvement of professional legal interpreting and translation services.
3. The alleviation of disadvantage produced by language in legal processes.

4. The provision of forensic linguistic evidence that is based on the best linguistic expertise.
5. The provision of linguistic expertise in issues of legal drafting and interpretation, including plain drafting.

As is well known, the language of the law and of legal documents (area 1 in the above list) is sometimes so complex that it has to be translated into 'plain English' to be understood, as in the following example (from Gibbons 2003: 183 after J. C. Redish):

Original version of part of a hire-purchase agreement: The buyer further promises to pay the holder thereof a delinquency and collection charge for default in the payment of any instalments above recited, where such default has continued for a period of ten days [...]

Plain language version: You also promise to pay a late fee if your payment is more than 10 days overdue.

A typical task where 'the best linguistic expertise' (area 4) is needed involves finding linguistic evidence on **authorship** (Gibbons 2003: 296–309). By analysing specific linguistic features, it may be possible to identify senders of threatening telephone calls or letters. Senders of threatening messages (or messages of embezzlement) can thus be narrowed down by the linguist as to their region of origin, their social class or other idiosyncratic language patterns. Linguistic expertise is also needed in the discovery of **plagiarism**, proof of which can be found in stylistic idiosyncrasies. Among the areas affected by plagiarism are at least the following: internet, education, literature and translation (see the discussion in Turell 2008: 267–271). Today, for testing written texts as to authorship computer programs are widely used (see also Coulthard 1994; Asp 2000). (For more on 'Language and the Law' see Kniffka ed. 1996; Gibbons and Turell eds. 2008 and the journal *Forensic Linguistics*, published by Birmingham University Press.)

Note

1. *AILA (Association internationale de linguistique appliquée)*, the International Association of Applied Linguistics, does not have Scientific Commissions any more, but is now (2010) divided into 15 divisions. The areas of Forensic Linguistics listed are nevertheless valid.

15. The Impact of Texts

'Text' (Lat. < *textum* = what is interwoven) is sometimes used synonymously with 'discourse', though there is a tendency to mean by 'text' a 'written piece of discourse'. In this study, we will use 'text' to mean a specific unit of discourse or, in accordance with the definition of De Beaugrande and Dressler (1981: 3) 'a communicative occurrence which meets seven standards of textuality', or indeed, in David Crystal's definition (1997: 438): 'a stretch of spoken or written language with a definable communicative function (news report, poem, road sign, etc.)' (see also Fairclough 1995a: 187–213 about 'discourse and text'). The seven standards of textuality according to De Beaugrande and Dressler are cohesion, coherence, intentionality, acceptability, informativity, situationality and intertextuality (for details see 1981: 3–11).

More relevant to our topic of language impact are studies of the use and effect of the different text types – a topic which is also addressed in some of the work produced in **text-linguistics**. Adrian Beard, in *How Texts Work* (cf. 2003: 25 ff.), distinguishes four categories of purpose into which most texts fall (author's italics):

> Texts produced to *persuade*
>
> Texts produced to *instruct or advise*
>
> Texts produced to *entertain*
>
> Texts produced to *inform.*

Texts may have one or more of these purposes, sometimes even a *primary* and a *secondary* purpose, but much depends on the context, and frequently the intended purpose is not the purpose understood (e.g. a polite request may be misunderstood as a sinister threat, cf. Beard 2003: 26).

A specific branch of text-linguistics deals with the text-type '**conversation**', in which the negotiation of topics and subtopics, as well as the role of speech-acts and turn-taking, are specific areas of research (for 'conversation analysis' see, for instance Coulthard 1977; Crystal and Davy 1981; Bublitz 1988; Brinker and Sager 1996; Mey 2001: 134–170; see also above Chapter 13). Most interesting for our topic are those analyses of conversation in which the creativity of 'common talk' (Carter 2004) and the problem-solving function of talking together (Mercer 2000) are investigated. Carter's main point is that linguistic creativity is not something found only in literary (or advertising, etc.) texts, but that it is a common feature of everyday conversation and dialogue, in which punning, verbal play and the creation of alternative realities go hand in hand with morphological and lexical inventiveness

(2004: 11–13). Mercer stresses that 'language provides us with a means for *thinking together*, for jointly creating knowledge and understanding' (2000: 15; emphasis by Mercer), which enables us to solve problems collectively.

Studies of '**Language in Politics**' and '**Language in Advertising**' have mushroomed since the beginning of text-linguistics and Pragmatics (see for instance Atkinson 1984; Kettemann ed. 1998; Beard 2000; Partington 2003; Alexander 2009: 163–214, etc. for politics; Leech 1966; Myers 1994; Myers 1997; Stöckl 1997; Goddard 1998; Cook 2001 for advertising). The use of language to create **A**ttention, **I**nterest, **M**emorability and **D**esire, which finally 'prompts the right kind of action' (Leech 1966: 27), has been discussed in many publications.

With Norman Fairclough's book *Language and Power* (1989/2001), the analysis of texts and discourse became 'critical', i.e. the hidden ideologies in texts began to be uncovered. Studies of manipulation and the exertion of power through language were made before Fairclough (e.g. by Mackensen 1973; Lay 1980 and others), but by becoming 'critical', linguistic analysis was linked with social criticism, media studies (Fairclough 1995) and even a particular political direction (Fairclough 2000). Though still in a way a branch of 'text-pragmatics', **Critical Discourse Analysis** (CDA) assumed a life of its own which will be given due attention in Chapter 18 below.

15.1 The Impact of the Internet

The invention of the internet has led to a number of text types and text uses which have brought with them a new kind of impact on the world, an impact which is still becoming stronger and steadily extending to new ontological areas. The main forms of this impact are due to the following activities made possible by the internet:

(a) Making ideas known globally
(b) Sending messages at any time to addressees all over the world
(c) Receiving answers to questions from people anywhere on the earth
(d) 'Chatting' with people one has never met in person
(e) Providing dictionary information for everyone (through *Wikipedia*, etc.)
(f) Dialogic teaching and learning (across cultures)
(g) Offering friendship and finding friends across borders (through social networking services such as *MySpace, Facebook* and *Twitter*)
(h) Storing knowledge and producing it at any time.

The mere possibility of carrying out activities like the ones listed has raised the effect language has on the human community to a level never attained before.

In the second edition of *Language and the Internet* (2006: 238), David Crystal comments on the developments which took place since the first edition of his book (2001, author's italics):

I had anticipated that the four domains of e-mail, chat, virtual worlds and the Web would evolve in interesting directions, but I did not expect to have to add an additional domain to this – and certainly not two. Yet that is what has happened. […] the activities generally referred to as *blogging* and *instant messaging* have developed a linguistic character sufficiently distinctive as to require separate treatment. And other activities, especially in Internet telephony, are becoming apparent just over the linguistic horizon.

The '**blog**' (the word was clipped from 'weblog' around 1999) is a text-type whose impact on the views and attitudes of the general public has grown at an incredible pace in the last few years. Blogs – which include diary entries, comments on news items, and short-lived snippets of news – already have a huge readership, but the growth rate of their influence on public opinion is difficult to assess. In the American Presidential campaigns of 2008, blogs played a major role in influencing the views of millions of voters – to such an extent that blogging is predicted to become a serious danger to traditional journalism (on 'blogging', see O'Brien 2004; Kline and Burstein 2005; Crystal 2006: 238–247).

> Blogging has introduced a new era of interactivity to websites. It has already provided a new means of publishing and distributing information on the Internet, and as the technology develops it could be the next stage in the evolution of online chat. There will be implications for the character of e-mail, too, if bloggers increasingly use the option to have their updates sent out as mail. And the multimedia developments in audio and video blogging will inevitably have consequences, in the form of new linguistic convention, as usage grows. (Crystal 2006: 247)

Most of what is promulgated over the internet is conveyed through **written language** or **language in combination with other media**, but spoken discourse is rapidly gaining ground. Crystal compares the internet to a new way of dressing which may not entirely replace the traditional 'fashion', but makes it look somewhat 'outmoded'. 'I see the arrival of Netspeak as similarly enriching the range of communicative options available to us. And the Internet is going to record this linguistic diversity more fully and accurately than was ever possible before' (Crystal 2006: 276).

The **negative side** of these unlimited options is expressed in the following quotation from Boardman (2005: 40):

> This is what many people see as the negative side of the Web – a haven for illicit activity where innocent surfers are in constant danger of stumbling across something very ugly. There is not the same sense of deliberate channel selection as there is with a TV or radio broadcast; print publications require a great deal of active seeking and physical handling, so with print too there are several stages at which you could opt out of the viewing process.

Many also hold the view that, if anyone can publish anything on the Web for next to nothing, where is the quality control?

While the internet has clearly increased the number of text types and ways in which language is used as discourse, it is still a matter of controversy what the effect of the internet on national and global **language diversity** will be. Some authors (Crystal 2006: 22–24) stress the creativity which 'Netspeak' makes possible, with new spellings (*@home*, the smileys and abbreviations such as *lol* for 'laughing out loud') and neologisms (*blogosphere, clicktosis*) becoming popular. It has also been suggested that the web is multilingual and makes it possible for 'small' languages to be present all over the world. 'The web is increasingly reflecting the distribution of language presence in the real world, and there is a steadily growing set of sites which provide the evidence' (Crystal 2006: 231). On the other hand, the internet (with its still predominantly written texts) will no doubt exert a unifying influence on all languages and thus have an adverse effect on diversity.

Globally, the **predominance of English** on the web may have decreased since 1997, when 82.3% of the web pages were English (Crystal 2006: 230), but English is still the language represented most frequently (cf. Graddol 2006: 44 f.). It is true that awareness of many 'small' and dying languages can be raised all over the world through the internet; on the other hand, there is a tendency for endangered languages to have a 'home page' and a forum on the internet – in English! This will certainly not prevent these languages from dying out.

A different kind of impact of the internet is addressed by Fairclough (2001: viii f.), who writes the following comment on the **social and political consequences** of this new form of networking (2001: ix):

> [The internet] has led to a certain optimism about power inequalities, because it is freely accessible to those who have the necessary technology (though the division between technological 'haves' and 'have-nots' both within and between countries is a major problem in itself); it is a relatively egalitarian form of communication, and it allows forms of networking which promise new possibilities for social and political mobilization.

The following questions need to be posed: Will the internet destroy global language diversity or will it help to keep languages alive? Will it have a levelling effect on new ideas or will it foster creativity? And will it contribute to the disappearance of power inequalities or create a new division into 'haves' and 'have-nots'? These questions are at present (2010) difficult to answer. If one accepts Dawkins' (1976) theory of 'memes', i.e. cultural units handed on from brain to brain and from generation to generation, then the internet is the logical result of a cultural evolution aiming at propagating ideas as fast as possible.

From this perspective, the impact of language has, through the internet, reached a further dimension with the possibility of communicating without temporal and local limitation and spreading new ideas rapidly around the globe – a process in which state borders or demarcation lines between political and social systems do not play the slightest role. One could even speculate that through the internet, the impact of language (whether it be English or any other 'tongue') has reached a stage where language fulfils a new function: the unification of the human species and the globalization of cultural developments (cf. Abbate 2000). It will be up to us, the 'users', in what direction this process will take us.

15.2 The Impact of Language through Literary Texts (Literary and Media Pragmatics)

Language made literature possible. In literature, with its three genres of the epic, the dramatic and the lyrical, we find a specific type of language use with very specific effects. Among these are the following:

- Aesthetic effects (pleasure and entertainment; 'edification')
- Social effects (anger, aggression, sympathy, solidarity with underprivileged groups)
- Sexual effects (e.g. arousal, see Chapter 19.2 below)
- Provocation (e.g. in the novels of D. H. Lawrence) and, as a result,
- Changes of attitude in society.

The study of the effect of literature could be called 'literary pragmatics' – in analogy to linguistic Pragmatics, which studies the uses and effects of language in general. Somewhat surprisingly, this field of study is as yet barren ground. Jacob Mey has written a chapter with this title (Mey 2001: 236–261), in which, however, the main topics are narrative perspective, voice and point of view (see also Mey 1999 with a different conception of literary pragmatics). Among the questions to be asked in literary pragmatics are the following:

Did the **novels** of Dickens have an effect on thinking about social problems?

Did nineteenth-century novels have an effect in raising awareness of Evolution theory?

Did G. B. Shaw's *Pygmalion* make known to the public the role of language variation (standard vs. regiolect or sociolect)?

Did D. H. Lawrence's novels have an effect in changing attitudes towards sexuality?

Did Lawrence's nature **poems** (e.g. in *Birds, Beasts and Flowers*) contribute towards a more ecological understanding of animals and plants?

Did Salinger's *The Catcher in the Rye* create a better understanding of youth problems?

Did Virginia Woolf's novels and did Simone de Beauvoir's books contribute to a better understanding of feminist ideas?

Did George Orwell's novels create a more critical attitude towards authoritarianism and Communism?

Did Berthold Brecht's **plays** create an attitude more sympathetic towards Communism?

Does war literature (e.g. Erich M. Remarque's *All Quiet on the Western Front*) contribute to glorifying war or to making war abhorrent in the eyes of readers?

Have works of literature ever contributed to the overthrow of an authoritarian regime?

What is the effect of modern **films** on attitudes concerning partnership?

Have films ever contributed to a greater awareness of inequality in society?

These and many similar questions could be asked about the effect of literature (and film), and thus the language of literature (and film) on society. As is well known, Aristotle, in his *Poetics*, mentioned '**catharsis**' as one of the effects of drama: the spectator who sees cruelty and violence on stage becomes 'purified' and is unburdened of his/her own tendencies towards cruelty and violence (see 'Aristotle' in the list of philosophers below, Appendix II). To this day, there is a controversy about whether violence in literature (and, of course, especially in film and computer games) leads to cathartic effects or to **stimulation**. Young men who commit acts of cruelty are frequently reported to have watched films containing violence or played violent computer games before committing the act. One criminal who kidnapped a young woman and held her imprisoned for eight years is said to have read John Fowles' novel *The Collector,* in which a similar act is described, before committing the crime (Vienna, 2007). A question which might be added is whether cathartic (or stimulating) effects may be observed *in the mind of an author* who writes about cruelty and violence.

The effect of children's literature and films on character, intelligence, knowledge and the personality of children as readers, listeners and viewers could be another topic of literary and media pragmatics. Fantasy literature, now very popular not just with children, may have the effect of putting readers mentally into a different, perhaps better, world and giving them an agreeable sense of the magic. It may also teach children that words can have a **magic power**, but in addition it may do away with inhibitions and cause children and grown-ups to lose their sense of reality.

The power of the media (here understood as the 'mass media') is expressed very poignantly in the following list adapted from Norman Fairclough's book *Media Discourse* (1995: 2):

The media have the power:

- 'to shape government and parties'
- 'to transform the suffering of the South (rooted in exploitation by the North) into the entertainment of the North'
- 'to beam the popular culture of North America and Western Europe into Indian agricultural communities which still depend upon bullock power'
- 'to influence knowledge, beliefs, values, social relations and social identities.'

Since the power of the media is exercised chiefly through language, the impact of language has, with the rise of the new media, reached dimensions which can truly be called global and universal.

16. Discourse Ethics (Habermas, Apel) and Dialogue (Bohm)

> Rules of discourse can lay the foundation
> to an ethics, called discourse ethics. (Jürgen Habermas)

Our short survey of Pragmatics and related topics (Chapters 13 and 14 above) has dealt with thinkers who are not content to see in language a means to *represent* ideas, truths, reality and the world in general. They interpret language as an instrument for doing something, as a tool with which one can have an effect on others. Doing something with language, viz. using discourse to establish an ethics, is also one of the principles of Discourse Ethics, which was developed by the German philosophers **Jürgen Habermas** (*1929) and **Karl-Otto Apel** (*1922). Taking up an idea of **G. H. Mead** (1934), who criticized both Kantian and Utilitarian ethics, Habermas (1987: II, 141–147) positioned his Discourse Ethics in opposition to Kantian ethics as epitomized by the famous 'categorical imperative':

> Handle nur nach derjenigen Maxime, durch die Du zugleich wollen kannst, dass sie ein allgemeines Gesetz werde!

> *Act only in accordance with the maxim through which you can also wish that it may become a general law.*

This 'deontological' ('thou shalt [not] …') principle is replaced by Habermas with a co-operative search for **solutions by means of a discourse** in which only the quality of the arguments counts (cf. Habermas 1992: 13 f.). Instead of the categorical imperative, Discourse Ethics thus uses moral argumentation with the 'Principle D' (for *Discourse*), which says (Habermas 1992: 12):

(a) dass nur diejenigen Normen Geltung beanspruchen dürfen, die die Zustimmung aller Betroffenen als Teilnehmer eines praktischen Diskurses finden könnten,

 only those norms may claim validity which could find agreement among all the people involved as participants of a practical discourse.

(b) dass bei gültigen Normen Ergebnisse und Nebenfolgen, die sich voraussichtlich aus einer allgemeinen Befolgung für die Befriedigung der Interessen eines jeden ergeben, von allen zwanglos akzeptiert werden müssen.

 If valid norms exist, results and side-consequences (for the satisfaction of individual interests) which come from the general fulfilment of these norms have to be accepted by all as a matter of course.

An important point concerning discourse ethics is that it transcends Kant's 'monologic' approach which counts on each individual testing his or her maxim of action. In discourse ethics the decision about the generalization of maxims is the result of 'intersubjective' discourse whose structure is only determined by the principles of language use (cf. Habermas 1992: 20 f.).

Humans possess 'communicative competence', which requires that a speaker/ writer makes claims as to the 'validity' of his/her utterance. These claims are summarized by Chilton (2004: 43) as follows:

The claim to understandability (Habermas: *Verständlichkeit*)

What is being said is claimed to be intelligible. This could incorporate the Gricean maxim of manner (speak clearly, succinctly, etc.).

The claim to truth (Habermas: *Wahrheit*)

This is clearly connected with Grice's maxims of quality and quantity and refers to the objective truth, which may not be in accordance with the speaker's belief.

The claim to sincerity – telling the truth (Habermas: *Wahrhaftigkeit*)

This is the claim to be sincere and say what one thinks is true.

The claim to 'rightness' (Habermas: *Richtigkeit*)

Rightness means that the speaker has the 'authority to be performing the speech act in hand'. (Chilton 2004: 43), but 'a more perspicuous term would be "legitimacy"' (2004: 44).

Though the validity claims are universal, they may in practice not be met, because communication is frequently distorted by individual interests (see also Chilton and Schäffner 2002: 14–16).

Habermas developed Discourse Ethics together with **Hans-Otto Apel**, who suggested a two stage ethics of discourse (1988: 271 ff.): at stage one the principle of consensuality in discourse is agreed on, while at stage two the norms to be agreed upon (on both the content and the situation level) are negotiated. These two stages are necessary because today (in contrast to the time of Kant), moral norms can no longer be kept separate from the theoretical knowledge of 'normal' people – particularly knowledge about the consequences of our actions (say, in the area of environmentally relevant acts, e.g. burning fossil fuels). (For more on discourse ethics, see also the critical essays in Thompson and Held eds. 1982, and Habermas' reply to them in Habermas (1989: 475–570). Further literature on the use of language understood as a type of 'acting' can be found in Baumgärtner ed. (1977), Lenk ed. (1980) and Chilton (2004: 30–47) on 'interaction'.

16.1 Dialogue

A different kind of 'ethics through discourse' was developed by the mathematician **David Bohm** (1917–1992). In Bohm's theory, dialogue plays a decisive role in the shared search for solutions (1996). Dialogue (the word is derived from Greeek *dia* through – not two! – and *logos* word, language) produces the free flowing of meaning among us, through us and between us. Bohm distinguishes between discussion and dialogue. While in **discussion** (from Lat. *dis-* apart and *cutere* beat) different views are analysed critically, frequently with a winner and a loser emerging, in dialogue all participants are winners. **Dialogue** welds people together and makes the free flowing of opinions and a new understanding possible (1996: ch. 2). Dialogue is open and leisurely, people sit in a circle and do not have to come to a 'result'. The give and take of opinions is the important thing, there is no 'dialogue leader', only someone who guides and accompanies the dialogue. In this, Bohm's idea of dialogue is different from the Socratic dialogue, in which someone (usually Socrates) is dominant – although the two concepts have much in common. The dynamic aspect of dialogue is also stressed in Markovà and Foppa's book *The Dynamics of Dialogue* (1990) and in Eggins and Slade's *Analysing Casual Conversation* (1997).

Bohm's theory of dialogue is similar to the concept of 'collective thinking' as suggested by Mercer (2000: 131–166; see also Bublitz 1988 on 'cooperative conversation'). For us humans, language is a tool with which we can think aloud together (i.e. do 'interthinking', Mercer 2000: 1) in order to solve problems, come to decisions and agree on shared action. But interthinking will not always lead to success:

> Two heads may be better sometimes, but we also say that 'too many cooks spoil the broth'. That is, we find that people frequently misunderstand each other, and that joint activity can generate confusion, stifle individual creativity and achieve only mediocrity. Studying how we normally use language to think together may help us to understand how effective collaboration can be more reliably achieved. (Mercer 2000: 3)

Mercer's words of warning are more than justified. That this function of language (viz. thinking together) needs to be investigated further is clear to anyone who has experience with committee meetings, in which solutions acceptable to all participants are seriously sought but frequently missed. There are investigations on group efficiency which suggest that individual thinking is more creative and leads to solutions more quickly than deliberating together in a group (see the article by Diehl and Stroebe 'Why groups are less effective than their members', 1994).

'Dialogue' is also a key word in the philosophy of Mikhail Bakhtin, the Russian literary scholar. In every work of literature, for Bakhtin, several voices speak. This is the case particularly in the novel, in which author, narrator, characters, and perhaps even readers simultaneously raise their voices (Bachtin 1979; see also Mey 1999: 241–261). Bakhtin's philosophy of literature is sometimes even called 'dialogism', which refers to a way of thinking in which existence itself is seen as dialogue (cf. Holquist 2002: 14 and Mey 1999: 235).

17. Discourse Strategies

When John F. Kennedy, speaking in front of the Berlin Wall in 1963, began his speech with the (now famous) words:

> Two thousand years ago, the proudest boast was 'civis Romanus sum'.
> Today, in the world of freedom, the proudest boast is 'ich bin ein Berliner',

he used an attention raising strategy based on contrast, purr words, foreign elements and extolling his host city. Linguistic strategies can involve purely formal elements (like contrasts, lists and quotations), semantic elements (such as naming strategies, e.g. euphemism), and pragmatic elements such as suppressing information, using arguments for and against, making value judgements, etc. Strategies are not to be judged negatively from the outset as forms of '**manipulation**' (see 17.4 below), although of course the point of a strategy is that it is not recognized as such. A 'transparent strategy' may even have the opposite effect from that intended. Klemperer (1987) gives the example of Hitler's Reichstag, for which the ruling party at elections was called 'Einheitsliste' (*unity list*) and stickers were sold with 'Ja' (*Yes*). Klemperer calls this strategy (1987: 43) 'eine solche Vergewaltigung des Publikums, daß sie eigentlich das Gegenteil der beabsichtigten Wirkung hervorbringen müsste' [*doing such violence to the public that actually the opposite effect to the intended one should be the result*].

As the example from Kennedy's speech shows, strategies can also have a certain aesthetic value, particularly for the analyst who is not the goal of the strategy. Besides, certain strategic elements tend to be linked 'forever' with certain personages, like Martin Luther King's 'I have a dream' and Lincoln's 'of the people, by the people, for the people', from his Gettysburg Address.

The philosophical background to Discourse Strategies can be found again in **Jürgen Habermas**' philosophy of 'acting through language' ('*sprachliches Handeln*'). In his two volume *Theorie des kommunikativen Handelns* (1987), Habermas starts from the concept of 'teleological acting' (= purpose oriented acting), which since Aristotle has been at the centre of philosophical action theory (cf. 1987, I 126). Teleological acting is directed towards the realization of a purpose through action guided by certain maxims. The model of teleological acting can be extended into a *strategic* model if the success of the acting is linked to the expectation of decisions by another actor (cf. 1987, I 127). Apart from strategic, acting can also be:

- 'regulated by norms' (*normenreguliert*), i.e. guided by shared values;
- communicative (establishing interpersonal relation, e.g. in conversation); and
- dramaturgic (focused on the presentation of the self). (Habermas 1987, I 127 f.)

While these three types of acting are oriented towards information and agreement (*verständigungsorientiert*), strategic acting is **success-oriented** and finds its claim for validity (*Geltungsanspruch*) in its **effectiveness** (*Wirksamkeit*) (cf. Habermas 1987, I 439, Fig. 16).

Acting can be openly strategic or covertly strategic, in which case one of the actants is secretly success oriented while s/he makes other participants believe that all conditions of communicative acting are fulfilled (Habermas 1987, I 445). If this 'deception' is done consciously, Habermas speaks of **manipulation**, if unconsciously, the deception will be accompanied by disturbances on the 'intrapsychic' and the interpersonal level (1987, I 445 f.). Habermas' diagram 18 (1987, I 446, shown in Fig. 17.1 with my translation of his terms) shows the different types of social acts, and in particular the types of strategic acting.

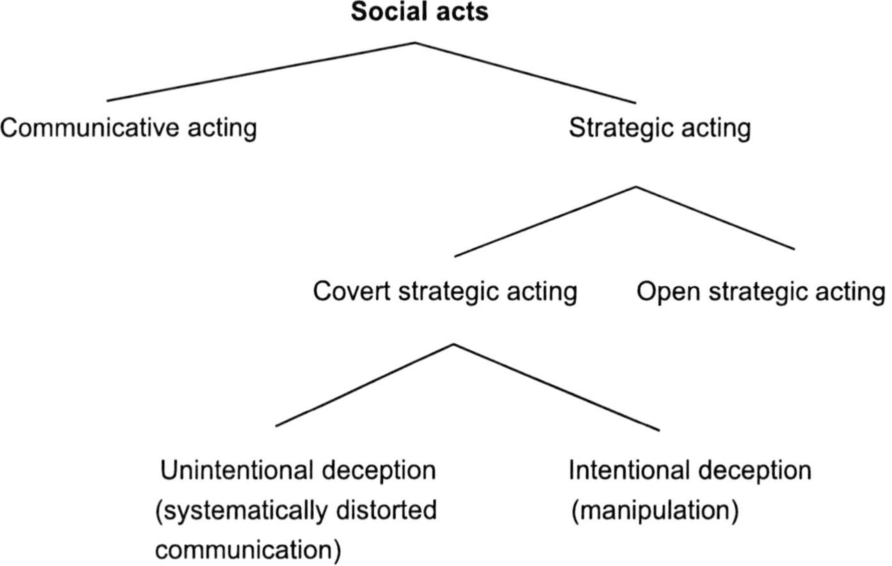

Figure 17.1

The distinction between actions which are success oriented (*'erfolgsorientiert'*) and those which are communicative (*'kommunikativ'* or *'verständigungsorientiert'*) is an important element in Habermas' theory of linguistic acting (1987, I 385–397). The two do not exclude each other: the same action can be described as success oriented and directed at influencing others, and *at the same time* as a process of communication between members of the same situational community (*'Lebenswelt'*); on the other hand, the participants may take *either* a success oriented *or* a communicative attitude towards the action, so that types of acting may also be distinct (1987, I 385 f.).

Reisigl and Wodak (2001: 44 ff.) list five types of **discursive strategies** involved in the **positive self and negative other representation**. 'By "strategy" we generally mean a more or less accurate and more or less intentional plan of practices (including discursive practices) adopted to achieve a particular social, political, psychological or linguistic aim.' Reisigl and Wodak (cf. 2001: 45) distinguish between the following strategies which may be used to discriminate against others:

- Referential or naming strategies;
- Predicational strategies, which label social actors negatively or positively;
- Argumentation strategies (e.g. justifying the exclusion of certain groups);
- Perspectivation or framing (e.g. the narration or quotation of discriminatory events or utterances);
- Intensifying and mitigating strategies, which enhance or modify the illocutionary force of discriminatory utterances.

While this distinction is geared towards Reisigl and Wodak's topic ('discrimination in discourse'), the following divisions are meant to comprise *all* linguistic strategies, no matter what purpose they may serve. A **strategy** is therefore very generally defined as the use of language with the aim of influencing or changing the views of others (or making others act in a certain way) in a manner which however does not make this aim visible.

For some authors, strategic is synonymous with manipulatory; for others, manipulation is a specific strategy of deception. Utz Maas (1974) uses this narrower definition of '**manipulation**: a strategy is manipulatory, if it results in deception by means of a true assertion' (Maas 1974: 245, original emphasis). For instance, 'X avoids carrying out illegal actions' may be a true statement meaning 'X does not carry out illegal actions'; however, *avoids* implies 'X is in a position to carry out illegal actions' and therefore in a 'manipulatory' way throws unfavourable light on X (1974: 245). There will be more on 'manipulation' in section 17.4 below and in the section on **Eristics** (17.5).

17.1 Categories of Discourse Strategies

Discourse strategies can be categorized in a number of ways. The simplest categorization is a division of strategies into:

1. (a) those operating with elements of form (which mainly serve the purpose of attention attraction and memory support);
   (b) those operating with content elements; and
   (c) those combining language with other media (e.g. text with picture).

Another categorization (crossing that in [1]) derives from the units at the different 'levels of language'. The strategic elements may be different in written and spoken texts, in the following way:

2. • **spoken texts**: delivery (intonation, rhythm, voice quantity and quality, combination with music, paralinguistic features);
    • **written texts**: typography, link with pictures, etc., iconicity;
    • **written and spoken**: strategies using the different units of language, viz. speech-sounds, morphemes, words, phrases/sentences, speech-acts, text-pragmatic elements;
    • the meta-level (using language to speak/write about language).

Since a comprehensive discussion of linguistic strategies would fill a treatise of more than one volume, the following treatment will be in the form of a list based on division (1) above. A few strategies will be highlighted and illustrated with typical examples (see also 17.2 below on euphemism and 18.2 on strategies in the discourse of discrimination).

Strategies operating on the level of form

Most **rhetorical figures** (tropes) are based on formal elements. Their function is attention attraction, creation of pleasure and memory assistance. Rhetoric sometimes conceals a lack of content. Rhetorical elements were already described in Antiquity (by Cicero, Quintilian and other rhetoricians). A well-known handbook is that of Heinrich Lausberg, in which numerous '*figurae*' (figures of speech) are discussed and illustrated (1971: 79–146). A comprehensive treatment of rhetoric through the ages is given by Brian Vickers (1988).

Attention attraction is particularly important in **politics** and **advertising**. All works on these two topics (see Chapter 15 above) contain sections on formal elements used strategically. Generally, strategies in political discourse can be said to be similar to those in advertising, since in both cases something is to be 'sold' using the strategy. The following are lists of formal strategies used in both politics and advertising to attract attention and support memory:

Written: typographical emphasis, iconicity; combination with pictures (Fischer 1999)

> Examples of **iconicity: strong** *and* weak (bold letters iconicizing strength);

> BIG and small (size of letters iconicizing the meaning 'different sizes')

Written and spoken: ordering words and sounds in a certain way (rhetoric), as in

• **lists of three** (see Atkinson 1984; examples: liberté, égalité, fraternité; 'Friends, Romans, Countrymen, lend me your ears', Shakespeare, *Julius Caesar*, III ii, 65)

- **enumerations** (lists of four, five and more)
- **contrasts**

  Example: Kennedy's Berlin speech (above) with three contrasts:

2000 years ago	:	today
The proudest boast was	:	the proudest boast is
Civis Romanus sum	:	Ich bin ein Berliner (languages contrasted)

- **surprising contrast**

  Example: Liberal leader David Steel (1979):

  '… there are two conservative parties in this election. *One* is offering the continuation of the policies we've had for the last five years, and *the other* is offering a *return to the policies of forty years ago.*'

  (Expected contrast: new policies which, however, will not work)

  (Source: Atkinson 1984: 41, my emphasis)

- **contrasting pronouns** (*they* vs. *we*)
- other figures of speech (chiasm, oxymoron, etc.)

Leech (1969: 36–52, 2008: 15–20) sees figures of speech as a type of deviation from everyday language and discusses deviation on eight levels (from the lexical to deviation by register). A figure of speech is 'foregrounded' against the background of everyday language – a metaphor, which according to Leech (2008: 18) was first used by the pre-war Prague School of Linguists. Plett (1979: 150–292) offers a discussion of more than 50 figures of speech on the levels of phonology, morphology, syntax, semantics and graphematics.

Further strategies using the level of form are the following:

- **Devices taken from poetry** (alliteration, assonance, rhyme, rhythm)
- **Phraseological elements** (idioms, parts of proverbs)
- **Quotation** and other forms of **intertextuality** (cf. Goatly 2000: 163–178)

  Examples of quotation:

  > 'to buy, or not to buy, that is the question' (echoing Hamlet's soliloquy)

  > 'Hier bin ich Mensch, hier kauf ich ein' (from Goethe's 'Hier bin ich Mensch, hier darf ich's sein')

- **Metaphor and simile**

  Example: 'we will open this window of opportunity'

  Example from a famous speech: 'to lift our nation from *the quicksands of racial injustice* to the *solid rock of brotherhood*' (Martin Luther King, 1963)

Example from advertising: An energy drink was suddenly successful when the following metaphor was used as its slogan: 'Red Bull verleiht Flügel' (*Red Bull lends you wings*)

- **Technical terms from the topic reported about used metaphorically** Example: 'airline in turbulence'

- **Puns** Example: 'a very happy outcome for the whites, the colours, and the *greens'* with pun on 'greens' – green colour, plants, environmentalists (from Myers 1994; see also the chapter 'Environmental advertising' in Mühlhäusler 2003: 161–171)

- **Playing with names** Example: '… who thinks himself a real shake-scene' (pun on *Shakespeare*)

(For further examples see Lausberg 1971 and Plett 1979: 150 ff. Harjung 2000 discusses 250 rhetorical devices illustrated with more than 1000 examples. For examples from political speeches see Atkinson 1984, Wächter 1996: 69 ff., Beard 2000 and other books on language and politics.)

Strategies operating on the content level

Strategies using the content level of language are those which concern word-meaning (particularly the naming function of the word) and those which use the linking and other functions of syntax; some strategies can be located on the textual or pragmatic level (speech acts), a few are found on the meta-level using comments *about* language.

Word level:

- **Naming strategies**: the best-known naming strategy is **euphemism** (see 17.2 below).

   Examples: *ethnic cleansing, collateral damage, their mission* for 'war'.

- **Dysphemism**, the less frequent opposite to euphemism (Bolinger 1980: 115–124).

   Examples: this is a *terrorist act*; I call this *war*.

- **Pejorative nomination**

   Examples: Calling a certain procedure 'provincial'.

   Using the 'Stone Age argument' (e.g. 'this would mean back to the caves').

- **'Purr words'** and 'sacred' words (see Alexander 2009: 140 ff. on purr words in the context of large agricultural corporations, e.g. *benefits, sharing, effective stewardship*; see Chapter 20.5 below).

- **'Snarl words'** and fear words (*rogue states, weapons of mass destruction*).

Level of the sentence:

- **Linking strategies**

  Examples: linking a product to be advertised with environmental issues:

  > 'All of it is biodegradable!'

  Linking the product with sex and love:

  > 'Pussycat by day. Bacardi by night.'

  (For more examples see *Sex in Advertising* by Reichert and Lambiase 2003).

- **Tu quoque**: responding to criticism by showing that the criticized act has been committed by the antagonist, too.

  Example: 'they criticize our activities in Iraq and in Afghanistan; but what about Ossetia? What about Berg Karabach?'

Text-pragmatic strategies (see also the section on Eristics below):

- **Giving a general answer to a specific question:**

  Example: A: What exactly are your strategies on inflation?

  B: The most important thing is to cooperate and not to give in to irrational fears …

- **Evading the issue** (related to the previous strategy)

  Example (from Fairclough 1995: 23 after D. Greatbatch):

  > Interviewer: D'you quite like him?

  > Interviewee: Well er I – think in politics you see – I – it's not a question of going about liking people or not, it's a question of dealing with people. And er I've always been able to deal perfectly well with Mr Wilson and er – indeed he has with me.

  The interviewee evades answering the question – indeed denies its relevance – but answers a somewhat different question that he himself has posed.

- **Spreading rumour by condemning its originators**

  This strategy (drawing attention to something by condemning it) has several variants. A frequent one is the condemnation of some trick or other illegal behaviour, e.g. when in a newspaper article 'the nasty tricks of the tax evaders' are condemned, but at the same time discussed in great detail.

  Another variant is to write of 'people who are looking for skeletons in the cupboard' (say, in the life of a certain politician). These people are then condemned as scavengers, but the possibility of such skeletons existing is not denied and remains a scar on the reputation of the politician.

- **Emotional language** (in extreme cases linked with breaking into tears).

- **Reporting atrocities**

  Frequently used to make another religion/culture/state, etc. appear hateful. It was also used (e.g. by Hitler) to justify military action against the alleged committers of atrocities.

- **I am one of you** ... Suggesting togetherness and intimacy.

- **Irony** (frequently used to make some/one/thing look ridiculous).

  Example: the new law testifies to the genius of the minister.

- **Critique dressed as praise**

  This strategy is alluded to by Alexander Pope in his 'Epistle to Dr. Arbuthnot' (1733):

  > Damn with faint praise, assent with civil leer,
  > And, without sneering, teach the rest to sneer.

This may, for instance, take the form of praising someone's 'intellectual honesty' and 'discreet charm', thereby implying that the person praised is somewhat boring and non-creative. Another variant is to mention that someone has many friends and then name a few which come from totally different camps – implying that the person praised is either a turn-coat or a person without firm convictions.

Strategies using the meta-level

- **Comments on one's own language** ('I'm not criticizing you ...').

- **Comments on the other's language** ('Are you in fact saying that ...').

- **Comments on the whole discourse** ('this discussion is one-sided'; 'let's not get emotional', *'sachlich bleiben'*, 'this topic needs to be discussed in more depth').

- **Silence**: failure to mention something; failure to report on something; quantitative differences in dealing with topics.

Example of quantitative differences in media coverage

Edward Herman and Noam Chomsky (in *Manufacturing Consent*, 2002: 37 ff.) show how the media manipulate opinions by reporting on certain topics – but *not* reporting on others. They show, for instance, that in reports about people abused in other states, reports about victims more welcome to the (say, US) government abound, while reports about unwelcome victims are few and far between. In a table (2002: 40 f.), they present how numerous the reports about the murder of a priest in Poland (Jerzy Popieluszko) were in an 18 month period after the murder, while media coverage about 'One Hundred Murdered Religious in Latin America' (including Archbishop Romero) was far smaller. The Polish priest was murdered in a (then)

Communist country, while murders in Latin America occurred in 'US client states'. These 'quantitative aspects of coverage' (2000: 38) seem to suggest that there are 'worthy and unworthy victims'.

Strategies operating with other media

Written: combination of text with picture

Text and picture are two different types of sign-system (text: symbolic, picture: iconic); as a result, their combination always attracts attention, particularly if tension between the two sign-systems is built up. In 1964, Roland Barthes raised the question of whether a picture accompanying a text repeated the information of the text and was therefore redundant or whether it added information. Barthes (1977: 38 ff.) made an often quoted distinction – between 'anchorage' (text and picture are firmly anchored in each other) and 'relay' (they are independent and complement each other). From both anchorage and relay a number of strategies can be derived in which the two sign systems are made use of for attention attracting and interest creating purposes (for further categories of the text picture relation see Nöth 1990: 454; Kress and Van Leeuwen 1996; Schierl 2001: 248 f.; Stöckl 2004: 249–253; Fill 2007: 137).

In written texts, attention value is frequently achieved through **iconicity**. This means that formal elements of the text (letters, other typographical features, images) echo the meaning. The following are three examples from Cook (2001: 84):

(a) An advert for spectacles uses blurred print.
(b) The words in an advert for tourism to Australia are upside down.
(c) A cat tip-toes along the top of three-dimensional letters spelling 'Kattomeat'.

Further examples can be found in Fischer (1999), Cook (2001: 84, 92) and Goddard (1998: 21 ff.). See also 21.1 and 21.2 below.

Spoken: combination with non-verbal elements or with music, film, etc.

'Intermodal strategies' occur in politics, advertising and art. The combination of verbal and gestural elements has been described, among others, by Atkinson (1984), Jane Lyle (1990) and Desmond Morris (2002). Morris calls signs which rhythmically accompany the verbal delivery '**baton signals**' (2002: 78–87). He describes 12 types, from the 'vacuum precision grip' to the 'foot baton'. In combination with speech they all have meaning, though this may vary according to culture, social class and individual temperament. '[The speaker] must win over the listener and to do this he must emphasize his words over and over again. Bearing this in mind, it suddenly becomes clear why public speakers addressing large groups of people gesticulate so much more than private conversationalists' (Morris 2002: 87). In her book *Body Politics* (1986: 2), Nancy Henley distinguishes two dimensions of nonverbal communication, the first one concerning closeness, intimacy, emotion and attitudes, the second one being about status, power, dominance and superiority.

The combination of speech with music is typical of radio and TV commercials. The music is chosen to fit the words or simply to create a pleasant atmosphere – though tension between words and music may enhance attention value (Fill 2007: 150–153).

17.2 Euphemism

Of all content strategies, those involving euphemisms of some kind are perhaps, if not the most frequent, then at least the ones most frequently commented on. A number of books (e.g. Rawson 1983; Ayto 1993, 2007) deal specifically with the topic of euphemism, some of them listing frequent examples, others (Ayto 2007) giving 'strategic' advice. Since euphemisms continuously have to be replaced by new euphemisms (a phenomenon called by Rawson 'the law of succession'), and since new political events require new euphemisms, the topic is in fact inexhaustible. The discussion here will therefore be restricted to a few instances topical at the time of writing.

Anita Wenden's definition of euphemism (also quoted by Alexander 2009: 171) will serve as a good starting point: 'A euphemism is an alternative choice of word used to disguise something unpleasant or undesirable' (Wenden 1995: 223). Unpleasant and undesirable things are found in a number of ontological areas including bodily functions, sexuality, illness, death, war and political activities (some of the words in this list are euphemisms themselves). Alexander (2009) discusses many examples from the latter two areas. Here are a few of them (2009: 202 f):

> pacification (for *war*);
>
> protective reactions/protective retaliation (for *bombing raids*);
>
> urbanization (for *the destruction of peasant villages*); and
>
> peacekeeping (for *annihilation of the enemy*).

Further frequently quoted examples from recent reports on 'military action' are 'collateral damage' (for 'civilian casualties and deaths'), 'friendly fire' (fire hitting one's own troops), 'ethnic cleansing' (expelling, perhaps killing members of certain ethnicities) and 'mission', 'operation' and 'military activity' (for *war*).

Euphemism is not just a phenomenon of the word-level; it also works on the level of phrases. The following example is from Alexander (2009: 197):

> A British general said on 'The World at One' – BBC Radio 4 (1999): 'If our troops are faced by life-threatening behaviour in any form they will respond in a robust and decisive fashion.' Alexander's translation of this into ordinary English: 'Our troops will kill anyone who they consider to be acting aggressively.'

Using down-toning (palliative), but even more typically downright mendicant language has been called (in a term derived from the novel *1984*) 'Orwellian language' (see Paul Chilton's book *Orwellian Language and the Media,* 1988). A corpus search carried out by Alexander (2009: 174–176) using the Collins Wordbanks Online corpus (45 million words) yielded 264 occurrences of 'Orwellian', many of them with collocations such as 'doublethink', 'corruption of language' and 'falsification of reality'. Indeed, examples from Orwell's novel such as 'joycamp' (for *concentration camp,* itself of course a euphemism), 'ministry of truth' (*of propaganda*) and 'newspeak' (*reduced language*) seem to justify this meaning of the word 'Orwellian'.

Chomsky, in his book *Knowledge of Language* (1986), speaks of 'Orwell's problem': by this he means the surprising fact that so many people are unable to see through linguistic 'smokescreens' and thus accept how a totalitarian system presents 'the truth' to them. Chomsky writes (1986: xxvii):

> Plato's problem, then, is to explain how we know so much, given that the evidence available to us is so sparse. Orwell's problem is to explain why we know and understand so little, even though the evidence available to us is so rich. Like many other twentieth-century intellectuals, Orwell was impressed with the ability of totalitarian systems to instil beliefs that are firmly held and widely accepted although they are completely without foundation and often plainly at variance with obvious facts about the world around us.

(See also Chomsky 1986: 276–287 and Alexander's chapter 'Language and Orwell's problem', 2009: 163–188.)

Concerning the role of language in generating Orwell's problem, Chomsky is undecided and even seems to warn us not to overestimate the influence of language. In the preface to *Knowledge of Language* (1986: xxix), he writes of 'the widespread belief, which I personally share only in part, that misuse or control of language is a central feature of the problem'. Chomsky hereby puts himself among those linguists who raise their warning voices against the simplistic view that control of *the language* means control of the people and that the public cannot see through linguistic strategies. (See also the quotation from Alexander below and the critique of Jung concerning euphemism and anthropocentrism quoted in 20.4 below.)

17.3 Obfuscation and Disinformation

The headline of this section is taken from the title of a chapter in Richard Alexander's book *Framing Discourse on the Environment* (2009: 189–214). Alexander shows how with various methods (e.g. euphemizing, metaphor, code-names for military operations such as 'Operation Rolling Thunder', 'Operation Freedom Train', 'Restore Hope' and many others, pp. 203 ff.) positive associations are created for lethal activities. Through a process called allusively 'semantic engineering' (2009: 205) the bombing of civilian targets and other military operations is either not allowed to reach the consciousness of the public or made to appear necessary, unavoidable or even harmless and normal.

By a similar process ('discourse engineering' 2009: 22), unecological and potentially dangerous practices such as using insect killers (called 'plant protectors') and genetic manipulation (under the guise of 'providing enough food for the poor') are made to appear harmless and even beneficial to the underprivileged. (Read more on this in Chapter 20.)

17.4 Manipulation through Language

The term *manipulation* with its negative connotations is usually used in connection with strategies which are not only undetected as such by the addressee (here frequently: victim), but which also specifically serve the interest of the 'manipulator' (see the definitions of Jürgen Habermas and Utz Maas discussed at the beginning of this chapter). In Habermas' system of strategic acts, manipulation appears as 'intentional deception' (Habermas 1987, I: 446). Similarly, Van Dijk defines manipulation as follows:

> Manipulation not only involves power, but specifically *abuse* of power, that is, *domination*. More specifically, manipulation implies the exercise of a form of *illegitimate* influence by means of discourse: manipulators make others believe or do things that are in the interest of the manipulator, and against the best interests of the manipulated. (Van Dijk 2006: 360; original emphasis)

A good example of this, according to Van Dijk, is the manipulation of US and world opinion after the attacks on the World Trade Centre of 11 September 2001. In speeches and other documents issued by the US Government (and divulgated through the mass media) the measures taken after this event (the dramatic rise in military spending, the invasion of another country, and restrictions of personal freedom) were represented exclusively as measures taken in the interest of peace, safety and security, while in reality other interests, too, lay behind them. In addition, the consequences of these measures were suppressed:

> That through anti-terrorist actions and military intervention not only the military and business corporations who produce arms and security outfits may profit, but more terrorism may actually be promoted, and hence security of the citizens further endangered, is obviously not part of the preferred attitudes that are the goals of such manipulation. (Van Dijk 2006: 370)

Among the manipulatory strategies, Van Dijk lists many which have to do with positive self-presentation and negative other-presentation, but also euphemisms, nominalizations and rhetorical figures, such as metaphors and metonymies (2006: 373; one might profitably compare Van Dijk's list with Fairclough's list of questions to be asked of a text, 1989/2001: 110 f./89 f., see Chapter 18 below). Though most manipulatory strategies concern 'the "content" of text and talk', the manipulation may be strengthened or weakened through specific syntax and rhetoric (in spoken texts: intonation, volume, speed; in written texts: text layout, font, photos, etc.) (cf. Van Dijk 2006: 376). Manipulation may also be effected through intermediality, i.e. the combination of text with pictures, movies or other media (2006: 360 f.).

A specific type of manipulation occurs through the mass media which may report or keep silent about certain events and thereby 'filter out the news fit to print, marginalize dissent, and allow the government and dominant private interests to get their messages across to the public' (Herman and Chomsky 2002: 2). Herman and Chomsky speak of five 'filters' through which the 'raw material of news' must pass so that only news in keeping with the interests of dominant power structures is divulged. These are the following, 'which interact with and reinforce each other' (2002: 2 ff., adapted):

1. The ownership of the dominant mass media firms.
2. Advertising as the primary income source of the mass media.
3. The reliance of the media on information provided by the government, business, and 'experts' funded and approved by these primary sources and agents of power.
4. 'Flak' as a means of disciplining the media – 'flak' meaning negative responses to reports in the form of letters, telegrams, phone calls, petitions, lawsuits, etc. (2002: 26).
5. 'Anticommunism' as a national religion and control mechanism.

These filters, according to Herman and Chomsky (cf. 2002: 31) restrict what can become news, particularly 'big' news, and thus in a country like the USA public opinion is brought in line with the interests of the government and of big business (see the example from Herman and Chomsky discussed in 17.1 above).

A specific type of manipulation can be observed in those situations where language is used to **hide** opinions. Talleyrand is reported to have said: 'Language is there to hide the thoughts of the diplomat' (quoted by Klemperer 1987: 16). The evolution of language must have included this purpose which can be achieved by talking in a roundabout way, 'waffling', announcing that one will 'say nothing', avoiding the issue and using other eristic devices as enumerated by Schopenhauer (see 17.5 below).

An important point made by Van Dijk (2006: 360) is that since '"manipulation" is a typical observer's category, e.g. of critical analysts, and not necessarily a participant category, few language users would call their own discourse "manipulative"'. In this context, the warning words of Jung (2001) and others not to overestimate the effect of manipulation should again be remembered (see section 20.4 below).

Among older publications on 'manipulation' through language, Mackensen (1973), Kaltenbrunner (ed. 1975) and Lay (1980) deserve to be mentioned here.

17.5 Eristics, or 'the Art of Always Being in the Right'

Eristics is the 'art' of fighting with language, of quarrelling and of gaining the upper hand in an argument. Some of the eristic tricks of the Sophists are already shown in Plato's dialogues (*Gorgias, Sophistes, Euthydemos*, see Plato in the list of philosophers, Appendix II) and in Aristotle's *Topica*. The Renaissance scholar Rudolph Agricola (1443–1485), in his three books *De invention dialectica* discusses 24 '*loci*', i.e. ways of arguing (see Agricola 1992), and the German philosopher **Arthur Schopenhauer** (1788–1860) collected 38 argumentative tricks, which were published after his death by Julius Frauenstädt under the title *Eristische Dialektik. Die Kunst, Recht zu behalten* (1864, now available as Schopenhauer 1983).

In eristic argumentation, Schopenhauer distinguishes between two modi:

(a) modus ad rem; and
(b) modus ad hominem.

While in the *modus ad rem*, the arguer tries to disprove the antagonist's argumentation by referring to the facts (objective truth), in the *modus ad hominem* an attempt is made to find contradictions in the other's arguments and to show that the other's argumentation does not agree with other statements of the opponent (subjective pronouncements). The 38 linguistic devices ('*Kunstgriffe*') are presented by Schopenhauer not as pieces of advice, but are meant to lay open how people manage to be 'in the right' '*per fas et nefas*' (by right or wrong).

The following is a brief discussion of the most interesting of Schopenhauer's eristic devices (the whole list can be found on Wikipedia, s.v. 'Kunstgriffe – Schopenhauer)'.

Device No. 1: expansion, narrowing

What one has said is expanded or narrowed down according to one's needs.
Schopenhauer's example (translated):

A: German Hanseatic towns regained their independence with the treaty of 1814.
B: But Danzig did not become independent, rather more restricted in its freedom.
A: I said German towns, Danzig is a Polish town.

Device No. 2: Homonymy

Extending the argument to a homonym of the original concept.

Schopenhauer's example, however, is based on metaphoric extension, not really on homonymy:

A: Omne lumen potest extingui. Intellectus est lumen. Ergo intellectus potest extingui.

[Every light can be extinguished. The intellect is a light. Therefore it can be extinguished.]

This device is also discussed by Agricola as the application of the *locus* 'de nomine rerum'.

Device No. 12: reversive nomination, using hateful words

Schopenhauer's examples: instead of 'religious zeal' say 'fanaticism', instead of 'in holy orders' say 'clerics' (*'Pfaffen'*) – a device which in modern terminology is called 'dysphemism'.

Device No. 29: diversion

Suddenly talk of something else pretending that this is to the point.

Device No. 30

Quote authorities instead of giving reasons (also called 'argumentum ad verecundiam' [argument from reverence]).

Device No. 31: Pretend ironically not to understand

Example: 'What you are saying transcends my weak comprehension.' According to Schopenhauer, this device was used against Kant by philosophers who pretended not to understand Kant's *Kritik der reinen Vernunft*.

Some of Schopenhauer's devices have nothing to do with argumentation, but are simply strategies intended to create confusion, e.g. No. 7 (ask a great deal at the same time), No. 8 (make your opponent angry), No. 36 (dazzle through high-sounding flood of words) and, as the last resort, No. 38 (offend the other in person, also called 'argumentum ad personam' in contrast to the 'argumentum ad hominem'). Almost hilarious is device No. 14: cry out triumphantly, when nothing else helps.[1]

That Schopenhauer did not offer his devices as advice for disputants, but rather meant them as a warning and as a help against sophistry is clear from his comment: 'damit man sie selbst erkenne und vernichte' [*so that they can be recognized and destroyed*]. At the end of his treatise, he advises us on the only way to avoid being exposed to eristic devices (or avoid having to use them): only argue with intelligent, sensible people who speak reasonably – in Schopenhauer's view hardly one in a hundred!

In modern manuals of rhetoric with titles such as *Say it more convincingly* or *Use the power of language,* eristic tricks also play a role, though they are not categorized as tricks or strategies of manipulation, but simply as ways how to argue more convincingly and powerfully. There have also been attempts at establishing an encyclopedia of Eristics on the web.

Note

1. Some of Schopenhauer's devices remind one of the linguistic 'gambits' presented in the satirical books by Stephen Potter. *Lifemanship* (1950) and *One-upmanship* (1952) are full of linguistic tricks intended to give one the upper hand in a discussion (make one be one-up!), such as answering every argument with 'Yes, but not in the South'. Potter's books are still available (e.g. *The Complete Upmanship,* London: Continuum).

18. Critical Discourse Analysis: Language, Ideology and Power

The most influential school of linguistics in which the influence of discourse on the world is investigated is a school of thought associated above all with Norman Fairclough, but also with Gunther Kress, Robert Hodge, Roger Fowler, Ruth Wodak, Theo van Leeuwen and Teun A. van Dijk. The representatives of this school (Critical Discourse Analysis, CDA) regard discourse as a form of social practice and analyse discourse from the point of view of its (hidden) effects on society.

The forerunners of CDA were **Critical Language Study** (CLS) and **Critical Linguistics**. The main idea behind Critical Language Study is expressed by Fairclough (1989, 2001: 5, 4) as follows:

> CLS analyses social interactions in a way which focuses upon their linguistic elements, and which sets out to show up their generally hidden determinants in the system of social relationships, as well as hidden effects they may have upon that system.

In 'Critical Linguistics', a close relation between **language and ideology** was established: 'If linguistic meaning is inseparable from ideology, and both depend on social structure, then linguistic analysis ought to be a powerful tool for the study of ideological processes which mediate relationships of power and control' (Fowler *et al.* 1979: 186). The closeness of 'ideology' to power is stressed particularly by the sociologist Anthony Giddens, who defines *ideology* as follows (1993: 722): 'values and beliefs which help secure the position of more powerful groups at the expense of less powerful ones'.

For both Critical Linguistics and CDA, 'language is an instrument of control as well as of communication' (Hodge and Kress 1993: 6). Hodge and Kress (*ibid.*) define 'ideology' in the following way:

> [as] a systematic body of ideas, organized from a particular point of view. Ideology is thus a subsuming category which includes the sciences and metaphysics, as well as political ideologies of various kinds, without implying anything about their status and reliability as guides to reality.

For Fowler it is important 'to get at the ideology coded implicitly behind the overt propositions' and to get at this ideology by combining Halliday's functional approach with other approaches, e.g. identifying speech acts (Fowler 1996: 3).

The 'Critical Linguists' were particularly *critical* of Chomskyan linguistics, in which the study of language structure is dissociated from that of language use. Hodge and Kress (1993: 2) write about the Chomskyan Revolution: 'Linguists came to assume that theoretical linguistics meant syntactic theory, and, for many, syntactic theory meant purely transformational theory. Inevitably this led to a drastic narrowing of the scope of linguistics.' The theory behind Critical Linguistics thus was not Transformationalism, but rather the functional model of Halliday (cf. Fowler *et al.* 1979: 3 and Goatly 2000: 5). One of its basic assumptions is 'that the relation between form and content is not arbitrary or conventional, but that form signifies content' (Fowler *et al.* 1979: 188). This assumption also holds for Critical Discourse Analysis.

CDA developed a number of methodological approaches, most of them based on a close analysis of texts. These are described in Fairclough and Wodak (1997) and in the different chapters of Wodak and Meyer (eds. 2001; see Fairclough's questions to be asked of a text, below). For a discussion of the relation between Critical Linguistics and Critical Discourse Analysis see Wodak (2001: 1–9).

18.1 Language and Power (Fairclough)

Possessing language may mean exerting power, i.e. 'the ability to influence other persons to do what one wants' (Henley 1986: 19). Knowing and pronouncing another person's name may mean having power over this person – as fairy-tales (e.g. 'Rumpelstilzchen') remind us. Through language, a magic power may be exerted over a person. Merely knowing the name of one's foe, in some cultures, meant having magic power over this person (cf. Russell 1973: 152).

The power of language discussed in this section is of a different kind. It is the power of discourse, of texts, to constitute society and shape a society's beliefs as well as its prejudices. This notion of the power of language as discourse is inspired by French socio-philosophy, in particular by the ideas of **Michel Foucault** and **Pierre Bourdieu**. Foucault's understanding of Discourse is that of a force that creates truth for a society. 'Each society has its regime of truth, its "general politics" of truth: that is the types of discourse it accepts and makes function as true' (Foucault 1980: 131). For Bourdieu, Language is (together with Art and Religion) a symbolic system which can exercise a 'structuring power' because it is structured itself (cf. Bourdieu 1991: 166). Symbolic power is an invisible power 'which can be exercised only with the complicity of those who do not want to know that they are subject to it or even that they themselves exercise it' (1991: 164).

Norman Fairclough stresses the **dialectical** nature of the relationship between discourse and social structure (cf. 1992: 65). 'On the one hand, discourse is shaped and constrained by social structure in the widest sense and at all levels' (1992: 64), on the other hand, discourse constitutes and constructs society in many ways (cf. Fairclough 1992: 64 f.):

> Discourse constructs 'social identities'.
> Discourse 'helps construct social relationships between people'.
> Discourse 'contributes to the construction of systems of knowledge and belief'.
> Discourse also 'contributes to transforming society'.

The latter power of discourse is the most interesting for our topic of language impact. Beliefs concerning class, race and gender can be transformed radically through discourse – but can also be stabilized and fossilized. An example of this is the different attitudes of societies towards gender inequalities, which are very much dependent on the discourse about gender (see Chapter 19 below).

Discourse – as media discourse, but also as individual text – may influence us ideologically, *mostly without our noticing it*. Fairclough makes this important point when he explains what a *critical* approach to language is:

> Critical approaches differ from non-critical approaches in not just describing discursive practices, but also showing how discourse is shaped by relations of power and ideologies, and the constructive effects discourse has upon social identities, social relations and systems of knowledge and belief, *neither of which is normally apparent to discourse participants.* (Fairclough 1992: 12; original italics)

In *Language and Power* (1989, 2001: 110–139, 92–120), Norman Fairclough presents and discusses ten questions to be asked of a text – questions on the levels of the lexicon, of syntax and of textual structure. These ten general questions, of which most have more specific sub-questions, are meant to bring to light ways in which texts exert power over us. They have provided the theoretical framework for many studies on language in politics, in advertising, in the media as well as on a more general level in public discourse. The most important of these questions and sub-questions for our topic seem to be the following (cf. Fairclough 1989, 2001: 110 f., 92 f.; original italics):

Lexical level:
Are there words which are ideologically contested?
Is there *rewording* or *overwording*?
What ideologically significant meaning relations (*synonymy, hyponymy, antonymy*) are there between words?
Are there euphemistic expressions?
Are there markedly formal or informal words?
What metaphors are used?

Level of Grammar:
Is agency unclear?
Are *nominalizations* used?
Are sentences active or passive?
Are sentences positive or negative?
What *modes* (*declarative, grammatical question, imperative*) are used?
Are the pronouns *we* and *you* used, and if so, how?
How are simple sentences linked together?
What logical connectors are used?
Are complex sentences characterized by *coordination* or *subordination*?
What means are used for referring inside and outside the text?

Level of textual structure:
What interactional conventions are used?
Are there ways in which one participant controls the turns of others?
What large-scale structure does the text have?

Some of the above questions may at first sight seem somewhat trivial or even irrelevant as far as ideology and power are concerned. But for a critical analysis of texts they are important, since one of the main tenets of CDA is that nothing in discourse is arbitrary. No formal feature is accidental (cf. Fowler *et al.* 1979: 188, see above), and even apparently small changes (from active to passive – agency! – or from positive to negative) may make a substantial difference and contain hidden meaning.

The following examples may make the importance of seemingly small features of syntax, vocabulary and textuality clear:

(1) In 1975, police in Harare fired into a crowd of people and killed 13 of them. The following headlines from papers of different political orientation produce different 'truths' concerning this event:

> *The Times:* 'Rioting Blacks Shot Dead by Police' [passive clause]
>
> The victims are in subject position, the **agent** ('police') is indicated with a prepositional phrase. The number of victims is not given. 'Rioting blacks' is the textual 'theme'.
>
> *The Guardian:* 'Police shot 13 dead in Salisbury Riot' [active clause]
>
> The agent ('police') is in subject position; the number of people shot is given.
>
> *Rhodesia Herald:* 'A political clash has led to death and injury' [non-commital]
>
> Neutral report: neither the agent not the victims are expressly mentioned.
>
> *Tanzanian Daily News:* 'Rhodesia's white supremacist police ... opened fire and killed thirteen unarmed Africans' [active clause with two verbs]
>
> The agent ('police') is in subject position and is characterized as 'white' and 'supremacist'. The victims are characterized as 'unarmed'. Their number is given.
>
> (Example from van Leeuwen 2009: 281, adapted, after Tony Trew)

(2) Changing from active to passive may make the **agent invisible**. An active sentence such as 'South African police have burnt down a black township' expresses the agent (police) and the experiencer/sufferer (black township), while in the passive voice the agent can be suppressed: ('a black township has been burnt down'), and the 'ergative' construction 'a black township has burnt

down' may even suggest that there is no agent at all. (Example from Fairclough 1989, 2001: 121, 101, adapted).

(3) Agency can also be suppressed through **nominalization** ('the killing of the whales' does not tell us who the killers were); on the other hand, the addressee (reader, hearer) can be made a party of harmful actions by the use of '**inclusive we**' ('*We* are using more and more fuel and producing more and more traffic'). The following extract from a White Paper on competitiveness (issued by the British Department of Trade and Industry in 1998) shows the two features of inclusive 'we' and agent suppressing passive (quoted from Fairclough 2000: 23; original italics):

> In the increasingly global economy of today, *we* cannot compete in the old way. *Capital* is mobile, *technology* can migrate quickly and goods *can be made* in *low cost countries* and *shipped* to *developed markets*.

The passage also contains some interesting lexical features: 'Capital' and 'technology' are used metonymically for 'industrialists' and 'production plants', while 'low cost countries' and 'developed markets' could be seen as euphemisms for 'third world/ poor countries' and 'Western industrialized countries'.

All these features combine to support the ideologies of Imperialism and Capitalism: they suppress agents and make cruel and unecological activities appear not to be the doings of the rich and powerful, but of everyone (including you and me). The inequality in the world is made out to be the inevitable and natural outcome of 'progress' in which 'we' all are involved.

In **politics**, the fine points of language are particularly important (Fairclough 2000: vii):

> Why for instance did the Labour Party change its name to 'New Labour'? According to one of its key advisers, Blair 'knew that only by contrasting "new" Labour with "old" Labour explicitly would the electorate believe that Labour had changed and could be trusted'. In other words, changing the name wasn't just reflecting a shift in political ideology, it was manipulating language to control public perception.

In politics, as in other areas, there is a great deal in a name. Special agencies advise politicians and whole parties which words to use ('which words work'). For example, 'climate change' is to be preferred over 'global warming', since it is less frightening and simply suggests a natural change (Alexander 2009: 209; Poole 2006: 42). "Genetic modification" (GM) is better than "genetic engineering", and "Kernenergie" (*nuclear energy*) is to be used rather than "Atomkraft" (*atomic power*), which still possesses associations with "Atombombe" (*atom bomb*) (cf. Fill 2001: 46 following M. Jung).

'**Framing**' (in the sense of G. Lakoff 2006, see Chapter 9.2 above) is largely a question of language. The US response to the terrorist acts of 11 September 2001, was first framed as a 'War on Terror', but later reframed as the 'Global struggle against violent extremism' (G. Lakoff 2006). The War frame emphasized the military aspect of this response too much, whereas the frame 'struggle' brought a number of advantages (cf. G. Lakoff 2006):

(a) It suggests an ideological controversy rather than a military battle.
(b) It does not suggest winning or losing.
(c) It suggests continuity rather than abrupt ending.
(d) It made people forget the failures of activities so far and made a new beginning possible.

This can also be illustrated with a more recent example: the election campaign of Barack Obama (2008) was carried out within the frame of 'change' and 'hope'. The campaign's success also exemplifies that a linguistic motto (in this case 'Yes we can') can be an important point of identification and a rallying device.

The rhetorical style of a politician is important too: it can produce emotionality, credibility, and signal personal involvement and commitment. Thus Tony Blair frequently asked questions ('Why not do so?', 'What's the point of …?') or pretended to be responding to a stimulus given by the audience. His speeches thus sounded like dialogue. He also used elements on the meta-level ('I say to you', 'I say unto the British people'), which added a sense of passion and conviction to his arguments (cf. Fairclough 2000: 113–114).

The representatives of CDA are also interested in recent changes in the way discourse occurs and how it affects society. Thus Fairclough (1992: 200–224) speaks of three major tendencies which discourse exhibits at the end of the twentieth century: **'democratization'**, **'commodification'** and **'technologization'**. One domain of 'democratization' concerns attempts at making visible the sexist elements in language and avoiding gender stereotypes (see Chapters 8.3 and 19). An example of 'commodification' is the tendency of educational institutions such as colleges and universities to treat their students as 'clients' or 'customers' and to advertise courses and degree programmes as commodities (cf. Fairclough 1992: 210–215). The 'technologization' of discourse is the tendency to teach (in manuals, seminars, special courses, etc.) certain 'discourse technologies' needed in various professions. Being skilled in 'interviewing', in 'managing conversation' and in controlling different types of rhetoric is suggested to be important for one's career and is therefore taught to employees and job applicants (Fairclough 1992: 215–218; see also Fairclough 1995a: 102–111).

Even more recently, there have been changes in the relation between discourse and society because of a development called 'globalization'. In Chapter 10 of *Language and Power* (2nd edn, 2001: 203–218), Fairclough takes account of this development and discusses the role of language in changes concerning aspects of economy and of communication. With 'global TV' (e.g. CNN) adopting a major role in world communication processes, 'what happens in one place happens against a global horizon' (Fairclough 2001: 205). In *Language and Globalization*, Fairclough calls this development the 'mediatization of politics' (2006: 101–108) and addresses the global discourse on the 'war on terror' (2006: 140–161).

18.2 Strategies in the Discourse of Discrimination

Representatives of the linguistic school of CDA have also investigated the role of language in perpetuating prejudice, particularly concerning racism, anti-Semitism and sexism. In this approach, 'stereotype' is defined as 'the verbal expression of a certain conviction or belief directed towards a social group or an individual as a member of that social group' (Reisigl and Wodak 2001: 19 quoting Uta Quasthoff; see also Reisigl and Wodak 2001: 224 ff.).

Reisigl and Wodak distinguish a number of strategies by which discrimination is brought about, the simplest being 'that of identifying persons or groups of persons linguistically by naming them derogatorily, debasingly or vituperatively' as in German *Neger, Zigeuner, Tschusch*, etc. (2001: 45). A second strategy is 'predication', through which (evaluatively) certain qualities are assigned to persons, e.g. 'Foreigners are aggressive and criminal' (2001: 54 f.). Discriminatory predications can also be expressed through metonymy and metaphor. Thus, immigration has been compared to natural disasters (*avalanche, flood*), fire (*smouldering conflicts*), pollution and impurity, disease/infection, food-growing (*wheat* to be separated from the *chaff*) and the overcrowding of a boat (cf. Reisigl and Wodak 2001: 59 f.). More subtle than predication is the effect of attribution: using adjectives in the attributive position (as in 'aggressive foreigners' and 'criminal refugees') does not state anything, but does imply that (at least some) foreigners are aggressive and some refugees are criminal.

Reisigl and Wodak also show how certain words, such as *Sozialschmarotzer* ('social parasites'), *Überfremdung* ('over-foreignization') and *nicht ortsüblich* ('not usual in this region'), create negative stereotypes about foreigners and refugees (2001: 19–21, based on Quasthoff 1973 and 1978). The authors suggest creating 'guidelines for journalists [...], which help to avoid the discriminatory linguistic presentation of specific groups of persons in the media' (2001: 269).

Social inequality and injustice, whose linguistic dimension is the province of CDA, affects women in different ways in different cultures. These ways are investigated in a specific branch of CDA called 'Feminist Critical Discourse Analysis'. The articles in Michelle Lazar's book of the same title (2005) look at discriminatory discourse in different cultures. How CDA can be applied to spoken and written texts from various sources is also shown in the articles in Caldas-Coulthard and Coulthard (eds. 1996) and in Goatly's coursebook *Critical Reading and Writing* (2000).

The social dimension of language is also investigated by a school of linguistics related to CDA, viz. 'Social Semiotics' (Halliday 1979; Hodge and Kress 1988). This school in some ways goes beyond CDA, since it considers not just language, but all media of communication (cf. *Semiotics Encyclopedia Online*, s.v. Social Semiotics; see also the articles in the journal *Social Semiotics*).

18.3 Critique of CDA: Overestimating Power in Discourse

Despite their belief in the negative effect of discriminatory linguistic presentation, Reisigl and Wodak (2001: 33) warn of naively overestimating the 'manipulative' power of language:

> To speak about 'manipulation' [...] could imply reductionist, hardly provable causal assumptions about the effects of language use, about a simple and direct relationship between discursive and other forms of social practices. Apart from that, the meaning of the expression risks incapacitating the recipients (hearers or readers) as autonomous, self-aware and self-reflective psycho-physical organisms.

This critique of an I-know-better attitude of the discourse analyst is reminiscent of Matthias Jung's warning of a naïve belief in the manipulative power of euphemisms in texts on the environment (2001: 277):

> Whoever imputes calculated intention to users and great manipulative power to the use of euphemisms excludes any manipulatory effect in him/herself – only the others are stupid enough not to see the manipulation! As a polemical cliché the accusation of euphemizing is therefore above all the expression of self-righteous moralizing intended to immunize against the consideration of differing views. Those who manipulate in a perfidious way cannot be in the right. To sum up: critical attentiveness as to public use of words, playful unmasking, explicit criticism – fine; stereotyped accusation of euphemizing – no!

In a similar vein, Alexander (2009: 197) warns us not to overestimate the power of euphemisms and the 'militarization' of language:

> After all, there is perhaps no area of human activity other than war, military violence and force which could demonstrate as compellingly and definitively how insubstantial language is when people are confronted with violently socialized (and brutalized) groups of human beings (aka soldiers) directing bombs and missiles at them.

Henry Widdowson's critique of CDA (1995) focuses on the point that CDA is committed to a specific cause (viz. showing the role of language in social inequality). CDA is thus not 'analysis' but 'interpretation' – from the subjective point-of-view of the interpreter; from their commitment it follows that CDA practitioners prefer to interpret a certain type of discourse, or rather, text:

There may be reasons for preferring one discourse to another, and if you are ideologically committed you will be inclined to imply that your interpretation of a text is the only one which is valid, that it is somehow *in* the text indeed, needing only to be discovered, uncovered, revealed by expert exegesis. What is actually revealed is the particular discourse perspective of the interpreter. (Widdowson 1995:171; original emphasis)

This critique led to a controversy between Widdowson and Fairclough, in which Fairclough defended 'commitment' – including commitment to linguistic analysis as a tool in social scientific analysis. (The articles by Widdowson and Fairclough are reprinted with an introduction in Seidlhofer ed. 2003: 125–168.)

18.4 Misunderstanding and Mistranslation

Pragmatics usually makes the tacit assumption that the uses and effects of language are those intended by the sender of the message: what is meant to be communicated by the speaker/writer is more or less what is understood by the hearer/reader. That this is rarely fully the case is stressed by the growing number of linguists who have concerned themselves with 'misunderstanding' and 'miscommunication'. Different forms of misunderstanding have been discussed, among others, by Tannen (1986, 1990, as differences in style), Falkner (1997), Tzanne (2000) and the authors in Grimshaw (ed. 1990).

Misunderstanding can occur on all levels of language (cf. Falkner 1997: 130–140):

The phonetic
The morphological
The lexico-semantic
The syntactic
The speech act level
Other pragmatic levels (politeness, irony, degrees of indirectness, etc.).

Misunderstanding occurs among speakers of the same language (intralinguistic misunderstanding), but also among speakers of different languages (cross-linguistic). Since each language has its own 'grip on reality', some degree of misunderstanding or rather mistranslation is the rule rather than the exception.

Misunderstanding (for instance, simple mis-hearing of numbers) has been the cause of serious accidents (air-travel, Czernobyl), but also (e.g. by misunderstanding speech-acts) of conflict, quarrel, perhaps even war. Misunderstanding can be a source of humour (examples in Falkner 1997), but also of confusion and aggression. Tzanne (2000: 234) speaks of 'the dynamics of miscommunication' through which conversation constructs its own interpretative context. However, when a compliment is misunderstood as criticism, a word wrongly interpreted in its derogatory meaning, or a joke 'misunderstood' as racist or sexist, this may have serious consequences on the 'dynamics' of personal relations and political careers.

The cause of the catastrophe at Czernobyl is said to have been a simple misunderstanding between two operators. Even more tragic was a misunderstanding between the Japanese Cabinet and the Allied forces in July, 1945: a Japanese word was allegedly intended by the Japanese to mean 'suspend the decision', but interpreted by the US forces as 'ignore the demand to capitulate' – a mistranslation which may have been responsible for the atom bombs falling on Hiroshima and Nagasaki (cf. Chase 1955: 16; see Chapter 7 above). (For more examples of mistranslation, some with comic effect, see Appendix III.)

18.5 Conclusion (CDA)

As has been shown, Critical Discourse Analysis is a still flourishing approach to discourse, in which the impact of discourse on society and on possible changes in society is emphasized. In spite of the critique summarized above, CDA can be regarded as an important contribution to showing the impact of language (as discourse) on human societies. CDA is also important because it emphasizes the dialectical and interactional quality of this influence, as expressed by Fairclough in the quotation printed at the beginning of this chapter.

What is needed is more data on the effect of discourse elements, such as euphemisms and dysphemisms, data which could be obtained only by using the method of informant questioning. For an early attempt at obtaining such data by using a word association test (*Kernenergie* vs. *Atomkraft*), see Fill (2001: 46 after M. Jung).

19. Women, Men and Discourse[1]

> Those who want to learn a foreign language will therefore always do well at the first stage to read many ladies' novels, because they will there continually meet with just those everyday words and combinations which the foreigner is above all in need of, what may be termed the indispensable small-change of a language.
>
> (Jespersen 1922: 248)

In Chapter 8.3, the topic of the construction of gender and sexuality in the language system was addressed. In the present chapter, the focus is on *discourse*, i.e. on language in use. Discourse has an impact on the position of women and men in society, but also on the relation between the two genders (for individuals as well as for communities). Changes in discourse habits may have consequences concerning gender roles and gender relations – just as changes in gender roles may in their turn have consequences on discourse. The 'gender issue' is thus a prime example of the interrelatedness of language and society.

'Discourse and gender' is a large thematic area, in which at least the following three topics can be distinguished: the discourse *of* women and men, discourse *between* women and men and discourse *about* women and men.

19.1 The Discourse of Women and Men: Women's Talk, Men's Talk

The most concise treatment of the differences between women's talk and men's talk may be found in the books by Jennifer Coates (1996, 2003 and 2004). In *Women Talk* (1996), Coates addresses the topic of talk among women friends, in *Men Talk* (2003) she discusses specifically the characteristics of conversations among men, and in *Women, Men and Language* she has a chapter on 'Same-sex talk' (2004: 125–144). In contrast, Judith Baxter (2003) uses an approach called 'Feminist Post-structuralist discourse analysis' (FPDA), which does not centre on male-female differences, but recognizes differences within and between females (2003: 182–186).

Coates (2004: 5–7) distinguishes four approaches to the topic of language and gender. The **deficit** approach sees women (and women's language, WL) as deficient in comparison to men. Otto Jespersen was a representative of this approach, but more recent authors such as Robin Lakoff (in *Language and Woman's Place*, 1975) still attribute a certain weakness and unassertiveness to women's language. 'This approach was challenged because of the implication that there was something wrong with women's language, and that women should learn to speak like men if they wanted to be taken seriously.' (This and the following quotations are from

Coates 2004: 6; see also Chapter 8.3 above.) The **dominance** approach 'sees women as an oppressed group and interprets linguistic differences in women's and men's speech in terms of men's dominance and women's subordination'. The **difference** approach is based on the different cultures theory of Maltz and Borker (1982) and is particularly evident in the books of Deborah Tannen (e.g. 1991). 'The advantage of the difference model is that it allows women's talk to be examined outside a framework of oppression or powerlessness. Instead, researchers have been able to show the strengths of linguistic strategies characteristic of women, and to celebrate women's way of talking.' On the other hand, this approach does not take the issue of **power** into consideration, a topic which is particularly important in mixed talk (see for instance Part II of Holmes and Meyerhoff eds. 2003). The most recent approach (although anticipated in the work of Simone de Beauvoir) is one in which gender identity 'is seen as a social construct rather than as a "given" social category'. This approach, called by Coates **dynamic** or **social constructionist**, sees speakers as '"doing gender" rather than statically "being" a particular gender'. (See the discussion of Judith Butler in Chapter 8.3 above.)

Otto Jespersen's chapter 'The Woman', in his book *Language, its Nature, Development and Origin* (1922: 237–254), was one of the earliest attempts to characterize women's talk in comparison with men's. The many **stereotypes about women** contained in this chapter have been rightly criticized, among others, by Spender (1985: 10 f.), Coates (2004: 10 f.) and Cameron (2007: 27–29). Although Jespersen writes of 'the greater rapidity of female thought' (1922: 252), he thinks that women are less creative in language, their vocabulary is smaller, they more often break off without finishing their sentences and they use hyperbole and adverbs of intensity 'with disregard of their proper meaning' (e.g. German *riesig klein*, English *awfully pretty, terribly nice*, and French *rudement joli, affreusement délicieuse*, 1922: 250). Jespersen blames the differences between women's and men's language on the 'division of labour enjoined in primitive tribes and to a great extent also among more civilized peoples' (1922: 254). He speaks of great social changes going on in his time 'which may eventually modify even the linguistic relations of the two sexes' (1922: 254).

More than 50 years later, the '**division of labour**' between women and men was made a topic of research concerning **conversation**. Pamela Fishman (1977, 1978) investigated the failure or success in topic introduction by women and men and the support work women do in cross-gender conversation (see also the chapter "Conversation: The Sexual Division of Labour" in Graddol and Swann 1989: 69–94). Don Zimmerman and Candace West (1975) examined minimal responses (*mhm, ok, right*, etc.) and interruptions. They found that men interrupted three times as often as women, and their interruptions were also closer to the beginning of the interlocutor's turn (cf. Graddol and Swann 1989: 78 f.).

More recently, researchers have been less inclined to see fundamental differences between the way women and men talk. Deborah Cameron (2007: 7 f.) writes of **'the myth of Mars and Venus'**, which is 'the proposition that men and women differ fundamentally in the way they use language to communicate'. Cameron lists **five claims which uphold this myth**. These are (cf. 2007: 7 f.):

(a) Communication matters more to women than to men, and women talk more.
(b) Women are more verbally skilled than men.
(c) Men's interests are things and facts, women are interested in relations.
(d) Men talk competitively, women cooperatively.
(e) These differences lead to miscommunication between the sexes; problems arise especially in heterosexual relationships.

According to Cameron, none of these statements are true, nor are men from Mars, women from Venus; rather, 'Men are from Earth, Women are from Earth. Deal with it' (2007: 181).

From the point-of-view of language impact, the issues of communication and possible *mis*communication *between* the sexes (perhaps based on an unequal distribution of power), are of specific relevance. The next sub-chapter will therefore discuss different aspects of cross-gender (or mixed) talk, with a section on talk in pair-relations and another one on miscommunication.

19.2 Discourse between Women and Men

Discourse between individuals plays a great role in shaping the relationship between them. How this discourse influences future actions is one of the topics of Pragmatics as it is understood by Watzlawick *et al.* (1967, see above, Chapter 14.1). A specific form of this discourse is the discourse between women and men. Many topics in this research area have been addressed in the literature, for example:

* Do men and women speak the same language? Can they ever really communicate? (Cameron 2007: 1; see also the articles in Coates ed. 1998).
* Which gender is dominant concerning (1) topics, (2) speech acts and (3) turn-taking? (R. Lakoff 1975; Spender 1985: 41–51).
* Which gender does more to support a conversation? (Fishman 1977, 1978).
* Do women and men have different politeness strategies? Do they have different perceptions of rudeness and politeness? (Holmes 1995).
* Which gender interrupts more? (Zimmerman and West 1975).
* How do children acquire 'gender-appropriate speech'? (Coates 2004: 150–155).
* What non-verbal elements (touch, posture, gesture, body movement, eye contact) come into play? (Henley 1986: 94–167).

Discourse between women and men may occur based on a number of text-types (letters, e-mails, professional debates, etc.; see Part V of Holmes and Meyerhoff eds 2003). However, the most thoroughly researched type of cross-gender discourse is **conversation** (see, for instance Graddol and Swann 1989: 69–94; Heath 1991; Coates 2004: 85–124; see also the list of ten features of cross-gender conversation in D. Lee 1992: 122). Coates (2004: 113) writes of three ways in which a man or a woman may be dominant in conversation (emphasis by Coates):

> First, a speaker may break the 'one speaker speaks at a time' rule by interrupting the current speaker and **grabbing the floor**. Secondly, a speaker may contravene the norm of 'speaker change recurs' by taking a very long turn, ignoring the other speakers' bids for the floor, and **hogging the floor**. Thirdly, and paradoxically, a speaker may talk too little, in effect withdrawing from conversational interaction; such non-cooperative behaviour will often lead to the breakdown of conversation.

Although gender roles have changed in the last few decades and men are in general less dominant than they were in the past, Coates (2004: 124) still finds that 'women and men do not have equal rights to the conversational floor'. According to Coates, this is true for most conversational settings, but also for professional ones such as the classroom, the work-place and the public domain, where women are in a Catch 22 situation: 'They are expected to adopt the more adversarial, information-focused style characteristic of all-male talk, and typical of talk in the public domain, but if they do [...], they run the risk of being perceived as aggressive and confrontational, as un-feminine' (Coates 2004: 201).

19.3 Discourse in Pair Relations

A specific kind of cross-gender communication is the discourse between a woman and a man[2] in a pair-relationship. **Ernst Leisi**'s book *Paar und Sprache* (1983) is an early attempt to show the role of language specifically in pair-relations with a particular focus on the development of the relation and its quality later on. The following is a short summary of the Swiss linguist's ideas on this topic.

The importance of language in female male relations is described by Leisi (1983: 7) in the following way:

> Die Beziehung wird weitgehend durch Sprache angebahnt; an ihrem weiteren Verlauf ist die Sprache stets beteiligt. Ob die Beziehung fortdauert oder zusammenbricht, kann von sprachlichen Dingen abhängen.
>
> *Relations are largely initiated through language, and language always plays a role in their further development. Whether a relation lasts or collapses may be dependent on linguistic factors.*

Leisi lists a number of qualities which characterize the language of pair relations. For our topic of discourse impact, four aspects, which all concern language as discourse, are of particular importance (cf. 1983: 8 f.; see the comments below):

1. Language can be an **erotic stimulant**.
2. Feelings and actions can be influenced by linguistic patterns expressed in **works of literature**, such as novels, poems and songs.
3. In long lasting relationships, language may serve as a means to **remember common experiences** and thus help to keep the relationship young.
4. **Disturbances** and conflicts in pair relations may have their origin in language. On the other hand, disturbances due to language may not harm the relation.

(1) Language can help to stimulate desire starting with playful talk, continuing with compliments ('verbal caress can be more stimulating than manual', Leisi 1983: 65), declarations of love and finishing with breach of taboo. Erotic jokes, naming parts of the body ('Your breasts are lovely') and revealing sexual intentions all need the medium of language. More recently, the chapters in *Language and Desire* (Harvey and Shalom eds 1997) have emphasized and illustrated the desire creating function of language (see also Kulick 2003). A branch of linguistics (not yet existing) called Ero-linguistics could study this topic in more detail.

(2) Literary texts have frequently helped to bring about sexual activity. Literary texts or the words of songs 'construe' for us experiences and feelings which before were nebulous, subconscious and thus unreal (cf. Leisi 1983: 91–93). Leisi (1983: 87 f.) gives the example of Paolo and Francesca from Dante's *Inferno* (Book 5): the two lovers (who later are murdered by Francesca's husband) were inspired to their loving action by reading together a novella about Lancelot, who gives a kiss to Queen Guinevere, King Arthur's wife. Another example of this instigation to love by the language of literature is *Madame Bovary,* a novel by Gustave Flaubert. In this novel, Emma, the heroine, finds in Léon a kindred spirit also interested in literature. From reading love novels she is then easily seduced by Rodolphe to being unfaithful to her husband.

From the *Song of Solomon* (Old Testament) and Ovid's *Ars Amatoria* to D. H. Lawrence's *Lady Chatterley's Lover* and the modern pornographic novel, literature which makes possible 'loving according to text' abounds in all languages.

> Licence my roving hands, and let them go
> Before, behind, between, above, below.

These lines (from John Donne's 'On his mistress going to bed') are an example which combines breach of taboo with describing sexual intentions (cf. Leisi 1983: 68). The role of films in making desires concrete has not yet received adequate attention (see, however, Kipnis 1998 and Robert Stam's chapter on 'Metamorphoses of *Madame Bovary*', 2005: 144–190). The internet (chatrooms, internet partner services, pornographic sites) is already becoming an object of research concerning this topic (see, for instance, Crystal 2006; Marko 2008). (For more on the effect of language through literature and film, see the section about literary and media pragmatics, Chapter 15.2 above.)

(3) Language (as discourse) can be a factor which helps to keep a relationship alive. Through discourse (dialogue!), shared experiences are remembered and brought to life again. Talking about pleasant experiences of the past can even be a strategy used to save a threatened relationship.

That language may help to remember past scenes, emotions and encounters is true not only in pair-relations. Language may have a co-constructive power which, optimistically, preserves the agreeable parts of past experiences and thus welds people together who would otherwise look for new partners. This recalling function of language continues after a partnership is dissolved: 'die Sprache erhält die Erinnerung an den Partner, auch an den verlorenen, in höherem Maße lebendig, als andere Mittel es könnten' [*Language keeps the memory of the partner alive more vividly than other means could*] (Leisi 1983: 152).

(4) The **communication of couples** can be **disturbed** on the speech act level or through differences in the code, although code differences need not necessarily disturb a relationship; in specific cases they may even support it. Leisi's example of this is Max Frisch's play *Als der Krieg zu Ende war*, in which a young German woman and a Russian captain fall in love with each other. Whatever separates them (ideology, culture) cannot be expressed in words since they do not know each other's language. Another example of this is Lady Chatterley and the game-keeper Mellors (from D. H. Lawrence's novel *Lady Chatterley's Lover*), whose code differences are a source of laughter and of an increased feeling of togetherness for them rather than a reason for separation.

19.4 Miscommunication between Women and Men

Another source of disturbance based on code difference can be found in the different degrees of indirectness. Women and men, though speaking the same 'language', may come from different parts of their country, may have different social and ethnic backgrounds and different family traditions concerning (in)directness. Generally, women are thought to be more indirect in their way of using language. In her books (particularly in *That's Not What I Meant* 1986, and *You Just Don't Understand* 1990), Deborah **Tannen** shows how this leads to different conversational styles which could be the cause of misunderstanding. Here is one of her examples (1990: 15, adapted):

Woman (*in the car, to her husband*): Would you like to stop for a drink?

Husband: No.

Woman (*later, annoyed*): *I* would have liked to stop for a drink.

Husband: Then why didn't you just say what you wanted? Why did you play games with me?

To understand 'Would you like to stop for a drink?' as '*I* would like to stop for a drink' would have needed a deeper understanding of indirect speech acts than the husband possessed.

A well-known theory which tries to explain problems of communication between women and men is the **different cultures theory** (already mentioned above), which was proposed by Daniel N. Maltz and Ruth A. Borker in 1982. This theory says that communication between women and men may break down because the two genders grow up in different cultures (different 'worlds of words'). Boys grow up in large groups with a hierarchical structure, mostly with a leader, while girls form small intimate groups or just pairs where they may have a 'best friend' and where status does not play a role. The two cultures theory is based on the idea that young people learn how to speak and behave not just from their parents, but even more so from their peers. Communication between women and men, according to this theory, is 'cross-cultural communication' (cf. Tannen 1990: 42–47).

Maltz and Borker's theory and Deborah Tannen's reference to it have been criticized by feminists because this theory perpetuates old gender stereotypes. Tannen's distinction between 'rapport-talk' (characteristic of females) and 'report-talk' (males) expresses these stereotypes very typically:

> For most women, the language of conversation is primarily a language of rapport: a way of establishing connections and negotiating relationships. Emphasis is placed on displaying similarities and matching experience.
>
> [...]
>
> For most men, talk is primarily a means to preserve independence and negotiate and maintain status in a hierarchical social order. This is done by exhibiting knowledge and skill, and by holding center stage through verbal performance such as story telling, joking, or imparting information. (Tannen 1990:77)

Tannen's distinction, which is based on the view that women feel more comfortable speaking in private, while men prefer public speaking (1990: 76 f.) seems somewhat outdated today and is not seriously supported by many linguists in the twenty-first century.

An important critic of Maltz and Borker and Tannen is Deborah **Cameron**, whose book *The Myth of Mars and Venus* (2007) was mentioned above. Cameron collected evidence that there are no basic differences between women's and men's talk. Consequently the belief in frequent misunderstandings between members of the two sexes (based on these differences) also belongs into the realm of myth:

> Claims about male-female misunderstanding have proliferated since the 1980s, but many have never been tested in any rigorous way. They are based on speculation or on purely anecdotal evidence. A case in point is the claim that men favour a direct style of speaking and have difficulty understanding women who prefer to go about things more indirectly. (2007: 84 f.)

One situation in which **misunderstanding** was thought to be frequent was **agreeing to have sex together**. In particular, it was claimed that women's indirect way of refusing sexual offers was often misunderstood by men to mean 'yes'. Cameron reports research which shows that refusing an offer is done in the same way by both genders and that claims of misunderstandings are in fact myths (Cameron 2007: 80–99).

A disturbance on the speech act level may occur when speakers (say, husband and wife) use **meta-communication**, i.e. talk about their way of communicating together. From 'You shouldn't have said that' and 'unfortunately we seem to speak different languages' (cf. Leisi 1983: 143) to 'That was a very nice thing to say' and 'I knew immediately what you meant by this', the range of meta-communicative acts goes from utterances which may endanger a relationship to those which create togetherness and forgiveness. Tannen's book-titles (*That's Not What I Meant*, 1986 and *You Just Don't Understand*, 1990) are instances of frequently used meta-communicative utterances. Leisi (1983: 143 f.) gives examples, from literature and film, of failure to meta-communicate leading to disaster (e.g. Othello does not ask Desdemona about her conversations with Cassio). On the other hand, there may also be a surplus of meta-communication (examples are Ingmar Bergman's film *Scenes from a Marriage* and Edward Albee's play *Who's Afraid of Virginia Woolf*): here talking about the other's language leads to aggressive behaviour.

Jennifer Coates (2004: 204–206) discusses research on the role humour plays in linguistic interaction between women and men. 'Collaborative humour' was found to be more frequent in meetings where women participated or were in the majority. However, humour can also be an instrument of power as shown in some of the chapters in Kotthoff (ed. 1988). Humour in jokes directed against women (Trömel-Plötz 1988) has more recently found its counterpart in humour which ridicules men.

All in all, there seems to be a growing awareness (at any rate in the Western world) that the roles of the genders and the public perception of these roles are changing in the direction of more equality. The efforts of linguists who have pointed out asymmetries and implicit forms of oppression have played an important role in bringing about this change. The interaction between 'women, men and language' (title of Coates 2004) is an excellent example of the interconnectedness and the give-and-take-relationship between language, linguistics and the world.

19.5 Discourse about Women and Men: the Impact of Gender-Biased Language

Discourse about women and men may have a profound influence on how we see the roles of the two genders in a society and how we perceive individual persons, women and men. In recent years, feminist linguists have investigated the influence that gender-biased language has on our thinking about the two genders. The question addressed by these linguists is whether or not non-inclusive language makes our thoughts incline towards excluding women. Do English *man, he, his*, etc. direct our thoughts chiefly towards male persons – or do they really have a double function in representing (1) male persons or (2) '**generically**' persons of either gender, as is sometimes claimed (cf. Kalverkämper 1979)? In German, does a sentence such as 'Die *Ärzte* empfehlen diese Therapie' (*doctors recommend this therapy*), with the form *Ärzte* rather than *ÄrztInnen*, make us think chiefly of male doctors – or is there no gender specific thinking involved?

Concerning English, questions like these were addressed in several studies of the 1970s and 1980s by American psychologists. Thus, Moulton *et al.* (1978) carried out an experiment with 226 male and 264 female students and found that masculine pronouns (*he, his, him*) even in explicitly gender-neutral contexts caused the students to think of males significantly more often than did *he or she/his or her*. Cecilia M. Hamilton's experiments with asking subjects to complete sentence fragments by giving first names and thus specifying gender (1985, 1988) led to the same results. From the point of view of prototypicality, 'the most typical *he* is probably a man' (Hamilton 1988: 785). John Gastil (1990) made informants read sentences aloud and verbally describe the images that came to mind. While the plural pronoun *they* served as a generic pronoun for both males and females, 'generic' *he* was associated largely with male images. In her book *Pronoun Envy,* Anna Livia (2001) shows similar effects in the readers of English and French literary texts.

Studies concerning German were conducted in the 1990s and early 2000s. For instance, Dagmar Stahlberg and Sabine Sczesny (2001) carried out experiments concerning **three ways of naming persons** of either gender, viz. *Studenten* (generic form), *Studentinnen und Studenten* (naming both genders) and *StudentInnen* (capital *I* – Binnen-*I,* Versalien-*I*). The experiments involved for instance the naming of students, celebrities or candidates for the position of dean. The persons were to be named including their Christian names, to make gender identification possible. Here is an example which shows the three possibilities (the tasks required of the informants have been translated into English):[3]

(a) Mehrere *Studenten* beteiligten sich an der Diskussion – (list some names of these students).

(b) Dort trafen wir berühmte *Autorinnen und Autoren* – (give possible names of them).

(c) Wer wird DekanIn werden? – (give the name of a possible candidate).

All experiments showed that the generic form (Sentence a: *Studenten*) led to fewer namings of female persons than the alternatives (b and c).

In a similar study by Elke Heise (2000), 150 students were given short sentences in which persons were mentioned in different ways (generic masculine forms vs. capital *I* vs. slash). The students were asked to write stories about these persons and use Christian names for them. The results showed a marked influence of writing conventions: generic masculine forms (*Studenten*) led to an overrepresentation of male identification, while interior capital *I* (*StudentInnen*) favoured female identification. Only the use of slash (*Student/inn/en*) resulted in an equal representation of males and females.

'Role names' (e.g. *florist, captain, singer*) can have grammatical and/or conceptual gender. **Grammatical gender** is expressed through pronouns (*she* vs. *he*) and in some languages through suffixes. **Conceptual gender**, on the other hand, concerns the 'perceived' gender of persons who represent certain roles, such as professions, interests, pastimes:

> *florist*, perceived as female, vs.
> *captain*, perceived as male, vs.
> *singer*, neutral (see also the lists in Irmen 2007: 451).

Hellinger and Bußmann (2003: 149) make a similar distinction between grammatical gender and 'social gender', which is 'a non-linguistic category which reflects social and cultural stereotypes of female and male character traits, behaviors and roles'. Examples: *doctors* (social gender: m) and *nurses* (f), *boss* (m) and *secretary* (f).

Lisa Irmen's results show 'that both grammatical and conceptual gender cues affect the interpretation of linguistically conveyed person information' (Irmen 2007: 450). There is still 'a general mental "people = male" schema' present in our brains, so that 'reading about people activates male- more often than female-biased representations' (2007: 449).

Although it could be objected that in some of the studies discussed above it was the effect of writing, perhaps even spelling (thus not really 'language') which was investigated, it is still remarkable how unanimously the studies show a strong influence of supposedly formal features of language on our thinking about the gender of persons.

As concerns language and gender in general, it is to be hoped that **positive interaction between language and society** will take place in the near future: changes in the use of language which make both genders visible should lead to changes in thinking, which in their turn will lead to changes in society – with the possible result, among others, that more women are admitted to positions of power. This will again influence language, so that a 'benign circle' of changes is set in motion (cf. Klann-Delius 2005: 191). 'Women, men and language', this excellent example of the interaction between language and society, may thus prove that changes in language, which become evident in discourse, are part of the evolution towards greater well-being of an increasing number of groups.

Notes

1. Pace Jennifer Coates (2004, *Women, Men and Language*).
2. Other sexual orientations beside the heterosexual one will not be dealt with here; the reader is referred to books on queer language such as Leap (1996), Kulick (2000) and Campbell-Kibler *et al.* (eds 2002).
3. The English translations of the sentences would be gender-neutral: a. Several students took part in the discussion. b. There we met some famous authors. c. Who will be the next dean?

20. Interaction between Language and World (Ecological Linguistics)

Merritt Ruhlen (2001: 214) describes the interrelation between the development of human behaviour and modern culture (on the one hand) and language (on the other) as follows:

> 50,000 years ago there was a major (probably the major) transition in human evolution, as anatomically modern humans started, quite suddenly, to exhibit modern human behaviour. Artefacts that had changed little in hundreds of thousands of years, over vast geographical areas, suddenly became much more complex and began to change rapidly in both space and time. For the first time tools were made not just from stone, but also from bone, antler, tusks, shells, and other materials. It is at this time that the first clear indications of art appear, in both Australia and Europe. It was apparently also at this moment that these behaviourally modern people spread out of Africa, carrying with them the genes that attest to their recent African origin, and the language that has left traces […] A number of scholars have maintained that this sudden and profound change in human behaviour could hardly have been accomplished without modern human language […] Indeed, the emergence of fully modern human language at this time is often seen as the underlying mechanism behind the swift change to behavioural modernity and the subsequent occupation of the entire world.

This account expresses one of the main ideas to be elaborated in the present chapter: language was not there first, with tool-making, art and modern behaviour following from it; nor was there 'modern behaviour' first with language coming as its consequence: cause and effect merge, and the development of language and 'modern behaviour' (cooperation instead of confrontation) was an interactive process with small steps on both sides combining to bring about 'progress' (see also Chapter 1.1 above).

This chapter takes an 'ecological' look at the impact of language on the world. 'Ecology', as defined by Ernst Haeckel in 1866, is the study of the mutual interaction (*Wechselwirkung*) between organisms and between organisms and their environment. An ecological view of language thus means considering impact on both sides: languages are seen as organisms in an environment (a society, or even the earth as a whole): they have mutual influence on each other, but they also interact with their environment, since this environment (society) in its turn influences language – and vice versa. An 'ecological' understanding of language thus means not simply looking from a monolithic viewpoint at the effect of language on thinking and acting, but rather acknowledging a double-sided mutual influence, or even a circle in which each effect of language on the world may cause a responding effect of the world on language, which in turn again has an impact on the world and so on.

Here are two examples which illustrate this interaction.

(1) Our languages contain many elements of **anthropocentrism**, i.e. they describe Nature from the point of view of human use (see 20.3 below). This anthropocentrism is criticized by ecologists, who point out that such words as *herbs, pests, weeds* and *waste land* one-sidedly express (non-)usability for humans. This critique may lead speakers and writers to an avoidance of anthropocentrisms, which in its turn may lead to a sensitized perception of the relation between humans and Nature. Finally, there will be action which tries to preserve the diversity of species, of languages and cultures (on 'cultural ecosystems' see Finke 2001: 85–87).

(2) Languages contain elements of **sexism**, i.e. they either make women invisible or fix women and men in stereotyped roles (see Chapter 8.3 above). For some time, these sexist elements have been pointed out by feminists who have provided guidelines on how to avoid sexism in language. Many people will follow this advice and will therefore:

- avoid 'generic' *he/his* (*'a good doctor will always consider *his* patients' needs');
- avoid '-*man*' in designations for professions (*'policeman, fireman');
- avoid gender stereotypes (*'motorists: make sure your wife and children have fastened their seat belts', with motorists being understood as male).

One consequence of this might be a different image of (a possible) reality (in the hearer as well as in the speaker) and thus a change of attitude which may lead to action and finally to changes in society. A second consequence could of course be protests from traditionalists, which, however, give increased attention to the envisaged changes (see also 19.5 above).

A very similar idea of the interrelation between language and the world is expressed by Sune Vork Steffensen (2007) in his representation of 'Dialectical Linguistics'. Dialectical Linguistics recognizes three aspects of our existence: '(i) The ways we use language in communication; (ii) the reality of our global capitalist societies; (iii) the current ecological crisis that threatens the sustainability of human and non-human life forms'. The interrelation between these three aspects is described by Steffensen (2007: 3) as follows (italics in the original):

> there are *dialectical relations* between these three aspects of our existence. That is, our language and our communicative interactions influence and are influenced by the way our societies are organized, which in turn influences and is influenced by our environmental surroundings, which in turn influence and are influenced by our language and our communicative interactions.

The following sections will deal with a number of topics from this ecological point of view. We will consider both the relation between language and the world and the relation between different languages.

20.1 Language, Conflict and Peace – the Buffer Function of Language

Hätten wir das Wort –	*If we had the word –*
Hätten wir die Sprache –	*If we had language –*
Wir bräuchten die Waffen nicht.	*We would not need weapons.*

Ingeborg Bachmann

Ethologists and anthropologists have written extensively about the conflict-resolving and aggression-preventing power of language – but few *linguists* have as yet occupied themselves with this topic. 'Jaw, jaw is better than war, war': Churchill's phrase expresses succinctly what ethologists have found out about this use of language.

The peace-maintaining function of language is present, first of all, in bonding talk (Malinowski's 'phatic communion'), in which an atmosphere of belonging together is created, for instance by sharing opinions and establishing a common ground (cf. Schneider 1988: 185 f.). Even more important are those contexts in which language is deliberately enlisted as a device for keeping aggression at bay and for creating a 'buffer' against physical violence. This is for instance the case when language is used competitively to prevent physical aggression. Volker Heeschen (1989: 220 f.) has written about the 'song duels' of the Inuit, the speech tournaments of the Maori and the 'shouting matches' of the Yali – events which are staged in order to 'handle' conflicts peacefully. Eibl-Eibesfeldt (1984: 125–128) calls language used in this way a 'valve' and speaks of the 'Ventilsitten' (*valve customs*) of many nations by which aggression and physical violence are kept under control.

Power reversal (e.g. in carnival traditions), rural competitions, and – ideally – sports events as ritualized forms of fighting fulfil this **cathartic** function (cf. Lorenz 1984: 249 f.), as does 'enthusiasm' (*Begeisterung*) for a good cause. Language, too, plays an important role, e.g. with the custom of loud complaining (without naming the antagonist) among the bush-people (Eibl-Eibesfeldt 1991: 63) and – in 'western' cultures – with cursing, swearing, 'confessing', praying and similar 'language games' (such as the 'ritual insults' described by Labov 1972: 297–353; see 14.2 above). According to Eibl-Eibesfeldt (1986: 651), these 'social functions' of language were the decisive factor for its phylogenetic development and were, for a long time, the most important functions of language – until, in the modern technical age, transmitting knowledge and communicating 'facts' became the (seemingly) dominant uses of language (see the section on 'exaptation' above, Chapter 1.2). It is as if, in the evolution of the human species, an 'inter-world' had developed – the world of language – which positions itself between anger and aggression on the one hand and physical violence on the other. That this 'buffer-zone' does not always function properly and sometimes even leads to greater escalation will be dealt with in the next subsection.

Language and Conflict Escalation

Different cultures make different use of the peace-maintaining or peace-disturbing function of language. In *Black and White Styles in Conflict,* Thomas Kochman (1981: 43) cites the example of a meeting between community representatives and the university faculty (at a US American institution) in which a black faculty member made an angry remark to a white one. 'Then, upon seeing her frightened look, he softened his anger and said, "You don't need to worry, I'm still talking. When I *stop* talking, then you might need to worry."' Kochman describes the different definitions of blacks and whites concerning the beginning of a 'fight' as follows:

> for blacks the boundary between words and actions is clearly marked. Consequently they would say the parties involved were 'having an argument' or, if there were threats and insults and challenges to fight, they might be *woofing*. But arguing or woofing is still not 'fighting'. [...] Fighting does not begin until someone makes a provocative *movement*. (Kochman 1981: 46; original emphasis)

Whites, in contrast to this, tend to think that hostile words lead to violent action without any obvious transition. For whites, there is a 'word-actions continuum' (Kochman 1981: 48), a notion which may lead to misunderstanding and false accusation between black and white people.

The influence of different 'styles' on frictions in relations between groupings and individuals has already been mentioned as a topic addressed by Deborah Tannen. While in Tannen (1986) styles based on ethnic or family backgrounds were investigated with regard to their effect on 'making or breaking relationships', in her later publications (e.g. 1990) the topic of female vs. male styles became the focus of her attention. Tannen's books have done much to raise awareness among the (American) public of the influence of 'language' on the peaceful or conflictual relation between people (see also Chapter 19.2 above).

That language can contribute to the escalation of a conflict and even lead to violence and murder is a fact which runs counter to the evolutionary aims of the phylogeny of language. Language in its role as a conflict escalator is usually explained by the argument that 'something went wrong' with discourse, e.g. that the Gricean maxims were being violated (see, for instance, Schank and Schwitalla eds. 1987). Ernst Leisi's (1983) distinction between 'disturbance in the speech act' and 'disturbance through code difference' has already been mentioned (see 19.2 above). Nevertheless, there is something surprising in the fact that possessors of the same sign system for communication (which developed in an evolutionary process favouring their propagation and survival) can use this sign system to insult each other to the point of causing death.

We have to accept that it is possible, through language (as discourse), to threaten and 'injure' another person's '**face**', i.e. 'the positive social value a person effectively claims for him/herself' (adapted from Goffman 1967: 5). According to Brown and Levinson (1987: 13), there are two kinds of face:

> Central to our model is a highly abstract notion of 'face' which consists of two specific kinds of desires ('face-wants') attributed by interactants to one another: the desire to be unimpeded in one's actions (negative face), and the desire (in some respects) to be approved (positive face).

Both face-wants can be threatened through linguistic acts, such as ordering, suggesting, advising, reminding, threatening, warning or expressing negative emotions (threats to negative face) – and (threats to positive face) criticizing, complaining, offending, contradicting, interrupting, not paying attention, etc. (cf. Brown and Levinson 1987: 66 f.).

In Brown/Levinson's theory face-threatening acts (FTAs) can be mitigated through politeness strategies, such as being indirect, apologizing, joking, etc. Nevertheless, these acts lead to a kind of indirect 'disparagement' or 'devaluing' of the other person.

Linguistically, conflict escalation proceeds in at least two stages (cf. Fill 1993: 66–71):

1. **Indirect disparagement** can be regarded as the base level on which language may lead to a dispute or quarrel. Apart from face-threatening acts, the following speech events may be responsible for the indirect disparagement of a person:
   (a)　irony (example: 'ok, you are right, of course, and I am in the wrong.');
   (b)　generalization (example: 'you *never* put ice in my drink.');
   (c)　negative transfer to the meta-level (examples: 'this sounded like a reproach'/'it's a question of *how* you talk to me'/'you keep interrupting me');
   (d)　expressing lack of interest in the other (example: 'I haven't been listening to what you were saying').

   The indirect message of these speech events is: 'You are unimportant to me.'

   Negative transfer to the meta-level sometimes results in neglecting the original cause of the conflict with language becoming the topic of conflict, as in the following example from Tannen (1986: 27):

   A: You said so.
   B: I said no such thing.
   A: You did! I heard you.
   B: Don't tell me what I said.

Exchanges of this kind occur because we hear what we want to hear. Speakers' utterances are frequently formulated vaguely and speech-acts expressed indirectly; their meaning is then *construed* by the hearer so as to fit into the desired frame.

2. The next stage of a quarrel is reached with **direct disparagement** of the other person, which is brought about through offensive language about the other, calling them names and using deprecatory expressions such as *idiot, stupid, whore, you haven't the faintest idea,* etc.

Direct disparagement is frequently answered in kind, with expressions becoming more and more offensive. Whether the next stage (physical violence) is reached depends very much on the pre-history of the conflict and on individual factors of personality.

Even at the stage of direct disparagement, language may be used to **de-escalate** and even resolve the quarrel. Speech events serving this purpose are:

- Apology
- Humour and laughter
- Positive transfer to the meta-level (example: '*This* I can accept. Go on.').

That language can also be used to instigate people to perform aggressive acts and even make them accept and desire war is a sad fact which runs counter to the evolutionary plan behind the development of language, as explained above. How the instigation to accepting war was carried out in Germany around the time of the First World War in speeches, articles, and even poems, is shown by Fritz Pasierbsky in his book *Krieg und Frieden in der Sprache* (1983: 90, 113–130; see also Fill 1993: 76–78 and the articles in Stanzel and Löschnigg eds. 1993).

The role of language in the development and escalation of conflict is also discussed in the chapters of Grimshaw (ed. 1990). Following Dahrendorf (1972: 41 f.), we should keep the concepts of 'conflict' and 'quarrel' apart, conflict being merely a collision of interests which can be 'handled' and resolved – processes which may even contain elements of creativity. On the verbal level, conflict may lead to an 'argument', a 'dispute', or even escalate to a 'quarrel'. The 'handling' of conflict may require verbal skill, but its escalation to a quarrel is rarely an intentional process.

20.2 'Ecological' and 'Unecological' Elements in the Language System

The quantum physicist Hans-Peter Dürr (2007: 41) says that language (with its many contrasts, with 'yes' and 'no' as answers to questions) contains a two-valued logic which is immensely practical in everyday situations, because it helps us to make decisions vital for our lives. But this logic is not the logic of Nature, which is much better described by quantum physics: in quantum physics, not 'yes' and 'no', but 'both … and', '… as well as' and 'in between' are recognized (see also Chapter 7 above on the two-valued orientation).

Another physicist and mathematician, David Bohm (1980: Chapter 2), called for the creation of a new, not yet existing linguistic mode, which he dubbed the 'Rheomode': this mode would make it possible to speak of processes without having to mention a doer/agent, a cause, a result and an experiencer, as in the following sentence:

> Industry [agent] with its CO_2 emissions [cause] causes global warming [result], which is harmful to the quality of the air in the cities [experiencer].

David Bohm holds our thinking (based on our languages) responsible for our ecological problems – our thinking which is 'fragmented' and which presupposes the limitlessness of the earth and its resources.

Similarly to Dürr and Bohm, ecolinguists have criticized SAE languages because they represent reality 'unecologically', i.e. with a two-valued logic, but also in terms of subject/predicate/object, or, expressed semantically, Agent/Process/Affected Participants (cf. Goatly 2001: 213). Michael Halliday even puts the blame for the ecological crisis at least partly on language ('the grammar'). Our belief in the unboundedness of human resources (water, coal, oil), our emphasis on growth and the sharp distinction we make between us humans and other living and non-living beings is contained in the grammar of our Western languages (Halliday 2001: 194 f. see the full quotation in Chapter 8.2 above).

Halliday's point is that ideologies such as growthism, sexism, classism and speciesism are not just social and political issues, but linguistic ones as well. Language provides, among its 'resources', ways to express these ideologies, and we 'use these resources' to shape our thinking and acting. But at the same time, language provides for us **the resources to point out the existence of these ideologies**, and we should use these resources as well (cf. Halliday 2001: 198 f.). In other words, we should all be linguists 'working on language' (2001: 185):

> If language merely 'reflects' our experience of what is out there, by correspondence with the categories of the material world, it is hard to see how we could threaten or subvert the existing order by means of working on language. But this is what we are doing when we plan the grammar in order to combat sexism. That this makes sense is because language does not correspond; it construes.

That language 'construes' and does not just 'reflect' reality enhances the responsibility of the linguist, who is called upon to bring to light this constructive power – perhaps even use it to change society!

20.3 The Anthropocentrism of Language

In the 1920s, the Polish linguist Baudouin de Courtenay (*avant la lettre*) criticized the anthropocentrism inherent in human language (1984; see Chapter 5.2 above). According to him, it is the human faculty to speak (*le langage* in Saussure's sense) which is responsible for human *superbia*. Baudouin de Courtenay's criticism of language includes a critique of androcentrism (male-centred sexism) and linguistics itself, the manifestations of which are dependent on the native language of the linguist. In the context of the present chapter, however, his early critique of anthropocentrism is most interesting.

'Anthropocentric', according to Mühlhäusler (2003: 219), means 'regarding humans as the central fact of the universe, to which all surrounding facts have reference'. It seems logical and even 'natural' that the communication system developed by humans, language, is essentially determined by this attitude – it would be surprising if it were otherwise. Perhaps more astonishing is the fact that by using this communicational system, the human species can draw attention to this attitude expressed in this very system, criticize it and even make attempts to avoid it. The metalinguistic and self-referential function of language (which, after all, has made possible the discipline of 'linguistics') enables us to adopt a distancing view of language which singles out the shortcomings and limits of this system of communication – including an exaggerated focus on its creators and users.

The anthropocentrism of language (with a focus on English and German) has been made a point of criticism above all by Schultz (2001), Trampe (2001), Fill (1993: 104–115; 1995, 2007a), and Heuberger (2003, 2007).

'The future can be lost and won in the language used today,' Schultz (2001: 113) writes. Without using the term 'anthropocentric', she lists words and phrases which favour exploitation (of nature, of women, of people in general). Among the expressions criticized by her are the following, for which she proposes alternatives which do not emphasize usability (or uselessness) for humans (2001: 113 f.):

Express exploitation by humans	Alternatives
Degenerate tree, overmature tree	old *or* ancient tree
Hardwood	broadleaf *or* eucalyptus
Softwood	conifer, pine
The harvest	wood products, logs
Locked-up (or sterilized) land	land protected from destructive exploitation
Production forest	forest used for industrial forestry
A resource	a forest, land, people, a river, water, etc.
To clear land, clearing	to remove native vegetation from land
Drainage line	creek, river

Schultz's alternatives avoid representing nature only from the point of view of human use: a tree is anthropocentrically called 'degenerate', because it is no longer useful for humans; the alternatives (*old, ancient*) name it as a living being. Calling land which 'yields' wood or water 'a resource' stresses the fact that it is there only to be used by humans. The alternatives (*a forest, land, people, a river, water,* etc.) name nature as nature, not as things usable for humans.

Wilhelm Trampe, who himself runs an ecologically oriented farm, gives in his 'Extracts from a Dictionary of Industrial Agriculture', a list of 65 words and phrases which describe animals, plants and landscape/soil as raw materials for, and products of, industrial agriculture (2001: 236 f.). Typical examples are *Schädlingsbekämpfung*/ 'pest control', *Tierproduktionsanlage*/'animal production plant' and *Flächenstilllegung*/'closing down areas'. Among the 'language-political tendencies' observed by Trampe (2001: 238) are 'reification' (living beings are treated like objects: they are *produced, managed, optimized* and *utilized*) and the concealment of facts: words such as *death, destruction, extermination* and *poison* are avoided and replaced by euphemistic expressions such as *biocide* and *plant protection*. 'When tons of fruit are destroyed, this is referred to as "removal from the market"' (2001: 238). Trampe also reports linguistic reactions to the industrialization of agricultural terminology, as when these terms are prefaced with *so-called* (e.g. 'so-called plant protection') or when lexical creativity is invoked, which leads to formations such as *Ackerwildkraut* ('wild field plants') or *Kultursteppe* ('cultural desert').

Fill (1993: 105 ff.) distinguishes different types of anthropocentrism, the most typical being '**utility naming**', i.e. naming natural phenomena from the point-of-view of their usefulness for humans (as Schultz's examples illustrate). The German language is particularly rich in compounds in which the 'determinant' (first element) expresses the use (or non-use) humans make of an animal, plant or piece of land (examples: *Zug-tiere, Speise-pilze, Bau-holz, Öd-land;* for more examples see Fill 1993: 105–107). A second type of anthropocentrism, called **distancing**, is a form of speciesism, with which a dividing line between humans and 'other animals' is drawn, as when different words are used to express analogous phenomena (*schwanger/pregnant* for humans, *trächtig/gravid* for animals). A third type is constituted by the **euphemizing** of our use (this frequently means our killing and eating) of 'other animals'. 'Meat production' is a euphemism for a use of animals which in reality amounts to 'killing, dissecting and selling as food'. 'Tierversuche' (*animal experimentation, toxicological tests*) is another euphemism which makes the 'use' (infecting with diseases, killing) of animals look harmless.

'Hunting' is an activity where the chasing and killing of animals as a sport is hidden linguistically by using such words as 'harvesting', 'the quarry' (= the animals hunted), 'the bag' (= the animals killed) and by the use of object names for parts of the animal body ('*Lichter*', literally 'lights', for *eyes*, '*Löffel*', literally 'spoons', for *ears,* 'mask' for a fox's head, 'slot' for a deer's foot, 'brush' for the tail of a fox and 'trophies' for all cut-off body-parts). (For more examples see Fill 1993: 105–109, 1995: 504–509.)

A particularly interesting piece of research into anthropocentrism was carried out by Reinhard Heuberger (2003, 2007), who investigated the definitions of animals and plants in monolingual English dictionaries. Heuberger went through ten dictionaries (including the *OED*, the *OALD*, the *Longman Dictionary of Contemporary English [LDOCE]* and *Chambers Essential English Dictionary [CEED]*) and found that many entries concerning animals stress the use humans make of the animals. For some reason, this is particularly evident in the lexical field of 'marine wildlife', where the lexicographers seem to conceptualize the referents chiefly as 'seafood'. 'Most definitions fail to depict the inherent physical features of the animals adequately, focusing on the function which humanity has assigned to them' (Heuberger 2003: 95).

Thus *sardine* is defined in the *OALD* as 'a young pilchard or a similar fish, cooked and eaten fresh or preserved in tins in oil or tomato sauce'. The following are a few more examples of 'utility naming' in the dictionary definitions of sweet (!) and salt water animals (Heuberger 2003: 96):

Trout: a fish that lives in rivers, lakes etc. and is good to eat. […] (*OALD*)

Shrimp: a small pink sea creature that you can eat, with ten legs and with a soft shell. (*LDOCE*)

Prawn: a prawn is a type of shellfish similar to a shrimp but larger. Prawns are eaten as food and they turn pink when you cook them. (*CEED*)

While with these definitions of 'seafood' the usefulness for humans is stressed, the definitions of *locust, shark, wasp, cockroach* and others emphasize the harm that these animals do to humans and their crops (cf. Heuberger 2003: 99).

An interesting observation made by Heuberger is that anthropocentrism frequently takes the form of pronouncing aesthetic judgements on animals, such as *graceful, beautiful, sweet* or *ugly*. These are obviously based on human conceptions of beauty, which may originally have had something to do with usefulness. The following are examples of this taken from Heuberger (2003):

Gazelle: a type of small deer which jumps very gracefully and has large beautiful eyes. (*LDOCE*)

Lark: a lark is a small brown bird that nests on the ground and sings sweetly as it flies overhead. (*CEED*)

Vulture: a large ugly bird with an almost featherless head and neck, which feeds on dead animals. (*Longman Interactive English Dictionary*)

The dictionary definitions show (and may reinforce) people's attitudes towards Nature. While it is not the task of dictionaries to change attitudes or be moral authorities, it would be possible for dictionary writers to avoid definitions purely based on human use and adopt a neutral or even physiocentric viewpoint, as in the following example:

> **Frog**: a small tailless amphibious animal with smooth moist skin, webbed feet and long back legs used for jumping. (*ENCARTA*)

This definition (which mentions the frog's use of its legs) stands in contrast to other dictionary descriptions in which the human use of the frog's legs (as food) is stressed (cf. Heuberger 2003: 98; see also Heuberger 2007: 120).

Attempts at counteracting linguistic anthropocentrism include word-coinage (*Baummord*/'tree murder') and ecological renaming, which can be illustrated with some of the examples of 'alternatives' given by Schultz, above; further examples such as replacing 'environment' by 'convironment', 'trophies' by 'body parts of animals' and 'cutlet' by 'animal muscle piece' are given in Fill (1993: 109–111). The latter two examples are already close to the word coinages of 'Political Correctness' as given, for instance in Beard and Cerf (1992).

In his book *Washing the Brain*, Goatly discusses *Gaia* theory, which was established by James Lovelock (1988), who claims 'that the world, including the atmosphere, the oceans, the biota, the rocks and minerals of the crust, functions as one large self-regulating system' (Goatly 2007: 301 f.). Goatly shows (2007: 305–315) how a language based on grammatical metaphor may show nature not as static and inert, but as dynamic and animate. Here are two of his examples (2007: 307):

> Activation of tokens, e.g.
>> Instead of *There is a boulder on top of the hill* > *a boulder tops the hill.*
> Activation of experiences, e.g.
>> Instead of *We noticed the river* > *the river arrested our gaze.*

Goatly speculates on how certain changes in English syntax, e.g. the rise of 'ergative' constructions (e.g. *The rice cooked* vs. *Pat cooked the rice*) might be an 'adaptive response' of the English language to new scientific insights and particularly to a new more ecological thinking (cf. Goatly 2007: 311).

20.4 Critique of Eco-criticism

To what extent 'language' really supports ideologies such as speciesism and anthropocentrism is still a matter of controversy. The 'eco-criticism' summarized above has itself been subjected to serious criticism, above all by Jung (2001). Concerning anthropocentrism, Jung argues that the naming of the world through language is of necessity anthropocentric; 'even "ecological renaming" from the point of view of animals and plants [...] remains the expression of human projection, for how else could we reproduce the "consciousness" of animals and plants?'

(2001: 275). (One is reminded here of Wittgenstein's assertion that a lion expressing his world-view in human language would not be understood by humans.)

Second, some of the eco-criticism (such as the criticism of word-monsters and neologisms) comes dangerously close to a conservative critique of language which would suffocate the creativity it seems to advocate. Here, eco-criticism seems to fall into the tradition of complaints about the loss of language purity and about cultural decay (cf. Jung 2001: 273).

Third, it is naïve to assume that people do not see through renaming strategies and euphemisms. Whoever assumes a manipulatory effect of euphemisms is excluding such an effect on him/herself and is therefore putting him/herself above other language users. 'As a polemical cliché the accusation of euphemizing is therefore above all the expression of self-righteous moralizing intended to immunize against the consideration of differing views' (Jung 2001: 277). The words *Atommüll* ('nuclear waste') and *Strahlenbelastung* ('radiation load') are denounced by some authors as 'lies', because they seem to make dangerous radiation look harmless, while others would regard them as metaphors which only the ignorant could misunderstand. Many instances of renaming and euphemism could be regarded as neologisms which show the creativity of language users and increase the diversity of a language (cf. Jung 2001: 274). (See also the section 'Critique of CDA', 18.3 above.)

20.5 Discourse on the Environment

In *Framing Discourse on the Environment* (2009), **Richard J. Alexander** shows how politicians and, in their service, the media treat the 'truth'. When reading texts about the environment – or listening to speeches - we have to look for '"where people are coming from", that is to say, what real interests underlie texts in both scientific and journalistic genres, as well as in business and politics' (2009: 3).

In his chapter 'Engineering Agriculture', Alexander (2009: 134–162) shows how large firms active in the area of 'genetically modified crops' (GM crops) use 'discourse engineering' to make their activities look harmless, bring out the beneficial aspects and suppress the harmful ones of their work. He notes, for instance, that on the website of one of these companies the word 'pledge' figures prominently. The company also talks about 'better understanding public expectations' and about their 'corporate social responsibility' concerning 'leading-edge agriculture' (2009: 137). In addition to 'pledge' itself, the words 'commitment' ('values-based/science-based commitment') and 'stewardship' add to the impression of an (almost religious) devotion to the public good. Frequent use of 'our' and 'we' (as in 'our commitment as capable stewards') and 'you/your' (as in 'your feedback', 'your comments') create an atmosphere of dialogicality and sharing between company and customer. (The use of *our,* in this context, is 'exclusive', i.e. it does not include the addressees, the public, but refers only to the company, see Fairclough 1989/2001: 111/106)

Other 'purr-words' employed by this company include *sharing, integrated solutions* and *benefits*. The aim of these linguistic strategies is throughout to divert the reader's (and potential customer's) attention from such ideas as 'profit', 'unnatural' and 'dangerous', and to create an atmosphere of togetherness, common good and sharing advantages.

Alexander's method to reveal implied ideological meaning and to uncover the strategies employed in discourse on the environment is a combination of CDA and corpus analysis. Thus the results of the mainly qualitative methodology of CDA can be confirmed with the quantitative data yielded by a corpus. Using this method, six Reith lectures from the year 2000 are analysed and the data compared (Alexander 2009: 66–111). (Among the lecturers were Gro Harlem Brundtland, former Prime Minister of Norway, Vandana Shiva, Indian scientist and environmental activist, and Prince Charles, owner of an organic farm and actively interested in environmentalism.) All the speakers work (to varying degrees) with purr words (e.g. *sustainable development*), and four of the six (excepting Shiva and the Prince of Wales) replace *global warming* with the less threatening *climate change* (Alexander 2009: 100, 108).

Discourse on the Environment is also discussed from various perspectives by **Peter Mühlhäusler**, who shows 'how perceptions of the environment are linguistically constructed' (2003: 45). This is done, for instance, through classification systems and metaphors. Of particular importance is Mühlhäusler's chapter 'Environmental discourse of others' (2003: 143–160), in which he poses the following questions: 'Is the language about the environment employed by speakers of indigenous languages better suited to environmentally friendly/sustainable ways of life? – Is it right to "ransack" other cultures for knowledge that might benefit our economy?' (2003: 143) His answer to the latter question is as follows: 'The conclusion is that diversity of perspectives is not only morally justified but also economically rewarding and one of the very few reliable ways of adding to human knowledge' (2003: 152). Mühlhäusler presents several examples of how the lexicon, the grammar and the discourse structure of non-Western languages express alternative ideas about Nature and the 'Environment'. For instance, Tok Pisin (New Guinea) has many words connected with the fine aspects of coconut growing, which in our languages can be rendered only insufficiently with the help of phrases (Mühlhäusler 2003: 152).

The study of the 'environmental' discourse of indigenous people will provide a rewarding task for linguists of the future. How 'hunting' and eating animals are worded in indigenous languages, what classification systems of animals, plants and minerals are used, how 'useful/useless for humans' is expressed and many similar questions remain to be answered (cf. Mühlhäusler 2003: 156 f.). The environmental discourse of others could teach *us* a great deal about both the environment and language. One problem concerning this is the following: will there still be enough indigenous languages and cultures to study in the future – or will everything have succumbed to 'Western' influence?

20.6 The Functions of Linguistic Diversity

> Arguments for the preservation of linguistic diversity divide roughly into two clusters that, for convenience of exposition, we can label the ecology of language cluster and the identity cluster. (Ferguson 2006: 77)

Linguistic diversity is actually a bit of a surprise. From the evolutionary point of view one would expect the most favourable situation to be having the same language all over the world. From this perspective, all developments towards the unification of communicational systems on this globe could be regarded as manifestations of an evolution in which the languages (or language!) best suited for global communication will be 'victorious'. Thus the debate about 'the spread of English' is in Darwinian terms a debate about whether evolution and natural selection also operate on the level of languages. (Similar ideas are expressed by George Steiner in *After Babel*, 1975: 49–51.)

In 1985, Braj Kachru established his well-known model of the three concentric circles, which show the English language spreading through cultures and functional domains. These are the inner circle (the UK, USA, Australia, etc.), the outer circle (India, the Philippines, etc.) and the expanding circle – the latter being the areas where English is a foreign language now developing *lingua franca* varieties (see also *The Handbook of World Englishes,* ed. by Kachru *et al.* 2006). In 1992 Robert Phillipson's book *Linguistic Imperialism* came out, in which tendencies to make English the *lingua franca* of the world are condemned. When, in 1997, David Crystal's *English as a Global Language* was published (2nd edn, 2003), a controversy about the role of English in the world arose, which is still continuing. On the one hand, the need for a global language to act as a *lingua franca* (in business, academia, politics, etc.) cannot be denied; on the other hand, the dangers of using *one specific* language globally (with a clear position of power of its native speakers and the possible death of small languages) are equally apparent (cf. Crystal 2003: 14–25). The most interesting papers from this controversy (up until 2003) are printed in Seidlhofer (ed. 2003: 7–75; see also Phillipson 2003 on the situation in the EU, and Graddol 2006 on recent global trends).

The surprising phenomenon of linguistic diversity must have advantages which at first sight do not appear on the surface. These are connected with the need to identify and delimit groups of people, but also with creativity and synergetic effects which a many-faceted system produces – as the next subsection will show.

Identification, delimitation and climate

Many millions of different species live on this earth, influence each other and are influenced by their environment. 5000 to 6000 languages are spoken on this planet which influence each other and have an influence on the fate of the planet. The relation between biodiversity and linguistic diversity is not just a metaphorical one, as this section will show.

Don Laycock writes about language diversity in Papua New Guinea (2001: 169):

> It has more than once been said to me around the Sepik that 'it wouldn't be any good if we all talked the same; we like to know where people come from'. In other words, linguistic diversity, of however minor a kind, is perpetuated as a badge of identification. Such an attitude is, I suggest, at the heart of the multiplicity of languages and dialects in Melanesia.

A 'small' language may be maintained only for the purpose of identifying speakers and making manifest that they belong to a certain group. Speakers possess 'deliberate linguistic markers of their origins' (Laycock 2001: 169), and language diversity serves to give people an identity and make them different from others.

Laycock shows that it is possible for a few hundred people to maintain their language – if they also speak another (more widely spoken) language which may serve as a *lingua franca* in communication with surrounding populations. This is confirmed by Kenneth Sumbuk (personal communication, 2005), who says that a creole like Tok Pisin may help to save the many small languages of Papua New Guinea, since people like to speak a different language at home from the one they speak in commerce with other villages.

Diversity may thus have arisen and been maintained from the necessity to identify speaker origins. With the migration of the different tribes to different parts of the world, other functions of diversity may have been added.

As the example of Papua New Guinea shows, language is not just a means of communication, but also of delimitation. Cockney rhyming slang and back-slang may have arisen as a means to prevent total transparency, when London workers did not want Irish workmen to understand them in every situation. This 'delimitatory function' of language also comes into play when code-switching is practised. As parents may use a different language to prevent their children from overhearing their talk, bilingual speakers may switch codes (apart from many other reasons!) for the purpose of maintaining a certain group awareness and protecting their privacy against uninitiated hearers (cf. Franceschini 1998 and other articles in Auer ed. 1998). Bilingualism thus gives its possessor a certain power – to restrict being understood to a select audience and to delimit communication to certain recipients.

In this context the question as to the effect of **language variation** might be addressed. No doubt using the standard variety (e.g. English 'Received' Standard) gives a speaker a privileged position in society. The same may be true of using special (professional) languages. On the other hand, using dialect (a regiolect or a sociolect) may have effects ranging from creating a cosy atmosphere to frightening listeners, who may be afraid of becoming the victims of coarse manners or even verbal violence. As is well-known, in advertising texts dialect is used to advertise certain goods (beer, agricultural products), while in politics a short code-switch to dialect may help to create a chummy atmosphere, with the message: this politician is one of us.

Other causes of linguistic diversity are discussed by **Daniel Nettle** (1999) and Nettle and Romaine (2000). Among these are physical isolation (because of the topography of an area) as well as factors concerning the agricultural productivity of a region. Linguistic diversity may thus have something to do with the *climate* of an area, as Nettle maintains (1999: 74):

> In New Guinea language groups are very small and localized. [...] Groupings larger than the household are formed and maintained by ritual and exchange and seem to be motivated at least partly by the need for defensive alliances. Basically, however, the small extent of primary social networks is a product of the ecology of New Guinea: continuous rainfall makes for continuous food production through the year, which in turn allows great self-sufficiency.

The greatest linguistic diversity is in areas near the equator or just north of it, where rainfall is continuous (see the maps in Nettle 1999: 62, and Nettle and Romaine 2000: 33–44). Language diversity stands in direct relation to species diversity ('biodiversity') which also decreases with greater distance from the equator. According to Nettle (1999: 61), the following 17 countries harbour 60% of the world's languages (i.e. more than 3900), although their total population amounts to only 23% of the earth's and their land surface area to only 9%:

> The Ivory Coast, Ghana, Togo, Benin, Nigeria, Cameroon, Zaire, Tanzania, India, Vietnam, Laos, the Philippines, Malaysia, Indonesia, Papua New Guinea, Vanuatu and the Solomon Islands.

Clearly, Africa, Asia and the Pacific Area are the parts of the earth with the greatest linguistic diversity.

That 'language' may have the power to build a nation is a topic addressed by Robert McColl Millar in his chapter 'language and nation-building' (2005: 154–198). One of the tasks of '**language planning**' is to contribute, among the inhabitants of a state, to a feeling of identification with the nation and of pride in its linguistic identity. Unfortunately, language planning frequently results in one dominant language getting standardized 'at the expense of other dialects and languages' (Millar 2005: 171). From the ecological point of view, language planning should involve the recognition of linguistic diversity and the creation of a situation in which several languages are officially recognized.

20.7 Diversity as a Resource and Prerequisite for Creativity

> To say that human minds have an ability to be original, or creative, is to say that
> they engender ideas that fall outside any range that could be predicted by studying
> past ideas or by possible study of mental mechanisms. (Sampson 2005: 168)

Mühlhäusler (2001: 159) writes about the story of the Tower of Babel: 'This story, which portrays linguistic diversity as a divine punishment, has dominated Western thinking about languages for centuries and as a result many people believe that a multiplicity of languages is undesirable.' For Mühlhäusler, language diversity should not be regarded as a problem, but as an essential resource which gives us the chance 'to learn from the cumulative insights, successes and errors of a large proportion of the human species' (2001: 159, cf. Chapter 3 above).

Mühlhäusler discusses the view that having a single language all over the earth would unite all separations and create a peaceful world. This view was held by some seventeenth- and eighteenth-century thinkers (e.g. Dr Samuel Johnson) and by the creators of artificial languages in the nineteenth century. Esperanto, Volapük and the roughly 800 planned languages (cf. Hüllen 1989: 174 f.) were created from the theoretical standpoint that having the same language (as the Babelians before the confusion of languages) would make infinite progress in commerce, technology and science possible and would lead to global peace.

Against this, Mühlhäusler holds that the belief in the attractions of a single language is based on a naïve and simplistic view of the world. Instead, 'each language may be seen as a provisional interpretation of a world so complex that the only hope for understanding it is to approach it from as many different perspectives as possible' (2001: 160). This can be done on the lexical level (examples: colour terms, kinship terms, plant names, human relations), but also on the grammatical one, where pronouns, grammatical endings expressing either immediateness or mediation, and verbalization (event-dominated) or nominalization (object-dominated) show different ways of experiencing the world. An area where the shared knowledge contained in different languages would be particularly important is the 'environment' and the current problems connected with it. '[T]he very term "environment" suggests a division between humans and what is around them, an idea that is not widely found in the languages of the world' (2001: 163 f.). Learning from non-Western languages to see the world as an undivided whole is indispensable to solving problems like global warming and its consequences. Mühlhäusler (2001: 164) suggests that:

> Westerners are trapped within the limitations imposed on them by their languages, and
> this is one of the principal reasons for the lack of genuine progress in the environmental
> sciences. This example of environmental discourse illuminates the dangers of
> monolingualism and monoculturalism and shows how many different interpretations –
> and many different languages – are necessary to solve the problems facing the world.

Mühlhäusler's answer to the question as to whether 'ransacking non-Western culture' for knowledge is morally justified (2003: 143–157) was discussed in 20.5 above.

An even more unconventional theory sees language diversity as one of the causes of, and even preconditions for, **creativity** and for the emergence of 'the new'. In this view, language diversity is the result of an evolution which wisely made people talk differently all over the world to produce 'creative misunderstandings'. The creative misunderstanding is at the root of much new thought even among people speaking the 'same' language (though according to Davidson (2006) there are no people speaking the same language). According to this 'creativity theory', there is no progress without previously 'having to interpret' and no communication without possible misunderstanding, and all developments owe their origin to the interplay between different languages and cultures. A world in which everyone speaks the same language is imaginable, but in this world there would be no movement, no 'progress' and no change (see Carter, 2004: 172–175 – following B. Rampton – on creativity through 'language crossing', and Tzanne 2000: 234 on the dynamics of 'miscommunication').

Creativity from Individual Bilingualism

There was a long period in which bilingualism was actually regarded as harmful to cognition and creativity. Weinreich (1968: 116–122) reports a number of investigations (the earliest from 1909) in which the supposedly negative effects of bilingualism on (1) intelligence, (2) group identification, (3) character formation and (4) education in general were outlined. Most early studies found that monoglots surpass bilinguals in intelligence (as reported by Weinreich 1968: 116 f.) and that bilinguals have more emotional problems – and may even be 'morally depraved because they do not receive effective religious instruction in their mother-tongue in childhood!' (1968: 119). In some studies it was conceded that 'it is the higher frequency and intensity of family conflicts in bilingual homes – not the child's "mental conflict" resulting from speaking two languages – which produces maladjustment' (1968: 120), but until about 1950 adverse consequences of bilingualism were taken as a fact.

In the second half of the twentieth century the value of bilingualism began to be recognized. In studies by Vildomec (1971), Wode (1980), Romaine (1989) and Bialystok (2001) the topics of creativity and cognition are addressed. Bialystok devotes a section of her book (2001: 203–206) to creativity and problem-solving in bilingual children. She comes to the conclusion that 'the primary index of bilingual advantage involves a measure of creativity' (2001: 204), although this is also a question of degree of bilingualism, fully bilingual children scoring higher than partly bilingual ones (cf. Bialystok 2001: 206). In *Life with Two Languages*, François Grosjean (1982: 284–288) lists famous people from the spheres of politics, philosophy, literature, music, etc. who were bilingual. Todd I. Lubart (1999: 344 f.) discusses 'the channelling influence of language on creativity'. If our native language makes us think in a certain way, having two or more languages at one's disposal may break the restrictions imposed by monolingualism and, by way of synergetic effects, open the door to creativity. The majority of modern studies on bilingualism and creativity attest to the greater creativity of bilinguals, although a certain level of bilingual proficiency must be reached (cf. Lubart 1999: 344 quoting Ricciardelli 1992).

Lubart (cf. 1999: 344 f.) names at least four reasons for the greater creativity of bilinguals:

(a) a more flexible approach to the world due to greater metalinguistic awareness of the importance of context, given the arbitrariness of words;
(b) greater diversity of associations, because each concept is situated in two different networks;
(c) greater tolerance for ambiguity and the co-existence of incompatible elements;
(d) extralinguistic causes, such as taking part in activities of more than one cultural group.

Lubart stresses that creativity may not only be a question of having two languages at one's disposal. The cultural aspects should always be considered as well: 'Creativity may be stimulated or hindered by cultural features such as worldview and the value placed on conformity or tradition' (Lubart 1999: 345).

Diversity makes possible **interaction**, and according to Csikszentmihalyi (1999: 314 f.) interaction is one of the prerequisites for creativity. Interaction may take place between producer and receiver, and on a higher level between 'field', 'domain' and 'individual'. In Csikszentmihalyi's systemic view of creativity, this means interaction between society, culture and personal background (1999: 315). We might add to this system's view that interaction between two or more constructions of reality (i.e. languages) in a society or in an individual is more likely to engender new ideas than staying within the boundaries of one cultural or linguistic network.

20.8 Revival of Small Languages

In the twenty-first century, we still live in an age in which many 'small' languages are disappearing and a few 'large' ones (particularly English) are becoming more and more dominant. But there are now a few initial signs that language diversity is beginning to be recognized as something good (in Europe!) and that small languages are being rescued and even revived. The arguments in favour of this development are as follows (cf. Fill, forthcoming):

(a) People who speak small languages are mostly bilingual, i.e. they also have a 'large' language at their disposal. Their job opportunities (and even salaries) may thus be better (see for instance Gazzola and Grin 2007; Henley and Jones

2005). There may be a 'premium' for speakers of a minority language (Rendon 2003).

(b) Other economic reasons may come into play, e.g. considerations concerning the development of cultural and linguistic tourism (see Mühlhäusler and Damania 2004).

(c) Young people have taken up the cause of the small language. Speaking a small language makes one special and causes a feeling of pride. In recent years, young people have increasingly developed a 'minority identity'. Under the guidance of YEN (Youth of European Nationalities), meetings and cultural events such as song contests have been organized exclusively for members of minorities (and speakers of so-called 'less widely used languages', LWULs). In June, 2008, the EUROPEADA, a football tournament for minority nationalities, took place in Graubünden, Switzerland, and brought together young people from 18 minorities. In the same month, the 'Network to Promote Linguistic Diversity' (NPLD) was founded in Brussels.

The future of 'small' languages is still uncertain. However, at least in Europe a certain pride in the continent's language diversity is becoming noticeable. Although, on the one hand, English is being pushed (e.g. in the form of English as a *lingua franca*, see, for instance, Seidlhofer 2005 and 20.6 above), a group within Leonard Orben's EU commission for languages advocates doing without English. EU citizens should all have a second mother tongue as their 'language of personal adoption', and Europe should be proud of its language diversity and do everything to cultivate it. There are also efforts being made towards a revival of small European languages (the attempts at revitalizing Welsh and Breton are discussed in some detail in Ferguson 2006: 71–109). While economic and socio-political factors may be most important for the fate of 'minority languages' (LWULs), the attitude of the speakers towards their language is also decisive (cf. Ferguson 2006: 107 f.). Pride in being a member of a minority should be generated in speakers of LWULs, perhaps even pride in speaking a language which few people understand.

21. Language Combined with Other Modes and Media

After the linguistic turn in philosophy (see Rorty ed. 1967), in the 1990s two 'turns' of communication were observed – a 'pictorial' one (Mitchell 1994: 11–34) and an 'iconic' one (Boehm 1994: 13). While the term 'pictorial turn' refers to attempts at making thinking in pictures respectable again (versus thinking in language), the term 'iconic turn' refers to the phenomenon that in printed messages there is a shift from verbal to visual transmission of information. In the 1990s, there was a feeling that images were becoming more important and verbal text less significant. Because of this 'Wiederkehr der Bilder' [*return of images*] (title of Boehm 1994), attempts were made to find in pictures structures similar to those of language. Kress and Van Leeuwen (1996: 1) claim that:

> Just as grammars of language describe how words combine in clauses, sentences and texts, so our visual 'grammars' will describe the way in which depicted people, places and things combine in visual 'statements' of greater or lesser complexity and extension.

On the other hand, pictures can also be instruments of cognition (Boehm 2008: 94). Clearly, ever since the invention of printing (and even before), the combination of text with image has been used for a variety of effects. In 17.1 above, the strategic effects of 'text and image' are described, which above all concern attention attraction and memory support. In this section, various combinations of modes and media will be regarded from an ecological point of view, i.e. from the point of view of the interaction among modes and media.

In addition, the aesthetic and didactic effects of text picture combination should be mentioned. Accompanying a text with pictures may make the text aesthetically more pleasing and, in the case of a didactic text, support the learning effect since the learning contents are transmitted over two channels. The combination of text with picture is a type of 'intermodality' – since two 'modes' of communication are involved.

21.1 Intermodality

Intermodality and intermediality (see below) have become major topics in both linguistics and literary studies. With the invention of photography and film, visual signs are not simply used any more just to convey information: messages containing various ideologies have become possible through these media. Walter Benjamin's work on photography raises the question of whether photography is a fine art or rather a new technical form to convey ideological messages. 'If Marx thought of ideology as a camera obscura, Benjamin regarded the camera as both the material incarnation of ideology and as a symbol of the "historical life-process" that would bring an end to ideology' (Mitchell 1986: 181).

Ever since the invention of the computer, the idea that photography and film convey realistic pictures of the world has had to be dismissed. There are countless ways to manipulate 'reality', and the manipulatory power of visual signs has grown in accordance with this.

In work on language and image, it is usually the differences between the two sign systems which are stressed, language being a symbolic, image an iconic one (cf. Goodman 1976: 40–43). For impact linguistics, the most important question is the effect that language and picture produce together. Several theoretical models have been suggested. Roland Barthes' distinction between anchorage and relay has already been mentioned (see 17.1 above). Nöth (1990: 454) and Stöckl (1997: 120–125, 2004: 242–300) have presented theories of the 'collaboration' of text with picture. The following is a model adapted from Fill (2007: 137), which is based on five different degrees of tension between the two modes when they cooperate:

1. Text describes picture; picture not given (**description**).
2. Text and picture give the same information, each through its specific sign system (**repetition**).
3. Text and picture complement each other. One of them contains additional information (**addition**).
4. Text and picture contradict each other (**contradiction**).
5. Text and picture seemingly have no relation to each other (**irrelevance**).

Description (1) and repetition (2) provide little tension, addition (3) somewhat more. Most tension arises in cases (4) and (5), where the reader/viewer has to search for possible meanings – a search on which some forms of art are based. The paintings of the Belgian painter René Magritte frequently show relation (5), insofar as the title of the painting does not seem to have any relevance to the picture. Generally, it can be claimed that whenever two modes are being used, contradiction and irrelevance will have the greatest effect as far as attention value and 'memorability' but also the search for meaning are concerned.

The five relational possibilities listed above (from description to irrelevance) can be applied to any situation in which two modes, such as the following, are operating together:

> Text and music (see Wolf 1999 and Bernhart and Wolf eds. 2001)
> Text and moving pictures (film: see Borringo 1980 and Reif 1984)
> Text and sculpture (see Kansteiner *et al.* eds. 2007)
> Text and architecture (see Cowling 1998 and Eriksen 2001)

In spoken language, the combination of verbal and non-verbal elements may also show agreement between the two modes (repetition or addition) – or disagreement (contradiction and irrelevance). The baton signs, with which speakers support their verbal message by making rhythmic gestures, have already been mentioned (see Morris 2002: 78–87 and 17.1 above). Generally, the effect of verbal language in combination with another mode may be more than the added effects of the two modes: through the workings of 'synergy', the effect of the two modes may be heightened and multiplied.

21.2 Intermediality

A work of art may use more than one medium; it may also be transferred from one to another medium. Thus a work of literature may find expression in a painting, or may be transferred into film. How text (say, a novel) is adapted to screen, and screen transferred into text (example: Jane Campion's *The Piano*) is discussed in the articles of the volume *Adaptations* (Cartmell and Whelehan eds. 1999; see also Stam 2005 on the effect of literature through film). The different types of intermediality (partial, total; primary, secondary) are described by Wolf (2004). The wealth of different media with which intermediality can be achieved is shown in the articles contained in Schnitzler and Spaude (eds) (2004).

For impact linguistics, those types of intermediality are significant in which a work of art is transferred into 'language', or more accurately into 'text'. This is the case, for instance, when music determines the structure of a work of literature, as in Aldous Huxley's novel *Point Counter Point*, or in a poetic description of a piece of music – as in the following text from the same novel, which describes Beethoven's 'string quartet in a minor' (Opus 132):

> Slowly, slowly, the melody unfolded itself. The archaic Lydian harmonies hung on the air. It was an unimpassioned music, transparent, pure and crystalline, like a tropical sea, an Alpine lake. (London: Granada 1978, p. 440; quoted from Wolf 1999: 168)

The effect of the language in this text, with its metaphors and similes (*unfolded itself, hung on the air, transparent, pure and crystalline, like a tropical sea, an Alpine lake*), is to create in the reader similar emotions as when hearing the music.[1]

A painting, too, or a magnificent building or sculpture, may be described with the help of language with the effect of making the reader 'see' the work of art and arouse emotions similar to those triggered by the visual impression. On the other hand, a building and a work of literature may 'draw on the same compositional ideals', as Eriksen (2001: xiii et passim) shows. Language, in combination with art, may have effects for whose study we still lack adequate methods. Fortunately, both intermodality and intermediality are topic areas in which at present a great deal of research is being carried out (see for instance the articles in Heusser *et al.* (eds) 2008).

Note

1. Music is sometimes metaphorically called 'the language understood everywhere'. Joseph Haydn is reported to have said: 'My music is a language understood all over the world.'

Summary: Expansion and Limitation

The purpose of this book has been to show the impact of language on individuals, societies and the community of living beings at the following three levels:

1. The level of species evolution (phylogenetic development of language).
2. The level of the linguistic system.
3. The level of discourse.

Level one concerns the 'existential' influence of language as a product of evolution: according to most authors, the development of this form of communication disrupted the continuity of the evolution of living beings on this planet and made one species more powerful than others – with the result of the spread of this species over the whole of the earth, of improved living conditions for this species and of what came to be called 'culture'. Another side of this impact was a disturbed equilibrium between the different species with its more recent consequence of an increased awareness in humans of a certain danger for all life forms on the planet.

The discussion on level two presupposes that the way humans communicate can be described as a system of sounds, meaningful units and combinations of these. The topic of Part II of the book is the influence of this 'system' of communication on human thought and consequently on human action. Thought may be helped on through the systemic elements of language, which make possible the conceptualization of abstract ontological areas. On the other hand, many thinkers have criticized this system of symbols called language, pointing out ways in which it may 'mislead' and disorient thought.

At Level three, the impact of speech and writing (now called discourse) in specific situations is considered. Discourse may be strategic, even manipulatory and 'obfuscating'. On the other hand, it may be used to cure disorders, create bonding and laughter and achieve other beneficial effects.

When considering these three levels, it becomes clear that 'language' has (had) a decisive influence on the fate of this planet, so that it seems justified to speak of an impact comparable to that of a meteor from the depths of the universe.

Our discussion of language and its impact on the world has in several places been **expanded** in the following way: it is not just language which exercises power; talking and writing *about* language, too, have an impact not to be underestimated. The meta-linguistic function of language (which must have evolved after the other functions) made the study of language, **linguistics**, possible, which had an influence on the world at the first meta-level and also led to an awareness of this influence (second meta-level). For example, when Structuralism was developed for the study of language (by Saussure and others), this approach was soon used in other fields of scholarship (such as literary studies and sociology). When Chomsky distinguished deep structures from surface structures, this distinction was transferred to literature, psychology and other fields. The meta-linguistic function also made **criticism of language and discourse** possible, the first instance of which can be found in the writings of the Pre-Socratic philosopher Parmenides (see Chapter 3 above), the most recent in the school of Critical Discourse Analysis (see Chapter 18 above).

Another expansion of our discussion of 'language impact' concerns the combined effects of language (as discourse) and other modes and media. In particular, the combination of text with image has provided the topic for a discussion of an 'intermodal impact' on individuals and societies. The impact of the internet (Chapter 15.1 above) relies very much on the effects of this combination.

While the book necessarily starts from the assumption that language is an all encompassing, extremely powerful tool (and process), the author has taken care not to overrate this power. He has, at various points, given space to voices which **warn of overestimating** the impact of language, particularly at Levels 2 and 3. Awareness of the limits of this power is particularly important when manipulation and obfuscation through 'linguistic strategies' (euphemism, devices of rhetoric, etc.) are being discussed. Making students of language avoid the fallacy of blaming on language *all* the problems of the world (conflicts of various kinds, war, racism, unequal treatment of the genders, environmental problems, etc.) is an important concern of the book. Future research will tell us more about those ontological areas where the impact of language is overrated and those where it is perhaps even underestimated.

References

Note: the date of the original publication of a book or article is added in square brackets if it deviates markedly from the version used here.
All internet sources were accessed 30 January 2010.

Aarsleff, Hans (1982). *From Locke to Saussure*. London: Athlone.
Abbate, Janet (2000). *Inventing the Internet*. Cambridge, MA: The MIT Press.
Agar, Michael (1994). *Language Shock. Understanding the Culture of Conversation*. New York: William Morrow.
Agricola, Rudolf (1992). *De inventione dialectica libri tres. Drei Bücher über die Inventio dialectica. Auf der Grundlage der Edition von Alardus von Amsterdam (1539) kritisch herausgegeben, übersetzt und kommentiert von Lothar Mundt.* (Latin and German). Tübingen: Niemeyer. (1539) [written around 1480].
Aitchison, Jean (1989). *The Articulate Mammal. An Introduction to Psycholinguistics*, 3rd edn. London: Unwin Hyman.
Aitchison, Jean (1994). *Words in the Mind. An Introduction to the Mental Lexicon*, 2nd edn. Oxford: Blackwell.
Aitchison, Jean (1996). *The Seeds of Speech: Language Origin and Evolution*. Cambridge: Cambridge University Press.
Alexander, Richard J. (1973). Towards a multidisciplinary view of language: some biolinguistic reflections. *Linguistische Berichte* 25, 1–21.
Alexander, Richard J. (1997). *Aspects of Verbal Humour in English*. Tübingen: Gunter Narr.
Alexander, Richard J. (2009). *Framing Discourse on the Environment. A Critical Discourse Approach.* New York, London: Routledge.
Anshen, Ruth Nanda (ed.) (1957). *Language: An Enquiry into its Meaning and Function*. Port Washington, NY, London: Kennikat Press.
Apel, Karl-Otto (1988). *Diskurs und Verantwortung. Das Problem des Übergangs zur postkonventionellen Moral*. Frankfurt/Main: Suhrkamp.
Argyle, Michael (1972). Non-verbal communication in human social interaction. In R. A. Hinde (ed.), 243–268.
Asp, Elissa (2000). Legal victims. In: E. Ventola (ed.), 30–46.
Atkinson, Max (1984). *Our Masters' Voices. The Language and Body-language of Politics*. London, New York: Methuen.
Attardo, Salvatore (1994). *Linguistic Theories of Humor*. Berlin, New York: Mouton de Gruyter.
Auer, Peter (ed.) (1998). *Code-Switching. Language, Interaction and Identity*. London, New York: Routledge.
Auroux, Sylvain and Djamel Kouloughli (1993). Why is there no 'true' philosophy of linguistics? In: R. Harré and R. Harris (eds), 21–41.
Austin, John L. (1962). *How to Do Things with Words*. Cambridge, MA: Harvard University Press.
Ayto, John (1993). *Dictionary of Euphemisms*. London: Bloomsbury.
Ayto, John (2007). *Wobbly Bits and Other Euphemisms: over 3,000 Ways to Avoid Speaking your Mind*. London: A. & C. Black.
Bacon, Francis (1900). *The Advancement of Learning and Novum Organum*. ed. James E. Creighton. London, New York: The Colonial Press [1605; 1620].
Bachtin, Michail M. (1979). *Die Ästhetik des Wortes*. Trans., ed. and with an introduction by Rainer Grübel. Frankfurt/Main: Suhrkamp [1924, etc.].
Bally, Charles (1950). *Linguistique générale et linguistique française*. 3rd edn. Berne: A. Francke [1932].

Bang, Jørgen Christian and Jørgen Døor (2007). *Language, Ecology and Society. A Dialectical Approach*, eds Sune Vork Steffensen and Joshua Nash. London: Continuum.

Barnard, Alan (2009). Social origins: sharing, exchange, kinship. In R. Botha and C. Knight (eds), 219–235.

Barthes, Roland (1977). *Image – Music – Text. Essays Selected and Translated by Stephen Heath*. New York: Hill & Wing. ('Rhetoric of the Image' [1964] 32–51.)

Baudouin de Courtenay, Jan (1984). Einfluß der Sprache auf Weltanschauung und Stimmung. In J. Mugdan (ed.), *Ausgewählte Werke in deutscher Sprache*. Munich: Wilhelm Fink, 201–271 [1929].

Bauer, Joachim (2006). *Prinzip Menschlichkeit. Warum wir von Natur aus kooperieren*, 2nd edn. Hamburg: Hoffmann und Campe.

Baumgärtner, Klaus (ed.) (1977). *Sprachliches Handeln*. Heidelberg: Quelle & Meyer.

Baxter, Judith (2003). *Positioning Gender in Discourse. A Feminist Methodology*. London: Palgrave Macmillan.

Beard, Adrian (2000). *The Language of Politics*. London, New York: Routledge.

Beard, Adrian (2003). *How Texts Work*. London, New York: Routledge.

Beard, Henry and Christopher Cerf (1992). *The Official Politically Correct Dictionary and Handbook*. New York: Villard.

Benedict, Ruth (1959). *Patterns of Culture*. Boston: Houghton Mifflin [1934].

Berger, Peter L. and Thomas Luckmann (1966). *Die gesellschaftliche Konstruktion der Wirklichkeit. Eine Theorie der Wissenssoziologie*. Trans. Monika Plessner. Frankfurt/Main: S. Fischer. (*The Social Construction of Reality*, New York: Doubleday.)

Berkeley, George (n.d.). *A New Theory of Vision and other Select Philosophical Writings*, ed. and introduced by A. D. Lindsay. London: J. M. Dent, New York: E. P. Dutton. (Everyman's Library, 483) [contains *A Treatise Concerning the Principles of Human Knowledge*, 1710].

Berlin, Brent and Paul Kay (1969). *Basic Color Terms. Their Universality and Evolution*. Berkeley, CA: University of California Press.

Berlitz, Charles (1982). *Native Tongues*. New York: Perigee Trade. [German edition: *Die wunderbare Welt der Sprachen. Fakten, Kuriosa, Geheimnisse*. München: Knaur.]

Bernhart, Walter and Werner Wolf (eds) (2001). *Word and Music Studies: Essays on the Song Cycle and on Defining the Field. (Proceedings of the 2nd Int. Conference on Word and Music Studies. Ann Arbor, 1999)*. Amsterdam, Atlanta, GA: Rodopi.

Bialystok, Ellen (2001). *Bilingualism in Development. Language, Literacy and Cognition*. Cambridge: Cambridge University Press.

Bickerton, Derek (2000). How protolanguage became language. In C. Knight, M. Studdert-Kennedy and J. R. Hurford (eds), 264–284.

Bierwisch, Manfred (2001). The apparent paradox of language evolution: can Universal Grammar be explained by adaptive selection? In J. Trabant and S. Ward (eds), 55–79.

Bierwisch, Manfred (2008). Bedeuten die Grenzen meiner Sprache die Grenzen meiner Welt? In Heidrun Kämper and Ludwig M. Eichinger (eds). *Sprache – Kognition – Kultur. Sprache zwischen mentaler Struktur und kultureller Prägung*. Berlin, New York: de Gruyter.

Black, Max (1962). *Models and Metaphors. Studies in Language and Philosophy*. Ithaca, NY: Cornell University Press.

Black, Max (1967). Language and reality. In R. Rorty (ed.), 331–339.

Black, Max (1968). *The Labyrinth of Language*. Harmondsworth: Penguin.

Blommaert, Jan (2005). *Discourse. A Critical Introduction*. Cambridge: Cambridge University Press.

Boardman, Mark (2005). *The Language of Websites*. London, New York: Routledge.

Boas, Franz (2002/1911). *Handbook of American Indian Languages*, 4 vols. Bristol: Thoemmes [1911].

Boas, Franz (1938). *The Mind of Primitive Man*. New York, etc.: Macmillan [1911].

Boas, Franz (1966). *Race, Language and Culture*. New York: The Free Press [1940].

Boas, Franz (1968). Introduction to *Handbook of American Indian Languages*. In D. E. Hayden *et al.* (eds), 155–234.

Boas, Franz (2002). *Indian Myths and Legends from the North Pacific Coast of America.* Edited and Annotated by Randy Bouchard and Dorothy Kennedy, trans. Dietrich Bertz. Vancouver: Talonbooks [1895].

Boehm, Gottfried (1994). Die Wiederkehr der Bilder. In G. Boehm (ed.), *Was ist ein Bild?*, 11–38. München: Wilhelm Fink.

Boehm, Gottfried (2008). *Wie Bilder Sinn erzeugen. Die Macht des Zeigens.* 2nd edn. Berlin: Berlin UP.

Bogen, James (1972). *Wittgenstein's Philosophy of Language. Some Aspects of its Development.* London: Routledge and Kegan Paul.

Bohm, David (1980), *Wholeness and the Implicate Order.* London: Routledge.

Bohm, David (1996). *On Dialogue,* ed. Lee Nichol. London, New York: Routledge. [German edition: *Der Dialog. Das offene Gespräch am Ende der Diskussionen,* trans. Anke Grube, 4th edn. Stuttgart: Klett-Cotta, 2005.]

Bolinger, Dwight (1980). *Language – the Loaded Weapon. The Use and Abuse of Language Today.* London, New York: Longman.

Borringo, Heinz-Lothar (1980). *Spannung in Text und Film. Spannung und Suspense als Textverarbeitungskategorien.* Düsseldorf: Schwann.

Botha, Rudolf and Chris Knight (eds) (2009). *The Cradle of Language.* Oxford: Oxford University Press.

Bouchard, Randy and Dorothy Kennedy (eds) (2002). *Introduction to Indian Myths and Legends from the North Pacific Coast of America.* 21–49. Translation of Franz Boas' 1895 edition of Indianische Sagen, eds. R. Bouchard and D. Kennedy. Vancouver: Talonbooks.

Bourdieu, Pierre (1991). *Language and Symbolic Power,* ed. John B. Thompson; trans. Gino Raymond and Matthew Adamson. Cambridge: Polity Press.

Bréal, Michel (1899). *Essai de Sémantique. (Science des significations).* Paris: Hachette.

Brinker, Klaus and Sven F. Sager (1996). *Linguistische Gesprächsanalyse. Eine Einführung.* 2nd edn. Berlin: Erich Schmidt.

Brown, Gillian and George Yule (1983). *Discourse Analysis.* Cambridge: Cambridge University Press.

Brown, Penelope and Stephen Levinson (1987). *Politeness. Some Universals in Language Usage.* Cambridge: Cambridge University Press.

Bublitz, Wolfram (1988). *Supportive Fellow-Speakers and Cooperative Conversations.* Amsterdam/ Philadelphia PA: John Benjamins.

Bublitz, Wolfram (2001). *Englische Pragmatik. Eine Einführung.* Berlin: Erich Schmidt.

Bühler, Karl (1934). *Sprachtheorie. Die Darstellungsfunktion der Sprache.* Jena: Gustav Fischer.

Butler, Judith (1999). *Gender Trouble. Feminism and the Subversion of Identity,* 10th anniversary edition. New York, London: Routledge [1990].

Caldas-Coulthard, Carmen Rosa and Malcolm Coulthard (eds) (1996). *Texts and Practices. Readings in Critical Discourse Analysis.* London, New York: Routledge.

Cameron, Deborah (1985). *Feminism and Linguistic Theory.* London: Macmillan.

Cameron, Deborah (2000). *Good to Talk? Living and Working in a Communication Culture.* London: Sage.

Cameron, Deborah (2007). *The Myth of Mars and Venus. Do Men and Women Really Speak Different Languages?* Oxford: Oxford University Press.

Campbell-Kibler, Kathryn, Robert J. Podesra, Sarah J. Roberts and Andrew Wong (eds) (2002). *Language and Sexuality. Contesting Meaning in Theory and Practice.* Stanford, CA: CSLI Publications.

Carnap, Rudolf (1934/36). *Logische Syntax der Sprache.* Wien: Springer.

Carroll, J. B. (1956). Introduction to Whorf (1956), pp. 1–34.

Carston, Robyn (2005). Relevance theory and the saying/implicating distinction. In L. R. Horn and G. Ward (eds), 633–656.

Carter, Ronald (2004). *Language and Creativity. The Art of Common Talk*. London, New York: Routledge.

Cartmell, Deborah and Imelda Whelehan (eds) (1999). *Adaptations. From Text to Screen, Screen to Text*. London, New York: Routledge.

Cassirer, Ernst (1923). *Philosophie der symbolischen Formen*, 3 vols. Vol 1: *Die Sprache*. Berlin: Bruno Cassirer Verlag.

Cassirer, Ernst (1944). *An Essay on Man. An Introduction to a Philosophy of Human Culture*. New Haven, CT: Yale University Press.

Chase, Stuart (1954). *The Power of Words*. New York: Harcourt Brace Jovanovich.

Chase, Stuart (1955). *Wörter machen Weltgeschichte* (German translation of Chase 1954). München: Verlag Moderne Industrie.

Chase, Stuart (1959). *Guides to Straight Thinking – with Thirteen Common Fallacies*. London, New York: Harper.

Chase, Stuart (1966). *The Tyranny of Words*. New York: Harcourt, Brace & World [1938].

Chilton, Paul (1988). *Orwellian Language and the Media*. London: Pluto Press.

Chilton, Paul (2004). *Analysing Political Discourse. Theory and Practice*. London, New York: Routledge.

Chilton, Paul and Christina Schäffner (2002). Introduction. Themes and principles in the analysis of political discourse. In P. A. Chilton and C. Schäffner (eds), *Politics as Text and Talk. Analytic Approaches to Political Discourse*, 1–41. Amsterdam/Philadelphia, PA: John Benjamins.

Chomsky, Noam (1957). *Syntactic Structures*. The Hague, Paris: Mouton.

Chomsky, Noam (1969). Some empirical assumptions in modern philosophy of language. In S. Morgenbesser, P. Suppes and M. White (eds), *Philosophy, Science, and Method*, 260-285. New York: St Martin's Press. (German translation in: G. Grewendorf and G. Meggle (eds) (1974), *Linguistik und Philosophie*, 313–352. Frankfurt/M.: Suhrkamp.)

Chomsky, Noam (1986). *Knowledge of Language. Its Nature, Origin, and Use*. New York: Praeger.

Christiansen, Morten H. and Simon Kirby (2003). Language evolution: The hardest problem in science? In M. H. Christiansen and S. Kirby (eds.), 1–15.

Christiansen, Morten H. and Simon Kirby (eds) (2003). *Language Evolution*. Oxford: Oxford University Press.

Coates, Jennifer (1996). *Women Talk. Conversation between Women Friends*. Oxford: Blackwell.

Coates, Jennifer (2003). *Men Talk. Stories in the Making of Masculinities*. Oxford: Blackwell.

Coates, Jennifer (2004). *Women, Men and Language. A Sociolinguistic Account of Gender Differences in Language*, 3rd edn. London: Pearson Longman. [1st edition 1986].

Coates, Jennifer (ed.) (1998). *Language and Gender: A Reader*. Oxford: Blackwell.

Cook, Guy (2001). *The Discourse of Advertising*, 2nd edn. London, New York: Routledge. [1992].

Cooper, Robert L. and Bernard Spolsky (eds) (1991). *The Influence of Language on Culture and Thought. Essays in Honor of Joshua A. Fishman's Sixty-Fifth Birthday*. Berlin, New York: Mouton de Gruyter.

Corballis, Michael C. (1999). Phylogeny from apes to humans. In Michael C. Corballis and Stephen E. G. Lea (eds) *The Descent of Mind. Psychological Perspectives on Hominid Evolution*, 40–70. Oxford: Oxford University Press.

Corballis, Michael C. (2002). *From Hand to Mouth. The Origins of Language*. Princeton, NJ, Oxford: Princeton University Press.

Coulthard, Malcolm (1977). *An Introduction to Discourse Analysis*. London: Longman.

Coulthard, Malcolm (1994). On the use of corpora in the analysis of forensic texts. In: *Forensic Linguistics. The International Journal of Speech, Language and the Law*. Vol. 1, 25–43. London: Routledge.

Cowling, David (1998). *Building the Text: Architecture as Metaphor in Late Medieval and Early Modern France*. Oxford: Clarendon Press.

Crystal, David (1997). *The Cambridge Encyclopedia of Language*, 2nd edn. Cambridge: Cambridge University Press.

Crystal, David (2003). *English as a Global Language*, 2nd edn. Cambridge: Cambridge University Press [1997].

Crystal, David (2006). *Language and the Internet*, 2nd edn. Cambridge: Cambridge University Press [2001].

Crystal, David and Derek Davy (1981). *Advanced Conversational English*. London: Longman.

Csikszentmihalyi, Mihalyi (1999). Implications of a systems perspective for the study of creativity. In R. Sternberg (ed.), 313–335.

Cutting, Joan (2008). *Pragmatics and Discourse. A Resource Book for Students*, 2nd edn. London, New York: Routledge.

Dahrendorf, Ralf (1972). *Konflikt und Freiheit. Auf dem Weg zur Dienstklassengesellschaft*. München: Piper.

Darnell, Regna (2006). Benjamin Lee Whorf and the contemporary foundation of Boasian ethnolinguistics. In Christine Jourdan and Kevin Tuite (eds), *Language, Culture and Society*, 82–95. Cambridge: Cambridge University Press.

Daly, Mary (1975). God is a Verb. In Uta West (ed.), *Woman in a Changing World*, 153–170. New York: McGraw-Hill.

Darwin, Charles (1996). *The Origin of Species*, ed. Gillian Beer. Oxford, New York: Oxford University Press [1859].

Darwin, Charles (1908). *Die Abstammung des Menschen*. German translation by Heinrich Schmidt. Leipzig: Alfred Kröner. [*The Descent of Man*, 1871.]

Davidson, Donald (2006). A nice derangement of epitaphs. In Ernie Lepore and Kirk Ludwig (eds), *The Essential Davidson*, 251–265. Oxford: Clarendon Press [1986].

Dawkins, Richard (1976). *The Selfish Gene*. Oxford: Oxford University Press.

De Beaugrande, Robert and Wolfgang Dressler (1981). *Introduction to Text Linguistics*. London, New York: Longman. [English version of Dressler 1972.]

Deignan, Alice (1997). Metaphors of desire. In K. Harvey and C. Shalom (eds), 21–42.

De Laguna, Grace (1927). *Speech, its Function and Development*. New Haven, CT: Yale University Press.

Dessalles, Jean-Louis (1998). Altruism, status and the origin of relevance. In J. R. Hurford, M. Studdert-Kennedy and C. Knight (eds), 130–147.

Dessalles, Jean-Louis (2000). Language and hominid politics. In C. Knight, M. Studdert-Kennedy and J. R. Hurford (eds), 62–80.

Dessalles, Jean-Louis (2007). *Why We Talk. The Evolutionary Origins of Language*, trans. James Grieve. Oxford: Oxford University Press.

Deutscher, Guy (2005). *The Unfolding of Language. The Evolution of Mankind's Greatest Invention*. London: William Heinemann.

Devitt, Michael and Kim Sterelny (1999). *Language and Reality. An Introduction to the Philosophy of Language*. Cambridge, MA: MIT Press.

Diehl, Michael and Wolfgang Stroebe (1994). Why groups are less effective than their members. On productivity losses in idea-generating groups. In W. Stroebe and M. Hewstone (eds) *European Review of Social Psychology*, Vol 5, 271–303. Chichester: Wiley.

Diels, Hermann (ed.) (1934). *Die Fragmente der Vorsokratiker. Griechisch und Deutsch*. Vol. I. 5th edn. by Walther Kranz. Berlin: Weidmannsche Buchhandlung.

Dixon, Peter (1971). *Rhetoric*. London: Methuen.

Dominguez-Rodrigo, Manuel, Rebecca Barba and Charles P. Egeland (2007). *Deconstructing Olduvai: a Taphonomic Study of the Bed I Sites*. Berlin, Heidelberg: Springer.

Dressler, Wolfgang (1972). *Einführung in die Textlinguistik*. Tübingen: Niemeyer.

Dunbar, Robin (1996). *Grooming, Gossip and the Evolution of Language*. London: Faber & Faber. [German translation: *Klatsch und Tratsch. Warum Frauen die Sprache erfanden*, trans. Sebastian Vogel. (München: Bertelsmann 1998)].

Dunbar, Robin (2003). The origin and subsequent evolution of language. In M. H. Christiansen and S. Kirby (eds), 219–234.

Dürr, Hans-Peter (2007). Am Anfang war der Quantengeist. In *Peter Mooslechners Zeitschrift (PM)*, May 2007, 38–46.

Eden, Tania (1999). *Lebenswelt und Sprache. Eine Studie zu Husserl, Quine und Wittgenstein*. München: Wilhelm Fink. (*Phänomenologische Untersuchungen*, ed. B. Waldenfels, vol. 12.)

Edie, James M. (1987). *Merleau-Ponty's Philosophy of Language: Structuralism and Dialectics*. Washington, DC: Center for Advanced Research in Phenomenology & University Press of America.

Eggins, Suzanne and Diana Slade (1997). *Analysing Casual Conversation*. London, Washington, DC: Cassell.

Eibl-Eibesfeldt, Irenäus (1984). *Krieg und Frieden aus der Sicht der Verhaltensforschung* (new edition). München, Zürich: Piper.

Eibl-Eibesfeldt, Irenäus (1986). *Die Biologie des menschlichen Verhaltens. Grundriß der Humanethologie*, 2nd edn. München, Zürich: Piper.

Eibl-Eibesfeldt, Irenäus (1989). *Liebe und Haß. Zur Naturgeschichte elementarer Verhaltensweisen*, 14th edn. München, Zürich: Piper.

Eibl-Eibesfeldt, Irenäus (1991). *Das verbindende Erbe. Expeditionen zu den Wurzeln unseres Verhaltens*. Köln: Kiepenheuer & Witsch.

Eriksen, Roy T. (2001). *The Building in the Text: Alberti to Shakespeare and Milton*. University Park, PA: Pennsylvania State University Press.

Ervin-Tripp, Susan, Jiansheng Guo and Martin Lampert (1990). Politeness and persuasion in children's control acts. *Journal of Pragmatics* 14 (2): 307–331.

Fairclough, Norman (1992). *Discourse and Social Change*. Cambridge: Polity Press.

Fairclough, Norman (1995). *Media Discourse*. New York, etc.: Arnold.

Fairclough, Norman (1995a). *Critical Discourse Analysis. The Critical Study of Language*. Harlow: Longman.

Fairclough, Norman (2000). *New Labour, New Language?* London, New York: Routledge.

Fairclough, Norman (2001/1989). *Language and Power*. London, New York: Longman. (2nd edition with additional chapter.) [1st edition 1989.]

Fairclough, Norman (2006). *Language and Globalization*. London, New York: Routledge.

Fairclough, Norman (forthcoming). Language, reality and power. In J. Culpeper, F. Katamba, P. Kerswill, R. Wodak and T. McEnery (eds.) *English Language: Description, Variation and Context*. London: Palgrave.

Fairclough, Norman and Ruth Wodak (1997). Critical discourse analysis. In Teun Van Dijk (ed.), *Discourse as Social Interaction. Discourse Studies 2. A Multidisciplinary Introduction*. London and Thousand Oaks, CA: Sage.

Falkner, Wolfgang (1997). *Verstehen, Mißverstehen und Mißverständnisse. Untersuchungen an einem Korpus englischer und deutscher Beispiele*. Tübingen: Niemeyer.

Fasold, Ralph W. (1990). *Sociolinguistics of Language*. Oxford: Blackwell.

Fauconnier, Gilles and Mark Turner (2002). *The Way we Think: Conceptual Blending and the Mind's Hidden Complexities*. New York: Basic Books.

Fauconnier, Gilles and Mark Turner (2008). Rethinking metaphor. In R. W. Gibbs (ed.), 53–66.

Ferguson, Gibson (2006). *Language Planning and Education*. Edinburgh: Edinburgh University Press.

Fill, Alwin F. (1986). 'Divided Illocution' in conversational and other situations – and some of its implications. *IRAL*, xxiv (1): 27–34.

Fill, Alwin (1993). *Ökolinguistik. Eine Einführung*. Tübingen: Gunter Narr.

Fill, Alwin (1995). Contrastive ecolinguistics – a new field for linguistic ploughshares? In W. Riehle and H. Keiper (eds), *Anglistentag Graz 1994. Proceedings*, 501-511. Tübingen: Niemeyer.

Fill, Alwin (2001). Ecolinguistics. State of the art 1998. In A. Fill and P. Mühlhäusler (eds), 43–53 [1998].

Fill, Alwin (2007). *Das Prinzip Spannung. Sprachwissenschaftliche Betrachtungen zu einem universalen Phänomen* 2nd edn. Tübingen: Gunter Narr.

Fill, Alwin (2007a). Nomination and ecology. Anthropocentric, anthropomorphic and physiocentric naming. In Christian Todenhagen and Wolfgang Thiele (eds), *Nominalization, Nomination and Naming*, 11–26. Tübingen: Stauffenburg.

Fill, Alwin (forthcomimg). The economy of language ecology. Paper presented at the AILA conference, Essen 2008.

Fill, Alwin and Peter Mühlhäusler (eds) (2001). *The Ecolinguistics Reader. Language, Ecology and Environment*. London: Continuum.

Finke, Peter (2001). Identity and manifoldness. New perspectives in science, language and politics. In A. Fill and P. Mühlhäusler (eds), 84–90 [1996].

Firth, J. R. (1957). *Papers in Linguistics 1934–1951*. London: Oxford University Press.

Firth, J. R. (1957a). The technique of semantics. In J. R. Firth (1957), 7–33 [1935].

Firth, J. R. (1957b). A synopsis of linguistic theory 1930–1955. In J. R. Firth *et al.* eds. *Studies in Linguistic Analysis*, 1–32. Oxford: Blackwell.

Fischer, Andreas (1999). Graphological iconicity in print advertising: a typology. In Max Nänny and Olga Fischer (eds). *Form Miming Meaning. Iconicity in Language and Literature*, 251–283. Amsterdam, Philadelphia, PA: John Benjamins.

Fishman, Joshua (1991). *Language and Ethnicity*. Amsterdam, Philadelphia, PA: John Benjamins.

Fishman, Joshua (ed.) (2001). *Can Threatened Languages be Saved?* Clevedon: Multilingual Matters.

Fishman, Pamela (1977). Interactional shitwork. *Heresies* 2: 99–101.

Fishman, Pamela M. (1978). Interaction: the work women do. *Social Problems* 25 (4): 397–406.

Flader, Dieter (ed.) (1979). *Therapeutische Kommunikation. Ansätze zur Erforschung der Sprache im psychoanalytischen Prozess*. Kronberg, Taunus: Scriptor-Verlag.

Foerster, Heinz von (1994). Das Konstruieren einer Wirklichkeit. In P. Watzlawick (ed.) (1994), 39–60.

Formigari, Lia (2004). *A History of Language Philosophies,* trans. Gabriel Poole. Amsterdam, Philadelphia, PA: John Benjamins.

Foucault, Michel (1980). *Power/Knowledge. Selected Interviews and Other Writings 1972–1977*, ed. Colin Gordon, trans. C. Gordon, L. Marshall, J. Mepham and K. Soper. New York: Pantheon Books.

Fowler, Roger (1996). On critical linguistics. In C. R. Caldas-Coulthard and M. Coulthard (eds), 3–14 [1987].

Fowler, Roger, Bob Hodge, Gunther Kress and Tony Trew (1979). *Language and Control*. London: Routledge & Kegan Paul.

Franceschini, Rita (1998). Code-switching and the notion of code in linguistics. Proposals for a dual-focus model. In P. Auer (ed.), 51–75.

Frisch, Karl von (1950). *Du und das Leben. Eine moderne Biologie für jedermann*. Berlin: Tempelhof.

Gadamer, Hans-Georg (1990). *Hermeneutik I. Wahrheit und Methode. Grundzüge einer philosophischen Hermeneutik*. Tübingen: J. C. B. Mohr.

Gadamer, Hans-Georg (1993). *Hermeneutik II. Wahrheit und Methode. Ergänzungen, Register*. Tübingen: J. C. B. Mohr.

Gadamer, Hans-Georg (1993a). Mensch und Sprache. In *Hermeneutik II. Wahrheit und Methode,* 146–154 [1966].

Gadamer, Hans-Georg (1993b). Wie weit schreibt Sprache das Denken vor? In *Hermeneutik II. Wahrheit und Methode,* 199–206 [1970].

Gastil, John (1990). Generic pronouns and sexist language: the oxymoronic character of masculine generics. *Sex Roles* 23 (11–12): 629–643.

Gazzola, Michele and François Grin (2007). Assessing efficiency and fairness in multilingual communication. Towards a general analytical framework. *AILA Review* 20: 87–105.

Geeraerts, Dirk (ed.) (2006). *Cognitive Linguistics. Basic Readings*. Berlin, New York: Mouton de Gruyter.

Gerhardt, Marlis (ed.) (1974). *Linguistik und Sprachphilosophie*. München: List.

Gessinger, Joachim and Wolfert von Rahden (eds.) (1989). *Theorien vom Ursprung der Sprache*. 2 vols. Berlin, New York: de Gruyter.

Gibbons, John (2003). *Forensic Linguistics. An Introduction to Language in the Justice System*. Oxford: Blackwell Publishing.

Gibbons, John and M. Teresa Turell (eds) (2008). *Dimensions of Forensic Linguistics*. Amsterdam, etc.: Benjamins. (AILA Applied Linguistics Series, 5).

Gibbs, Raymond W., Jr. (ed.) (2008). *The Cambridge Handbook of Metaphor and Thought*. Cambridge: Cambridge University Press.

Giddens, Anthony (1993). *Sociology*. 2nd fully revised and updated edition. Cambridge: Polity Press.

Gipper, Helmut (1972). *Gibt es ein sprachliches Relativitätsprinzip? Untersuchungen zur Sapir-Whorf-Hypothese*. Frankfurt/Main: S. Fischer.

Glasersfeld, Ernst von (1994). Einführung in den radikalen Konstruktivismus. In P. Watzlawick (ed.), 16–38.

Goatly, Andrew (1997). *The Language of Metaphors*. London, New York: Routledge.

Goatly, Andrew (2000). *Critical Reading and Writing. An Introductory Coursebook*. London, New York: Routledge.

Goatly, Andrew (2001). Green grammar and grammatical metaphor, or language and the myth of power, or metaphors we die by. In A. Fill and P. Mühlhäusler (eds.), 203–225. [First published in *Journal of Pragmatics* 25, 1996, 537–560.]

Goatly, Andrew (2007). *Washing the Brain. Metaphor and Hidden Ideology*. Amsterdam/Philadelphia, PA: John Benjamins.

Goddard, Angela (1998). *The Language of Advertising*. London: Routledge.

Goffman, Erving (1967). *Interaction Ritual. Essays on Face-to-Face Behavior*. Harmondsworth: Penguin ('On Face Work', 1955).

Goldstein, Kurt (1957). The nature of language. In R. N. Anshen (ed.), 18–40.

Goodman, Nelson (1976). *Languages of Art. An Approach to a Theory of Symbols*. Indianapolis, IN: Hackett.

Göttert, Karl-Heinz (1994). *Einführung in die Rhetorik. Grundbegriffe – Geschichte – Rezeption*. 2nd edn. München: Wilhelm Fink.

Graddol, David (2006). *English Next. Why Global English May Mean the End of 'English as a Foreign Language'*. London: British Council.

Graddol, David and Joan Swann (1989). *Gender Voices*. Oxford: Basil Blackwell.

Gregory, Michael (2000). Doing forensic linguistics: Endangered people in the community. In E. Ventola (ed.), 19–27.

Grewendorf, Günther (1995). *Sprache als Organ – Sprache als Lebensform*. Frankfurt/Main: Suhrkamp.

Grice, H. P. (1975). Logic and Conversation. In P. Cole and J. Morgan (eds.), *Syntax and Semantics, 3: Speech Acts*, 41–58. New York: Academic Press.

Grimshaw, Allen D. (ed.) (1990). *Conflict Talk. Sociolinguistic Investigations of Arguments in Conversation*. Cambridge: Cambridge University Press.

Grosjean, François (1982). *Life with Two Languages. An Introduction to Bilingualism*. Cambridge, MA: Harvard University Press.

Grundy, Peter (2000). *Doing Pragmatics*. 2nd edn. London: Hodder Arnold.

Gunnarsson, Britt-Louise (1997). Women and men in the academic discourse community. In Helga Kotthoff and Ruth Wodak (eds), *Communicating Gender in Context*, 219–248. Amsterdam: John Benjamins.

Habermas, Jürgen (1987). *Theorie des kommunikativen Handelns*. 2 vols. 4th edn. Frankfurt/Main: Suhrkamp [1981].

Habermas, Jürgen (1989). *Vorstudien und Ergänzungen zur Theorie des kommunikativen Handelns*. 3rd edn. Frankfurt/Main: Suhrkamp.

Habermas, Jürgen (1992). *Erläuterungen zur Diskursethik*. 2nd edn. Frankfurt/Main: Suhrkamp.

Hall, Kira and Mary Bucholtz (eds) (1995). *Gender Articulated. Language and the Socially Constructed Self*. New York, London: Routledge.

Hall, Phil (2008). Policespeak. In J. Gibbons and M. T. Turell (eds), 67–94.

Haller, Rudolf (ed.) (1981). *Sprache und Erkenntnis als soziale Tatsache. Beiträge des Wittgenstein-Symposiums von Rom 1979*. Wien: Hölder-Pichler-Tempsky.

Halliday, M. A. K. (1973). *Explorations in the Functions of Language*. London: Edward Arnold.

Halliday, M. A. K. (1976). *System and Function in Language. Selected Papers*, ed. by G. R. Kress. London: Oxford University Press.

Halliday, M. A. K. (1979). *Language as Social Semiotic. The Social Interpretation of Language and Meaning*. London: Arnold.

Halliday, M. A. K. (1985). *An Introduction to Functional Grammar*. London: Edward Arnold.

Halliday, M. A. K. (2001). New ways of meaning. The challenge to applied linguistics. In A. Fill and P. Mühlhäusler (eds), 175–202. [First published in *Journal of Applied Linguistics*, 6 (1990), 7–36.]

Halliday, M. A. K. and Christian M. I. M. Matthiessen (1999). *Construing Experience through Meaning. A Language-based Approach to Cognition*. London, New York: Continuum.

Hamann, Johann Georg (1967). *Schriften zur Sprache*, ed. J. Simon. Frankfurt/Main: Suhrkamp [1759–1784].

Hamilton, Mykol Cecilia (1985). Linguistic Relativity and Sex Bias in Language. Effects of Masculine Generics on the Imagery of the Writer and the Perceptual Discrimination of the Reader. Dissertation, University of California. (Ann Arbor, MI) [quoted from Werlen 1989].

Hamilton, Mykol Cecilia (1988). Using masculine generics: Does generic *he* increase male bias in the user's imagery? *Sex Roles* 19 (11–12): 785–799.

Harjung, Dominik J. (2000). *Lexikon der Sprachkunst. Die rhetorischen Stilformen. Mit über 1000 Beispielen*. München: C. H. Beck.

Harré, Rom and Roy Harris (eds) (1993). *Linguistics and Philosophy. The Controversial Interface*. Oxford, etc.: Pergamon Press.

Harris, Roy (1993). Saussure, Wittgenstein and *la règle du jeu*. In R. Harré and R. Harris eds, 219–231.

Harris, Roy and Talbot J. Taylor (eds) (1997). *Landmarks in Linguistic Thought I. The Western Tradition from Socrates to Saussure*. 2nd edn. London, New York: Routledge.

Harvey, Keith and Celia Shalom (eds) (1997). *Language and Desire. Encoding Sex, Romance and Intimacy*. London, New York: Routledge.

Haugen, Einar (1977). Linguistic relativity. Myths and methods. In W. C. McCormack and S. A. Wurm (eds) (1977), 11–28.

Hauser, Marc D. (1996). *The Evolution of Communication*. Cambridge, MA: MIT Press.

Hauser, Marc D. and Mark Konishi (eds) (1999). *The Design of Animal Communication*. Cambridge, MA: MIT Press.

Hawa, Salam (n.d., online). *Language as Freedom in Sartre's Philosophy*. http://www.bu.edu/wcp/Papers/Lite/LiteHawa.htm

Hawkins, John (1986). *A Comparative Typology of English and German. Unifying the Contrasts*. London: Croom Helm.

Hayakawa, S. I. (1974). *Language in Thought and Action*. 3rd edn. London: Allen & Unwin. [Language in Action, 1941.]

Hayden, Donald E., E. Paul Alworth and Gary Tate (eds) (1968). *Classics in Linguistics*. London: Peter Owen.

Heath, Shirley Brice (1991). Women in conversation: Covert models in American language ideology. In R. L. Cooper and B. Spolsky (eds), 199–218.

Hébert, Louis (2006). *The Functions of Language*. Online: http://www.signosemio.com/jakobson/a_fonctions.asp

Heeschen, Volker (1989). Humanethologische Aspekte der Sprachevolution. In J. Gessinger and W. von Rahden (eds.), vol. II, 196–248.

Heeschen, Volker (2001). The narration 'instinct': signalling behaviour, communication, and the selective value of storytelling. In J. Trabant and S. Ward (eds), 179–196.

Heidegger, Martin (1947). *Über den Humanismus*. Frankfurt/Main: Klostermann.

Heidegger, Martin (1984). *Sein und Zeit*. Tübingen: Niemeyer [1927].

Heidegger, Martin (2007). *Unterwegs zur Sprache*. 14th edn. Stuttgart: Klett-Cotta. (Contains, among other essays: 'Das Wesen der Sprache' 1957, 'Das Wort' 1958 and 'Der Weg zur Sprache' 1959.)

Heintel, Erich (1972). *Einführung in die Sprachphilosophie*. Darmstadt: Wissenschaftliche Buchgesellschaft.

Heise, Elke (2000). Sind Frauen mitgemeint? Eine empirische Untersuchung zum Verständnis des generischen Maskulinums und seiner Alternativen. *Sprache & Kognition* 19 (1–2): 3–13.

Hellinger, Marlis (1990). *Kontrastive Feministische Linguistik. Mechanismen sprachlicher Diskriminierung im Englischen und Deutschen*. Ismaning: Hueber.

Hellinger, Marlis and Hadumod Bußmann (2003). Engendering female visibility in German. In M. Hellinger and H. Bußmann (eds), vol. 3, 141–174.

Hellinger, Marlis and Hadumod Bußmann (eds) (2001–2003). *Gender Across Languages. The Linguistic Representation of Women and Men*. 3 vols. Amsterdam, Philadelphia, PA: John Benjamins.

Henley, Andrew and Rhian Eleri Jones (2005). Earnings and linguistic proficiency in a bilingual economy. The University of Wales, Aberystwyth. Research paper No 2001-18.

Henley, Nancy M. (1986). *Body Politics. Power, Sex, and Nonverbal Communication*. New York, London, etc.: Simon & Schuster. Touchstone edition [1977].

Herder, Johann Gottfried (2001). *Abhandlung über den Ursprung der Sprache*. Stuttgart: Reclam [1772, Berlin: C. F. Foß].

Heringer, Hans Jürgen (1982). Sprachkritik – die Fortsetzung der Politik mit besseren Mitteln. In H. J. Heringer (ed.), 3–34.

Heringer, Hans Jürgen (ed.) (1982). *Holzfeuer im hölzernen Ofen. Aufsätze zur politischen Sprachkritik*. Tübingen: Gunter Narr.

Herman, Edward S. and Noam Chomsky (2002). *Manufacturing Consent. The Political Economy of the Mass Media*. 2nd edn with a new introduction by the authors. New York: Pantheon Books [1988].

Heuberger, Reinhard (2003). Anthropocentrism in monolingual English dictionaries. An ecolinguistic approach to the lexicographic treatment of faunal terminology. *Arbeiten aus Anglistik und Amerikanistik* 28 (1): 93–105.

Heuberger, Reinhard (2007). Language and ideology. A brief survey of anthropocentrism and speciesism in English. In A. Fill and H. Penz (eds), *Sustaining Language*, 105–124. Münster: LIT-Verlag.

Heusser, Martin, Andreas Fischer and Andreas H. Jucker (eds) (2008). *Mediality/Intermediality*. Tübingen: Gunter Narr (Swiss Papers in English Language and Literature, 21).

Hewes, Gordon W. (1973a). Primate communication and the gestural origin of language. *Current Anthropology*, 14 (1–2): 5–24.

Hewes, Gordon W. (1973b). An explicit formulation of the relationship between tool using, tool-making, and the emergence of language. *Visible Language*, VII (2) (Spring 1973): 101–127.

Hinde, Robert A. (1972). Comments on Part A. In: R. A. Hinde (ed.), 86–98.

Hinde, Robert A. (ed.) (1972). *Non-Verbal Communication*. Cambridge: Cambridge University Press.

Hjelmslev, Louis (1969). *Prolegomena to a Theory of Language*, trans. Francis J. Whitfield. 2nd edn. Madison, WI.: University of Madison Press.

Hodge, Jean-Jacques (1983). Neo-Cartesianism in Linguistics. From the point of view of its opposition to philosophical behaviorism. Dissertation (Fribourg). Colerne/Grande-Bretagne.

Hodge, Robert and Gunther Kress (1988). *Social Semiotics*. Cambridge: Polity Press.

Hodge, Robert and Gunther Kress (1993). *Language as Ideology*. 2nd edn. London, New York: Routledge [1979].

Hoijer, Harry (1954). The Sapir-Whorf Hypothesis. In *Language in Culture*, 554–573. Chicago, IL: University of Chicago Press.

Holmes, Janet (1995). *Women, Men and Politeness*. London, New York: Longman.

Holmes, Janet and Miriam Meyerhoff (eds) (2003). *The Handbook of Language and Gender*. Oxford: Blackwell.

Holquist, Michael (2002). *Dialogism. Bakhtin and his World*. 2nd edn. London, New York: Routledge [1990].

Horn, Laurence (2001). *A Natural History of Negation*. Stanford, CA: CSLI Publications [1989].

Horn, Laurence and Gregory Ward (eds) (2005). *The Handbook of Pragmatics*. Molden, MA: Blackwells.

Huang, Yan (2007). *Pragmatics*. Oxford: Oxford University Press.

Hüllen, Werner (1989). *'Their Manner of Discourse': Nachdenken über Sprache im Umkreis der Royal Society*. Tübingen: Gunter Narr.

Humboldt, Wilhelm von (1994). *Über die Sprache. Reden vor der Akademie*, ed. Jürgen Trabant. Tübingen, Basel: Francke [1820–1828].

Humboldt, Wilhelm von (1998). *Über die Verschiedenheit des menschlichen Sprachbaues und ihren Einfluß auf die geistige Entwicklung des Menschengeschlechts*, ed. Donatella Di Cesare. Paderborn, etc.: Schöningh [1836].

Hume, David (1902). *Enquiries Concerning the Human Understanding and Concerning the Principles of Morals*, ed. L.A. Selby-Bigge. 2nd edn. Oxford: Clarendon Press [1748, 1751].

Hurford, James R., Michael Studdert-Kennedy and Chris Knight (eds) (1998). *Approaches to the Evolution of Language. Social and Cognitive Bases*. Cambridge: Cambridge University Press.

Husserl, Edmund (1965). *Philosophie als strenge Wissenschaft*. Frankfurt/Main: Vittorio Klostermann [1910/11].

Hutchby, Ian and Robin Wooffitt (1998). *Conversation Analysis. Principles, Practices and Applications*. Cambridge: Polity Press.

Irmen, Lisa (2007). What's in a (role) name? Formal and conceptual aspects of comprehending personal nouns. *Journal of Psycholinguistic Research* 36: 431–456.

Ishiguro, Hidé (1992). Die Beziehung zwischen Sprache und Welt im früheren und späteren Wittgenstein. In W. Vossenkuhl (ed.), 13–28.

Jaenecke, Peter (2002). *Sprache und Denken*. Online: http://philo.at/pipermail/philweb/2002-December/001811.html

Jakobson, Roman (1957). The cardinal dichotomy in language. In R. N. Anshen (ed.), 155–178.

Jakobson, Roman (1960). Closing statement: Linguistics and poetics. In T. Sebeok (ed.), *Style in Language*, 350-377. Cambridge, MA: MIT Press.

Jespersen, Otto (1922). *Language, its Nature, Structure and Development*. London: Allen & Unwin.

Johansson, Sverker (2005). *Origins of Language. Constraints on Hypotheses*. Amsterdam/Philadelphia, PA: John Benjamins.

Jourdan, Christine and Kevin Tuite (eds) (2006). *Language, Culture, and Society. Key Topics in Linguistic Anthropology*. Cambridge: Cambridge University Press.

Juliard, Pierre (1970). *Philosophies of Language in Eighteenth-Century France*. The Hague, Paris: Mouton. (Janua Linguarum, series minor, 18.)

Jung, Matthias (2001). Ecological criticism of language. In A. Fill and P. Mühlhäusler (eds), 270–285. [German original published in 1996.]

Kachru, Braj (1985). Standards, codification and sociolinguistic realism: the English language in the outer circle. In R. Quirk and H. G. Widdowson (eds). *English in the World: Teaching and Learning the Language and Literatures*, 11–30. Cambridge: Cambridge University Press.

Kachru, Braj, Yamuna Kachru and Cecil L. Nelson (eds) (2006). *The Handbook of World Englishes*. Malden, MA and Oxford: Blackwell.

Kainz, Friedrich (1964). *Handbuch der Psychologie*. 2 vols. Göttingen: Vandenhoeck.

Kainz, Friedrich (1972). *Über die Sprachverführung des Denkens*. Berlin: Duncker & Humblot.

Kaltenbrunner, Gerd-Klaus (ed.) (1975). *Sprache und Herrschaft. Die umfunktionierten Wörter*. Freiburg, Basel, Wien: Herder.

Kalverkämper, H. (1979). Die Frauen und die Sprache. *Linguistische Berichte* 62: 55–71.

Kansteiner, Sascha, Lauri Lehmann, Bernd Seidensticker *et al.* (eds) (2007). *Text und Skulptur. Ausstellungskatalog*. Berlin: de Gruyter.

Katz, Jerrold J. (1972). *Linguistic Philosophy. The Underlying Reality of Language and its Philosophical Import*. London: Allen & Unwin.

Kemmerling, Andreas (1992). Bedeutung und Zweck der Sprache. In W. Vossenkuhl (ed.), 99–120.

Kennedy, George A. (1991). *Aristotle: On Rhetoric. A Theory of Civic Discourse*. New York, Oxford: Oxford University Press.

Kennedy, George A. (1994). *A New History of Classical Rhetoric*. Princeton, NJ: Princeton University Press.

Kennedy, George A. (1998). *Comparative Rhetoric. An Historical and Cross-cultural Introduction*. New York, Oxford: Oxford University Press.

Kettemann, Bernhard (ed.) (1998). *Sprache und Politik. Verbal-Werkstattgespräche*. Frankfurt/Main, Wien: Lang.

Kipnis, Laura (1998). Pornography. In John Hill and Pamela Church Gibson (eds), *The Oxford Guide to Film Studies*, 153–157. Oxford: Oxford University Press.

Kirk, Geoffrey S., John E. Raven and Malcolm Scofield (eds) (1994). *Die Vorsokratischen Philosophen. Einführung, Texte und Kommentare*, trans. Karlheinz Hülser. Stuttgart, Weimar: Metzler. (English editions 1957, 1983, Cambridge University Press.)

Klann-Delius, Gisela (2005). *Sprache und Geschlecht. Eine Einführung*. Stuttgart: Metzler.

Kleiber, Georges (1993). *Prototypensemantik. Eine Einführung*. Tübingen: Gunter Narr.

Klemperer, Viktor (1987). *LTI. Notizbuch eines Philologen*, 9th edn. Leipzig: Reclam [1946].

Kline, David and Dan Burstein (2005). *blog! how the newest media revolution is changing politics, business, and culture*. New York: CDS Books.

Kniffka, Hannes (ed.) (1996). *Recent Developments in Forensic Linguistics*. (In cooperation with Susan Blackwell and Malcolm Coulthard). Frankfurt/Main, etc.: Peter Lang.

Knight, Chris (1998). Ritual/speech coevolution: a solution to the problem of deception. In J. R. Hurford, M. Studdert-Kennedy and C. Knight (eds), 68–91.

Knight, Chris (2000). Play as precursor of phonology and syntax. In C. Knight, M. Studdert-Kennedy and J. R. Hurford (eds.), 99–119.

Knight, Chris, Michael Studdert-Kennedy and James R. Hurford (eds) (2000). *The Evolutionary Emergence of Language. Social Function and the Origins of Linguistic Form*. Cambridge: Cambridge University Press.

Kochman, Thomas (1981). *Black and White Styles in Conflict*. Chicago, IL and London: University of Chicago Press.

Kodish, Bruce I. (2003). What we do with language – what it does with us. *ETC* (winter 2003–04), 383–395.

Koerner, Ernst F. K. and R. E. Asher (eds) (1995). *Concise History of the Language Sciences. From the Sumerians to the Cognitivists*. Oxford: Pergamon Press.

Komlosi, L. I. (1997). *Inferential Pragmatics and Cognitive Structures: Situated Language Use and Cognitive Linguistics*. Budapest: Nemzeti Tankönyvkiadó.

König, Peter (2005). *Giambattista Vico*. München: C. H. Beck.

Korzybski, Alfred (1958). *Science and Sanity. An Introduction to Non-Aristotelian Systems and General Semantics,* 4th edition. Lakeville, CN: Institute of General Semantics.

Kotthoff, Helga (ed.) (1988). *Das Gelächter der Geschlechter. Humor und Macht in Gesprächen von Frauen und Männern*. Frankfurt/Main: Fischer Taschenbuch.

Kövecses, Zoltán (2006). *Language, Mind, and Culture. A Practical Introduction.* Oxford: Oxford University Press.

Kramarae, Cheris and Mercilee Jenkins (1985). Women changing words changing women. In M. Hellinger (ed.), *Sprachwandel und feministische Sprachpolitik. Internationale Perspektiven*, 10–22. Opladen: Westdeutscher Verlag.

Kraus, Manfred (1987). *Name und Sache. Ein Problem im frühgriechischen Denken.* Amsterdam: B. R. Grüner.

Kress, Gunther and Theo van Leeuwen (1996). *Reading Images. The Grammar of Visual Design.* London: Routledge.

Kuckenburg, Martin (2004). *Wer sprach das erste Wort? Die Entstehung von Sprache und Schrift.* Stuttgart: Konrad Theiss Verlag.

Kulick, Don (2000). Gay and lesbian language. *Annual Review of Anthropology* 29: 243–285.

Kulick, Don (2003). Language and Desire. In Holmes and Meyerhoff (eds), 119–141.

Labov, William (1972). *Language in the Inner City. Studies in the Black English Vernacular.* Philadelphia, PA: University of Pennsylvania Press.

Labov, William and David Fanshel (1977). *Therapeutic Discourse. Psychotherapy as Conversation.* New York, San Francisco, London: Academic Press.

Lakoff, George (1987). *Women, Fire, and Dangerous Things. What Categories Reveal about the Mind.* Chicago, IL, London: Chicago University Press.

Lakoff, George (1991). Metaphor and war. *Viet Nam Generation Journal Online*, 3 (3). http://www2.iath.virginia.edu/sixties/HTML_docs/Texts/Scholarly/Lakoff_Gulf_Metaphor_1.html

Lakoff, George (2004). *Don't Think of an Elephant. Know your Values and Frame the Debate.* White River Junction, VT: Chelsea Green, Vermont Press.

Lakoff, George (2006). *Thinking Points. Communicating our American Values* and *Vision. A Progressive Handbook.* Berkeley, CA: Rockridge Institute, Farrar Straus & Giroux.

Lakoff, George and Mark Johnson (1999). *Philosophy in the Flesh. The Embodied Mind and its Challenge to Western Thought.* New York: Basic Books.

Lakoff, George and Mark Johnson (2003). *Metaphors We Live By*, 2nd edn. Chicago, IL: University of Chicago Press [1st edn, 1980].

Lakoff, George and Mark Johnson (2003a). Afterword 2003. In Lakoff and Johnson 2003, 243–276.

Lakoff, Robin (1975). *Language and Woman's Place.* New York: Harper & Row.

Lakoff, Robin Tolmach (1990). *Talking Power. The Politics of Language in our Lives.* New York: HarperCollins.

Lakoff, Robin Tolmach (1995). Cries and whispers. The shattering of the silence. In K. Hall and M. Buchholtz (eds), 25–50.

Langer Susanne K. (1957). *Philosophy in a New Key. A Study in the Symbolism of Reason, Rite and Art*, 3rd edn. Cambridge, MA: Harvard UP [1942].

Lausberg, Heinrich (1971). *Elemente der literarischen Rhetorik*, 4th edn. Munich: Max Hueber.

Lay, Rupert (1980). *Manipulation durch die Sprache.* Hamburg: Rowohlt.

Laycock, D. C. (2001). Linguistic diversity in Melanesia. A tentative explanation. In A. Fill and P. Mühlhäusler (eds), 167–171 [1997].

Lazar, Michelle M. (ed.) (2005). *Feminist Critical Discourse Analysis: Gender, Power and Ideology in Discourse.* Basingstoke etc.: Palgrave Macmillan.

Leap, William (1996). *Word's Out. Gay Men's English.* Minneapolis, MN: University of Minneapolis Press.

Leavitt, John (2006). Linguistic relativities. In C. Jourdan and K. Tuite (eds), 47–81.

Lee, David (1992). *Competing Discourses. Perspective and Ideology in Language.* London, New York: Longman.

Lee, Irving J. (1941). *Language Habits in Human Affairs. An introduction to General Semantics.* New York: Harper.

Lee, Penny (1996). *The Whorf Theory Complex. A Critical Reconstruction.* Amsterdam/Philadelphia, PA: John Benjamins.

Leech, Geoffrey N. (1966). *English in Advertising: a Linguistic Study of Advertising in Great Britain.* London: Longman.

Leech, Geoffrey N. (1969). *A Linguistic Guide to English Poetry.* London: Longman.

Leech, Geoffrey N. (1983). *Principles of Pragmatics.* London, New York: Longman.

Leech, Geoffrey N. (2008). *Language in Literature. Style and Foregrounding.* Harlow: Pearson Education.

Leinfellner, Elisabeth (1995). Fritz Mauthner im historischen Kontext der empiristischen, analytischen und sprachkritischen Philosophie. In E. Leinfellner and H. Schleichert (eds), 145–163.

Leinfellner, Elisabeth (2000). *Fritz Mauthners Sprachkritik.* Online: http://ejournal.thing.at/Essay/leinels.html

Leinfellner, Elisabeth, Werner Leinfellner, Hal Berghel and Adolf Hübner (eds) (1978). *Wittgenstein and his Impact on Contemporary Thought. Proceedings of the 2nd Wittgenstein Symposium.* Vienna: Hölder-Pichler-Tempsky.

Leinfellner, Elisabeth and Hubert Schleichert (eds) (1995). *Fritz Mauthner. Das Werk eines kritischen Denkers.* Wien, etc.: Böhlau.

Leisi, Ernst (1971). *Der Wortinhalt. Seine Struktur im Deutschen und Englischen,* 4th edn. Heidelberg: Quelle & Meyer.

Leisi, Ernst (1973). *Praxis der englischen Semantik.* Heidelberg: Carl Winter Universitätsverlag.

Leisi, Ernst (1983). *Paar und Sprache. Linguistische Aspekte der Zweierbeziehung,* 2nd edn. Heidelberg: Quelle & Meyer.

Leiss, Elisabeth (2009). *Sprachphilosophie.* Berlin, New York: Walter de Gruyter.

Lenk, Hans (ed.) (1980). *Handlungstheorien – interdisziplinär. Vol. 1: Handlungslogik, formale und sprachwissenschaftliche Handlungstheorien.* Munich: Wilhelm Fink.

Lewis, Jerome (2009). As well as words: Congo Pygmy hunting, mimicry, and play. In R. Botha and C. Knight (eds), 236–256.

Livia, Anna (2001). *Pronoun Envy. Literary Uses of Linguistic Gender.* Oxford, etc.: Oxford University Press.

Locke, John (1947). *An Essay Concerning Human Understanding,* abr. and ed. Raymond Wilburn. London: J. M. Dent [1690].

Lorenz, Konrad (1984). *Das sogenannte Böse. Zur Naturgeschichte der Aggression,* 11th edn. München: dtv.

Lovelock, James (1988). *The Ages of Gaia.* Oxford: Oxford University Press.

Lubart, Todd I. (1999). Creativity across cultures. In R. J. Sternberg (ed.), 339–350.

Lucy, John A. (1992). *Language Diversity and Thought. A Reformulation of the Linguistic Relativity Hypothesis.* Cambridge: Cambridge University Press.

Lucy, John A. (1996). The scope of linguistic relativity: An analysis and review of empirical research. In J. Gumperz and S. C. Levinson (eds). *Rethinking Linguistic Relativity,* 37-69. Cambridge: Cambridge University Press.

Lucy, John A. (2000). Introductory comments. In Susanne Niemeier and René Dirven (eds). *Evidence for Linguistic Relativity. Papers presented at the 26th LAUD Symposium 'Humboldt and Whorf revisited', Duisburg 1998,* ix-xxi. Amsterdam/Philadelphia, PA: John Benjamins.

Luther, Wilhelm (1970). *Sprachphilosophie als Grundwissenschaft. Ihre Bedeutung für die wissenschaftliche Grundlagenbildung und die sozialpolitische Erziehung.* Heidelberg: Quelle & Meyer.

Lycan, William G. (2008). *Philosophy of Language: a Contemporary Introduction,* 2nd edn. New York and London: Routledge [1st edn. 2000].

Lyle, Jane (1990). *Body Language.* London: Paul Hamlyn.

Lyons, John (1972). Human language. In R. A. Hinde (ed.), 49–85.

Maas, Utz (1974). Grammatik und Handlungstheorie. In U. Maas and D. Wunderlich (eds), 189–276.

Maas, Utz and Dieter Wunderlich (eds) (1974). *Pragmatik und sprachliches Handeln. Mit einer Kritik am Funkkolleg Sprache*, 3rd edn. Frankfurt/Main: Athenaion.

Mackensen, Lutz (1973). *Verführung durch Sprache. Manipulation als Versuchung*. München: List.

Macnamara, John (1991). Linguistic relativity revisited. In R. L. Cooper and B. Spolsky (eds), 45–60.

Malinowski, Bronislaw (1969). The problem of meaning in primitive languages. Supplement I of C. K. Ogden and I. A. Richards (1969), 296–336 [1923].

Maltz, Daniel N. and Ruth A. Borker (1982). A cultural Approach to Male-Female Miscommunication. In J. Gumperz (ed.), *Language and Social Identity*, 196-216, Cambridge: Cambridge University Press. Reprinted in Coates (ed.) (1998), 417–434.

Marko, Georg (2008). *Penetrating Language. A Corpus-based Investigation of Erotic and Pornographic Texts*. Tübingen: Gunter Narr.

Markovà, Ivana and Klaus Foppa (eds) (1990). *The Dynamics of Dialogue*. New York, London, etc.: Harvester Wheatsheaf.

Marty, Anton (1950). *Über Wert und Methode einer allgemeinen beschreibenden Bedeutungslehre* (Nachgelassene Schriften, ed. Otto Funke). Bern: A. Francke. ('Vom Nutzen und Schaden der Sprache für das Denken', 79–85).

Maturana, Humberto and Francisco Varela (1987). *Der Baum der Erkenntnis. Die biologischen Wurzeln des menschlichen Erkennens*, 3rd edn, trans. Kurt Ludewig. Bern, München, Wien: Scherz Verlag [El àrbol del conocimiento, 1984].

Mauthner, Fritz (1921). *Beiträge zu einer Kritik der Sprache*. 3 vols. *Sprache und Psychologie* [1901]. *Zur Sprachwissenschaft* [1901]. *Zur Grammatik und Logik* [1902], 3rd edn. Stuttgart/Berlin: Cotta.

McCormack, William C. (1977). Introduction. In: W. C. McCormack and S. A. Wurm (eds), 3–8.

McCormack, William C. and Stephen A. Wurm (eds) (1977). *Language and Thought. Anthropological Issues*. The Hague, Paris: Mouton.

Mead, G. H. (1934). *Mind, Self and Society*, ed. Ch. W. Morris. Chicago, IL: University of Chicago Press. [German translation: Geist, Identität und Gesellschaft, 4th edn, Frankfurt/Main: Suhrkamp 1980.]

Mercer, Neil (2000). *Words and Minds. How we use Language to Think Together*. London, New York: Routledge.

Merleau-Ponty, Marcel (2005). *Phenomenology of Perception*, trans. Colin Smith. London: Routledge [1945].

Mey, Jacob (1999). *When Voices Clash. A Study in Literary Pragmatics*. Berlin: Mouton de Gruyter.

Mey, Jacob (2001). *Pragmatics. An Introduction*, 2nd edn. Malden, MA, and Oxford: Blackwell [1993].

Millar, Robert McColl (2005). *Language, Nation and Power. An Introduction*. Basingstoke, New York: Palgrave Macmillan.

Miller, Robert L. (1968). *The Linguistic Relativity Principle and Humboldtian Ethnolinguistics*. The Hague, Paris: Mouton.

Mills, Sara (2008). *Language and Sexism*. Cambridge: Cambridge University Press.

Mitchell, W. J. T. (1986). *Iconology. Image, Text, Ideology*. Chicago, IL, London: Chicago University Press.

Mitchell, W. J. T. (1994). *The Picture Theory. Essays on Verbal and Visual Representation*. Chicago, IL, London: University of Chicago Press.

Morris, Charles W. (1971). Foundations of the theory of signs. In C. W. Morris *Writings on The General Theory of Signs*, 17–74. The Hague: Mouton [1938].

Morris, Desmond (2002). *Peoplewatching*. London: Vintage [originally *Manwatching*, 1977].

Moulton, Janice, George M. Robinson and Cherin Elias (1978). Sex bias in language use: 'Neutral' pronouns that aren't. *American Psychologist* 33 (11): 1032–1036.

Mugdan, Joachim (1984). *Jan Baudouin de Courtenay (1845–1929). Leben und Werk*. München: Wilhelm Fink.

Mühlhäusler, Peter (1996). Linguistic adaptation to changed environmental conditions. Some lessons from the past. In A. Fill (ed.) *Sprachökologie und Ökolinguistik*, 106–130. Tübingen: Stauffenburg.

Mühlhäusler, Peter (2001). Babel revisited. In A. Fill and P. Mühlhäusler (eds), 159–164 [1994].

Mühlhäusler, Peter (2003). *Language of Environment – Environment of Language. A Course in Ecolinguistics*. London: Battlebridge.

Mühlhäusler, Peter and Richard Damania (2004). Economic costs and benefits of Australian indigenous languages: Discussion Paper. The University of Adelaide digital library.

Myers, Greg (1994). *Words in Ads*. London: Edward Arnold.

Myers, Greg (1997). *Ad Worlds*. London: Edward Arnold.

Myers, William Andrew (1995). Victoria, Lady Welby (1837–1912). In Mary Ellen Waithe (ed.), *A History of Women Philosophers*. Vol . 4: *Contemporary Women Philosophers 1900–today*, 1–24. Dordrecht, Boston, London: Kluwer Academic Publishers.

Nash, Walter (1985). *The Language of Humour*. London, New York: Longman.

Nerlich, Brigitte and David D. Clarke (1996). *Language, Action and Context: The Early History of Pragmatics in Europe and America 1780–1930*. Amsterdam: John Benjamins.

Nettle, Daniel (1999). *Linguistic Diversity*. Oxford: Oxford University Press.

Nettle, Daniel and Suzanne Romaine (2000). *Vanishing Voices. The Extinction of the World's Languages*. Oxford: Oxford University Press.

Newen, Albert and Markus A. Schrenk (2008). *Einführung in die Sprachphilosophie*. Darmstadt: Wiss. Buchgesellschaft.

Nöth, Winfried (1990). *Handbook of Semiotics*. Bloomington and Indianapolis, IN: Indiana University Press.

O'Brien, Barbara (2004). *Blogging America. Political discourse in a digital nation*. Wilsonville, OR: William, James & Co.

Ogden, C. K. and I. A. Richards (1969). *The Meaning of Meaning. A Study of the Influence of Language upon Thought and of the Science of Symbolism*. London: Routledge & Kegan Paul [1923].

Otto, Stephan (ed.) (1984). *Renaissance und frühe Neuzeit. (Geschichte der Philosophie in Text und Darstellung*, vol. 3). Stuttgart: Reclam.

Partington, Alan (2003). *The Linguistics of Political Argument. The Spin-doctor and the Wolf-pack at the White House*. London, New York: Routledge.

Pasierbsky, Fritz (1983). *Krieg und Frieden in der Sprache*. Frankfurt/Main: Fischer tb.

Peirce, Charles S. (1878). How to Make our Ideas Clear. *Popular Science Monthly* 12: 286–302.

Penn, Julia M. (1972). *Linguistic Relativity versus Innate Ideas. The Origins of the Sapir-Whorf Hypothesis in German Thought*. The Hague, Paris: Mouton.

Pennycook, Alastair (1994). *The Cultural Politics of English as an International Language*. London: Longman.

Penz, Hermine (1996). *Language and Control in American TV Talk Shows. An Analysis of Linguistic Strategies*. Tübingen: Gunter Narr.

Phillipson, Robert (1992). *Linguistic Imperialism*. Oxford: Oxford University Press.

Phillipson, Robert (2003). *English-only Europe? Challenging language policy*. London: Routledge.

Pinker, Steven (1994). *The Language Instinct. The New Science of Language and Mind*. London: Penguin.

Pinker, Steven (2003). Language as an adaptation to the cognitive niche. In M. H. Christiansen and S. Kirby (eds), 16–37.

Pinker, Steven and P. Bloom (1990). Natural language and natural selection. *Behavioral and Brain Sciences* 13: 707–784.

Plato (2004). *Gorgias,* trans. Benjamin Jowett. Online: http//:ebooks.adelaide.edu.au/p/plato/p71g/ [after 399 BC].

Platon (1973). *Werke in acht Bänden. Griechisch und Deutsch.* Vol. 2 (*Euthydemos, Gorgias,* etc.), ed. G. Eigler. Darmstadt: Wiss. Buchgesellschaft.

Platon (1994). *Sämtliche Werke. Vol. 3 (Kratylos etc.),* trans. F. Schleiermacher, ed. Ursula Wolf. Reinbek b. Hamburg: rowohlt.

Plett, Heinrich F. (1979). *Textwissenschaft und Textanalyse. Semiotik, Linguistik, Rhetorik,* 2nd edn. Heidelberg: Quelle & Meyer.

Plett, Heinrich F. (2000). *Systematische Rhetorik. Konzepte und Analysen.* München: Wilhelm Fink.

Plett, Heinrich F. (ed.) (1991). *Intertextuality.* Berlin, New York: Walter de Gruyter.

Poole, Steven (2006). *Unspeak. How Words Become Weapons, How Weapons Become a Message, and How that Message Becomes Reality.* London: Grove Press.

Portis Winner, Irene (1977). The semiotic character of the aesthetic function as defined by the Prague Linguistic Circle. In William C. McCormack and Stephen A. Wurm (eds), 407–440.

Porzig, Walter (1967). *Das Wunder der Sprache. Probleme, Methoden und Ergebnisse der modernen Sprachwissenschaft,* 4th edn. Bern, München, Francke [1950].

Potter, Jonathan (1996). *Representing Reality. Discourse, Rhetoric and Social Construction.* London: SAGE.

Power, Camilla (1998). Old Wives' Tales: The gossip hypothesis and the reliability of cheap signals. In: J. R. Hurford, M. Studdert-Kennedy and C. Knight (eds), 111–129.

Pusch, Luise (1984). *Das Deutsche als Männersprache. Aufsätze und Glossen zur feministischen Linguistik.* Frankfurt/Main: Suhrkamp.

Pusch, Luise (1990). *Alle Menschen werden Schwestern. Feministische Sprachkritik.* Frankfurt/Main: Suhrkamp.

Quasthoff, Uta (1973). *Soziales Vorurteil und Kommunikation. Eine sprachwissenschaftliche Analyse des Stereotyps.* Frankfurt/Main: Athenäum.

Quasthoff, Uta (1978). The uses of stereotype in everyday argument. *Journal of Pragmatics* 2 (1): 1–48.

Quine, Willard Van Orman (1960). *Word and Object. An Inquiry into the Linguistic Mechanism of Objective References.* Cambridge, MA: MIT Press.

Radcliffe-Brown, Alfred R. (1952). *Structure and Function in Primitive Society. Essays and Addresses.* London: Cohen & Unwin.

Raskin, Victor (1985). *Semantic Mechanisms of Humour.* Dordrecht: Reidel.

Rawson, Hugh (1983). *A Dictionary of Euphemism and other Doubletalk.* New York: Macdonald.

Reichert, Tom and Jacqueline Lambiase (2003). *Sex in Advertising. Perspectives in the Erotic Appeal.* Mahwah, NJ: Lawrence Erlbaum.

Reif, Monika (1984). *Film und Text. Zum Problem der Wahrnehmung und Vorstellung in Film und Literatur.* Tübingen: Gunter Narr.

Reisigl, Martin and Ruth Wodak (2001). *Discourse and Discrimination.* London, New York: Routledge.

Rendon, Silvio (2003). *The Catalan Premium: Language and Employment in Catalonia.* Online: http://ideas.repec.org/p/cte/werepe/we033410.html

Ricciardelli, Lina A. (1992). Creativity and bilingualism. *Journal of Creative Behavior* 26 (4): 242–254.

Ricoeur, Paul (1978). *The Rule of Metaphor. Multi-disciplinary Studies of the Creation of Meaning in Language,* trans. Robert Czerny. London, Henley: Routledge & Kegan Paul [*La métaphore vive,* 1975].

Romaine, Suzanne (1989). *Bilingualism.* Oxford: Blackwell.

Rorty, Richard (ed.) (1967). *The Linguistic Turn. Recent Essays in Philosophical Method.* Chicago, IL, London: University of Chicago Press.

Rosch, Eleanor (1975). Cognitive representations of semantic categories. *Journal of Experimental Psychology: General,* 104: 192–233.

Rosenkranz, Bernhard (1971). *Der Ursprung der Sprache. Ein linguistisch-anthropologischer Versuch.* 2nd edn. Heidelberg: Carl Winter.

Ross, Alison (1998). *The Language of Humour*. London, New York: Routledge.

Rothmund, Jutta and Brigitte Scheele (2004). Personenbezeichnungsmodelle auf dem Prüfstand. *Zeitschrift für Psychologie* 212 (1): 40–54.

Ruhlen, Merritt (2001). Taxonomic controversies in the twentieth century. In J. Trabant and S. Ward (eds), 197–214.

Russell, Bertrand (1903). *The Principles of Mathematics*. Cambridge: Cambridge University Press.

Russell, Bertrand (1959). *My Philosophical Development*. London: Allen & Unwin.

Russell, Bertrand (1973). *Philosophie. Die Entwicklung meines Denkens*, trans. Eberhard Bubser. München: Nymphenburger Verlagsbuchhandlung. [German translation of Russell 1959.]

Ryle, Gilbert (1967). Systematically misleading expressions. In R. Rorty (ed.), 85–100 [1931–32].

Sacks, Harvey, E. Schegloff and G. Jefferson (1974). A simplest systematics for the organization of turn-taking in conversation. *Language* 50: 696–735.

Salamun, Kurt (1985). *Karl Jaspers*. München: C. H. Beck.

Sampson, Geoffrey (1985). *Writing Systems. A Linguistic Introduction*. London, etc.: Hutchinson.

Sampson, Geoffrey (2005). *The 'Language Instinct' Debate*. Revised edition. London, New York: Continuum [1st edn *Educating Eve*, 1997].

Sapir, Edward (1921). *Language. An Introduction to the Study of Speech*. New York: Harcourt, Brace & World.

Sapir, Edward (1929). The status of linguistics as a science. In David G. Mandelbaum (ed.), *Selected Writings of Edward Sapir in Language, Culture and Personality*, 160–166, Berkeley, CA: University of California Press.

Saussure, Ferdinand de (1967). *Grundfragen der allgemeinen Sprachwissenschaft*, 2nd edn, eds Charles Bally and Albert Sechehaye (with Albert Riedlinger), trans Herman Lommel. Berlin: Walter de Gruyter [1916].

Saussure, Ferdinand de (1968). *Cours de linguistique générale. Edition critique par Rudolf Engler*. 2 vols. Wiesbaden: Otto Harrassowitz. [An edition of the original scripts of Saussure's pupils.]

Schank, Gerd and Johannes Schwitalla (eds) (1987). *Konflikte in Gesprächen*. Tübingen: Gunter Narr.

Schierl, Thomas (2001). *Text und Bild in der Werbung*. Köln: Herbert von Halem.

Schiewe, Jürgen (1998). *Die Macht der Sprache. Eine Geschichte der Sprachkritik von der Antike bis zur Gegenwart*. München: C. H. Beck.

Schiffrin, Deborah (1994). *Approaches to Discourse*. Oxford (UK), Cambridge, MA: Blackwell.

Schlesinger, I. M. (1991). The wax and wane of Whorfian views. In R. L. Cooper and B. Spolsky (eds), 7–44.

Schneider, Klaus P. (1988). *Small Talk. Analysing Phatic Discourse*. Marburg: Hitzeroth.

Schnitzler, Günter and Edelgard Spaude (eds) (2004). *Intermedialität. Studien zur Wechselwirkung zwischen den Künsten*. Freiburg/Br.: Rombach.

Schopenhauer, Arthur (1983). *Eristische Dialektik. Die Kunst, Recht zu behalten*, ed. Arthur Hübscher. Zürich: Haffmanns Verlag [1864].

Schopenhauer, Arthur (1987). *Die Welt als Wille und Vorstellung*, ed. Arthur Hübscher, 2 vols. Stuttgart: Reclam [1819].

Schrastetter, Rudolf (1988). Die Sprachursprungsfrage in Platons 'Kratylos'. In J. Gessinger and W. von Rahden (eds), 42–64.

Schrenk, Friedemann and Timothy G. Bromage (2002). *Adams Eltern. Expeditionen in die Welt der Frühmenschen*, ed. S. Müller. München: C. H. Beck.

Schultz, Beth (2001). Language and the natural environment. In A. Fill and P. Mühlhäusler (eds.), 109–114 [1992].

Schulz von Thun, Friedemann (1981). *Miteinander reden: Störungen und Klärungen. Psychologie der zwischenmenschlichen Kommunikation*. Reinbek/Hamburg: Rowohlt.

Schulze, Rainer (1985). *Höflichkeit im Englischen. Zur linguistischen Beschreibung und Analyse von Alltagsgesprächen. Mit einer Zusammenfassung in englischer Sprache*. Tübingen: Gunter Narr.

Schütz, Alfred (2003). *Theorie der Lebenswelt 2. Die kommunikative Ordnung der Lebenswelt.* (= *Werkausgabe*, vol. V.2, eds H. Knoblauch, R. Kurt, Hans-Georg Soeffner). Konstanz: UVK Verlagsgesellschaft [1925–1955].

Schweizer, Karin and Edgar Erdfelder (2005). Sprache und Denken: Neue Argumente und Befunde zu einem alten Thema. *Zeitschrift für Psychologie* 213 (3): 127–132.

Searle, John (1969). *Speech Acts. An Essay in the Philosophy of Language.* London: Cambridge University Press.

Searle, John (1975). Indirect Speech Acts. In Peter Cole and J. L. Morgan (eds), *Syntax and Semantics 3*, 59-82. New York: Academic Press.

Searle, John (1979). *Expression and Meaning.* Cambridge: Cambridge University Press.

Seidlhofer, Barbara (2005). English as a lingua franca. *ELT Journal* 59 (4): 339–341.

Seidlhofer, Barbara (ed.) (2003). *Controversies in Applied Linguistics.* Oxford: Oxford University Press.

Semiotics Encyclopedia Online, s.v. Social Semiotics. http://www.semioticon.com/seo/S/social_semiotics.html

Shapere, Dudley (1967). Philosophy and the analysis of language. In R. Rorty (ed.), 271–283 [1960].

Slobin, Dan I. (1971). *Psycholinguistics.* Glenview, IL: Scott Foresman.

Smith, Barry (1990). Towards a history of speech act theory. In Armin Burkhardt (ed.), *Speech Acts. Meaning and Intentions: Critical Approaches to the Philosophy of John R. Searle*, 29–61. Berlin: De Gruyter.

Spender, Dale (1985). *Man Made Language,* 2nd edn. London, Boston, MA, Henley: Routledge & Kegan Paul [1980].

Sperber, Dan and Deirdre Wilson (1986). *Relevance: Communication and Cognition.* Cambridge, MA: Harvard University Press.

Stahlberg, Dagmar and Sabine Sczesny (2001). Effekte des generischen Maskulinums und alternativer Sprachformen auf den gedanklichen Einbezug von Frauen. *Psychologische Rundschau* 52 (3): 131–140.

Stam, Robert (2005). *Literature through Film. Realism, Magic, and the Art of Adaptation.* Malden, MA and Oxford: Blackwell.

Stanzel, Franz K. and Martin Löschnigg (eds) (1993). *Intimate Enemies. English and German Literary Reactions to the Great War 1914–1918.* Heidelberg: Winter.

Steffensen, Sune Vork (2007). Language, ecology and society: an introduction to Dialectical Linguistics. Introduction to Bang, J. C. and J. Døør, 3–31.

Steiner, George (1975). *After Babel. Aspects of Language and Translation.* London, New York, Toronto: Oxford University Press.

Steinthal, Heymann (1985). *Die Sprachwissenschaft Wilhelm von Humboldts und die Hegel'sche Philosophie.* Hildesheim: Olms [1848].

Sternberg, Robert J. (ed.) (1999). *Handbook of Creativity.* Cambridge: Cambridge University Press.

Sternberger, Dolf, G. Storz and W. E. Süskind (1968). *Aus dem Wörterbuch des Unmenschen. Erweiterte Ausgabe mit Zeugnissen des Streits über die Sprachkritik,* 3rd edn. Hamburg: Claassen [1945].

Stöckl, Hartmut (1997). *Werbung in Wort und Bild. Textstil und Semiotik englischsprachiger Anzeigenwerbung.* Frankfurt/Main: Peter Lang.

Stöckl, Hartmut (2004). *Die Sprache im Bild – Das Bild in der Sprache. Zur Verknüpfung von Sprache und Bild im massenmedialen Text. Konzepte, Theorien, Analysemethoden.* Berlin, New York: Walter de Gruyter.

Störig, Hans Joachim (1987). *Kleine Weltgeschichte der Philosophie,* 13th edn. Frankfurt/Main: Fischer tb [1949].

Stubbs, Michael (1983). *Discourse Analysis. The Sociolinguistic Analysis of Natural Language.* Oxford: Blackwell.

Sukale, Michael (1988). *Denken, Sprechen und Wissen. Logische Untersuchungen zu Husserl und Quine.* Tübingen: J. C. B. Mohr.

Swann, Joan (1992). *Girls, Boys and Language*. Oxford: Blackwell.

Tannen, Deborah (1986). *That's Not What I Meant! How Conversational Style Makes or Breaks your Relations with Others*. New York: William Morrow.

Tannen, Deborah (1990). *You Just Don't Understand. Women and Men in Conversation*. New York: William Morrow.

Taylor, Insup (1976). *Introduction to Psycholinguistics*. New York, etc.: Holt, Rinehart and Winston.

Thomas, Jenny (1995). *Meaning in Interaction: an Introduction to Pragmatics*. London, New York: Longman.

Thompson, J. B. and D. Held (eds) (1982). *Habermas – Critical Debates*. London: Macmillan.

Threadgold, Terry, E. A. Grosz, Gunther Kress and M. A. K. Halliday (eds.) (1986). *Semiotics – Ideology – Language*. Sydney: Sydney Association for Studies in Society and Culture.

Thucydides (n.d.). *History of the Peloponnesian War,* trans. Richard Crawley. The Internet Classics Archive. http://classics.mit.edu/Thucydides/pelopwar.mb.txt

Thucydides (1981). *Geschichte des Peloponnesischen Krieges,* 3rd edn, ed. and trans. Georg Peter Landmann. München: dtb [ca. 431 BC].

Trabant, Jürgen (1990). *Traditionen Humboldts*. Frankfurt/Main: Suhrkamp.

Trabant, Jürgen (1994). Kommentare und Anmerkungen zu den einzelnen Reden. In Humboldt (1994), 228–268.

Trabant, Jürgen and Sean Ward (eds) (2001). *New Essays on the Origin of Language*. Berlin, New York: Mouton de Gruyter.

Trampe, Wilhelm (2001). Language and ecological crisis. Extracts from a dictionary of industrial agriculture. In A. Fill and P. Mühlhäusler (eds), 232–240 [1991].

Trömel-Plötz, Senta (1988). Vorwort. In H. Kotthoff (ed.), 7–17.

Turell, M. Teresa (2008). Plagiarism. In J. Gibbons and M. T. Turell (eds), 265–299.

Tzanne, Angeliki (2000). *Talking at Cross-Purposes. The Dynamics of Miscommunication*. Amsterdam, Philadelphia, PA: John Benjamins.

Ulbaek, Ib (1998). The origin of language and cognition. In J. R. Hurford, M. Studdert-Kennedy and C. Knight (eds), 30–43.

Ungerer, Friedrich and Hans-Jörg Schmid (1996). *An Introduction to Cognitive Linguistics*. Harlow: Longman.

Vachek, J. (1966). *The Linguistic School of Prague*. Bloomington, IN: Indiana University Press.

Van Dijk, Teun A. (2006). Discourse and manipulation. *Discourse and Society* 17 (2): 359–383.

Van Hooff, J. A. R. (1972). A comparative approach to the phylogeny of laughter and smiling. In R. A. Hinde (ed.), *Non-Verbal Communication*, 209–238. Cambridge: Cambridge University Press.

Van Leeuwen, Theo (2009). Critical discourse analysis. In Jan Renkema (ed.), *Discourse, of Course. An Overview of Research in Discourse Studies*, 277–292. Amsterdam/Philadelphia, PA: John Benjamins.

Ventola, Eija (ed.) (2000). *Discourse and Community. Doing Functional Linguistics*. Tübingen: Gunter Narr.

Vickers, Brian (1988). *In Defence of Rhetoric*. Oxford: Clarendon Press.

Vico, Giambattista (1858–65). *Opere*. 4 vols. Napoli: Stamperia dei Classici Latini [1725].

Vildomec, Vèroboj (1971). *Multilingualism*. Leiden: Sijthoff.

Vine, Bernadette (2004). *Getting Things Done at Work. The Discourse of Power in Workplace Interaction*. Amsterdam/Philadelphia, PA: John Benjamins.

Vossenkuhl, Wilhelm (ed.) (1992). *Von Wittgenstein lernen*. Berlin: Akad. Verlag.

Vossler, Karl (1960). *Geist und Kultur in der Sprache*. München: Dobbeck Verlag [1925].

Vygotsky, Lev S. (1962). *Thought and Language,* ed. and trans. Eugenia Hanfmann and Gertrude Vakar. Cambridge, MA: The MIT Press. [Russian original 1934.]

Wächter, Christine (1996). *Language is a Virus*. München, Wien: Profil-Verlag.

Wandruszka, Mario (1979). *Die Mehrsprachigkeit des Menschen*. München, Zürich: R. Piper.

Wandruszka, Mario (1983). Denken in Bildern. In Klaus Piper (ed.) *Lust am Denken. Ein Lesebuch aus Philosophie, Natur- und Humanwissenschaften 1947–1981*, 4th edn., 301-212. München, Zürich: Piper.

Watts, Richard (2003). *Politeness*. Cambridge: Cambridge University Press.

Watzlawick, Paul, Janet Beavin Bavelas and Don D. Jackson (1967). *Pragmatics of Human Communication. A Study of Interactional Patterns, Pathologies, and Paradoxes*. New York, London: W. W. Norton & Cie.

Watzlawick, Paul (1983). *Wie wirklich ist die Wirklichkeit? Wahn – Täuschung – Verstehen*. 10th edn. München, Zürich: R. Piper.

Watzlawick, Paul (1994). Preface and Introduction to Watzlawick (ed.) (1994), 9–15 [1981].

Watzlawick, Paul (1994a). Selbsterfüllende Prophezeihungen. In Watzlawick (ed.) (1994), 91–110.

Watzlawick, Paul (ed.) (1994). *Die erfundene Wirklichkeit. Wie wissen wir, was wir zu wissen glauben? Beiträge zum Konstruktivismus*, 8th edn. München, Zürich: R. Piper.

Wawra, Daniela (2004). *Männer und Frauen im Job Interview. Eine evolutionspsychologische Studie zu ihrem Sprachgebrauch im Englischen*. Münster. LIT Verlag.

Weber, Jörg (1993). *Die Erde ist nicht untertan. Grundrechte der Natur,* 2nd edn. Frankfurt/Main: Eichborn.

Wegener, Philipp (1885). *Untersuchungen über die Grundfragen des Sprachlebens*. Halle: Niemeyer.

Weiler, Bernd (1997). Die Kulturanthropologie von Franz Boas im ideengeschichtlichen und wissenssoziologischen Kontext. Master's thesis, Graz.

Weinreich, Uriel (1968). *Languages in Contact. Findings and Problems*. The Hague, Paris, New York: Mouton [1953].

Weisgerber, Leo (1961). *The South Tyrol Question. Imperfection of Translation in an Official Document,* trans. Edith Raybould. Innsbruck: Inst. f. Sprachwissenschaft. (IBK, Sonderheft 10).

Weisgerber, Leo (1963). *Die vier Stufen in der Erforschung der Sprache*. Düsseldorf: Schwann.

Welby, Lady Victoria (1983). *What is Meaning? Studies in the Development of Significance*. Amsterdam/ Philadelphia, PA: John Benjamins [1903].

Wenden, Anita (1995). Critical language education. In C. Schäffner and A. Wenden (eds), *Language and Peace*, 211–227. Aldershot: Dartmouth Books.

Werlen, Iwar (1989). *Sprache, Mensch und Welt. Geschichte und Bedeutung des Prinzips der sprachlichen Relativität*. Darmstadt: Wissenschaftliche Buchgesellschaft.

Whorf, Benjamin Lee (1956). *Language, Thought, and Reality. Selected Writings of Benjamin Lee Whorf,* ed. and with an introduction by J. B. Carroll. Foreword by Stuart Chase. Cambridge, MA: MIT Press.

Whorf, Benjamin Lee (1971). The Hopi language, Toreva dialect. In Harry Hoijer (ed.) *Linguistic Structures of Native America*, 158–183. New York/London: Johnson Reprint Corporation.

Widdowson, Henry (1995). Discourse analysis: a critical view. *Language and Literature* 4 (3): 157–172. [Reprinted in B. Seidlhofer (ed.) 2003, 132–145.]

Wilson, Deirdre and Dan Sperber (2005). Relevance theory. In L. R. Horn and G. Ward (eds), 607–632.

Wittgenstein, Ludwig (1963/1922). *Tractatus logico-philosophicus. Logisch-philosophische Abhandlung*. Frankfurt/Main: Suhrkamp [1922].

Wittgenstein, Ludwig (2003/1953). *Philosophische Untersuchungen*, ed. Joachim Schulte. Frankfurt/ Main: Suhrkamp [1953].

Wittig, Monique (1976). *The Lesbian Body,* trans. Peter Owen. New York: Avon [quoted from Butler 1999].

Wodak, Ruth (1981). *Das Wort in der Gruppe. Linguistische Studien zur therapeutischen Kommunikation*. Wien: Verlag Akademie der Wissenschaften.

Wodak, Ruth (2001). What critical discourse analysis is about. A summary of its history, important concepts and its developments. In R. Wodak and M. Meyer (eds), 1–9.

Wodak Ruth and Michael Meyer (eds) (2001). *Methods of Critical Discourse Analysis*. London, Thousand Oaks, CA, New Delhi: Sage.

Wodak, Ruth and Paul Chilton (eds) (2005). *A New Agenda in (Critical) Discourse Analysis*. Amsterdam/Philadelphia, PA: John Benjamins.

Wode, Henning (1980). *Learning a Second Language. An Integrated View of Language Acquisition*. Tübingen: Gunter Narr.

Wolf, Werner (1999). *The Musicalization of Fiction. A Study in the Theory and History of Intermediality*. Amsterdam/Atlanta, GA: Rodopi.

Wolf, Werner (2004). Intermedialität. In Ansgar Nünning (ed.). *Metzler Lexikon Literatur- und Kulturtheorie*, 3rd edn, 296–297. Stuttgart: Metzler.

Wood, Linda A. (2000). *Doing Discourse Analysis. Methods for Studying Action in Talk and Text*. Thousand Oaks, CA: Sage.

Wunderlich, Dieter (1980). Aspekte einer Theorie der Sprechhandlungen. In H. Lenk (ed.) 381–401.

Wunderlich, Dieter (ed.) (1972). *Linguistische Pragmatik*. Frankfurt/Main: Athenäum.

Wustmann, Gustav (1891). *Allerhand Sprachdummheiten. Kleine deutsche Grammatik des Zweifelhaften, des Falschen und des Hässlichen*. Leipzig: Grunow.

Yus, Francisco (2006). Relevance theory. In Edward K. Brown (ed.). *Encyclopedia of Language and Linguistics*, 512–519. Amsterdam: Elsevier.

Zimmerman, Don and Candace West (1975). Sex roles, interruptions and silences in conversation. In Barrie Thorne and Nancy Henley (eds.), *Language and Sex: Difference and Dominance*, 105–129. Rowley, MA: Newbury House.

Appendix I

Glossary of terms

Note: some of the terms may have more than one meaning. The meaning given here is the one relevant to language impact.

Analytical philosophy: a branch of philosophy developed in the wake of Wittgenstein which considers the use of everyday language as opposed to the use of language in scientific and scholarly contexts. Representatives of Analytical Philosophy are: John Austin, H. P. Grice and Donald Davidson (see Newen and Schrenk 2008: 56–62 on Davidson's theory of meaning).

Androcentrism (Greek *aner/andros* = man): the practice of regarding the world from an exclusively male perspective. Example: the word *penetration* describes the sexual act androcentrically, while *enclosure* would be the 'gynocentric' counterpart.

Anthropocentrism (Greek: *anthropos* = human being): views and attitudes which put humans at the centre of the universe. Everything is seen in relation to its function for the human species. Since language is the creation of humans, a certain degree of linguistic anthropocentrism is unavoidable, but awareness of it is essential.

Anthropomorphism: everything is seen in the shape (Greek: *morphé* = shape) of humans. Animals and plants are integrated into human society (e.g. rabbits have 'aunts' and 'uncles').

Biodiversity: diversity of species on the earth. Linguistic diversity is often compared with biodiversity; but there is also a direct relation between the two diversities (see Chapter 20.6).

Cognitive Linguistics (CL): a school of linguistics in which human linguistic ability is seen as linked to the rest of cognition. CL focuses on meaning, which is regarded as part of our experience as humans. Famous manifestations of CL are Eleanor Rosch's Prototype Semantics (q.v.) and books such as *Metaphors We Live by* (1980) by Lakoff and Johnson or *The Way We Think* (2002) by Fauconnier and

Turner. Cognitive linguists are not unanimous in their choice of methods or topics. Categories – and how they are stored in the brain – play an important part in Cognitive Linguistics (see the chapters in Geeraerts (ed.) 2006).

Conceptualism: the view that 'concepts' (mental representations of entities) are there first, before the words for them appear.

Constructivism: the view that reality does not exist, but is only 'construed' by us. In its most radical manifestation, Constructivism would lead to 'solipsism', the view that only the self exists. Linguistic Constructivism builds on the power of language to construe reality.

Critical Discourse Analysis (CDA): an approach to Discourse which sees Discourse 'critically', i.e. as a carrier of ideologies and a means to exert power. Initiated by Norman Fairclough's book *Language and Power* (first published 1989).

Dialectical: According to Hegel's dialectics, progress occurs through thesis, antithesis and synthesis. Today, 'dialectical' is frequently understood as meaning 'recognizing interconnectedness, interrelatedness and multidimensionality'.

Discourse: Generally speaking, discourse refers to the manifestation of language in concrete situations. 'Discourse' is sometimes used to mean only spoken language. More frequently nowadays, however, 'discourse' is taken to comprise both spoken and written texts. A frequent meaning of Discourse is the totality of texts (or at least a body of texts) about a certain topic, as in 'the Discourse of environmental degradation'. (See the definitions of discourse at the beginning of Part III.)

Discourse ethics: an attempt at using discourse (and its rules) to establish an ethics. Kantian ethics (act in such a way that the maxim of your action can be made a general maxim) and Utilitarian ethics (the greatest good to the greatest number) were supplemented by Jürgen Habermas and Ernst-Otto Apel through discourse ethics.

Eco-criticism: a critique of language which focuses on unecological elements in the language system and on strategic elements in discourse about environmental topics.

Ecolinguistics: A branch of linguistics (pioneered by Einar Haugen) which looks at language from the ecological point of view, i.e. from the point of view of interrelation. Topics covered by Ecolinguistics are the interrelation of languages with each other and with their 'environment' (viz. the mind or society in which they are used together) and the interrelation of language and the world, particularly concerning environmental topics.

Ecological: An ecological relation is one in which changes in one part of an entity influence other parts. Here is an example given by Watzlawick: in a certain area, an increase in the number of foxes may influence (reduce) the number of rabbits; this reduction may in turn influence (reduce) the number of foxes, a change which in turn may lead to an increase in rabbits, etc. See also 'dialectical'.

Eristics: (Greek *eris* = quarrel) the art of gaining the upper hand in an argument. Schopenhauer collected 38 devices which may be used for this purpose (see Chapter 17.5).

Euphemism: word or phrase (even sentence) which makes something unpleasant look more agreeable (e.g. *ministry of defence* for *war ministry*). Ontological areas where euphemisms are frequent are death, war, bodily functions and sexuality (see Chapter 17.2).

Evolution: the development of all life forms and their features through natural selection. The exemplars of a species best suited to their surroundings are thought to have the greatest number of offspring, so that their advantageous qualities are propagated and developed in the following generations. The concepts of Evolution and natural selection were proposed by Charles Darwin in *The Origin of Species* (1859).

Exaptation: a development within evolution, in which (physical or mental) features developed as the result of natural selection are used for different tasks from those for which they were originally selected. An example of this is the 'speech organs', which originally developed for breathing, smelling, tasting and other tasks not connected with communication.

Family resemblances: a concept suggested by Wittgenstein, who compares the members of categories (say, games) with the members of a family. There may not be a specific characteristic which is common to all games, but it is possible to go through the range of games and find similarities in neighbouring games which are not found in those further away.

Forensic linguistics (Lat. *forum* = platform for speakers): branch of linguistics which concerns law cases, crime and plagiarism (see Chapter 14.3).

Framing: a theory established in particular by George Lakoff: political action is thought to follow or be contained in certain 'frames', i.e. situational contexts. Examples of frames: WAR, THEATRE, CONVERSATION.

Iconicity: an instance of form imitating meaning. In spoken language, onomatopoeic words are iconic, since the word form is expressive of its meaning (*splash, crack, creak*); in written language, typographical iconicity is frequent (example: LARGE and small)

Ideology: a specific way of thinking about groups of people, animals, etc.: 'a systematic body of ideas, organized from a particular point of view' (Hodge and Kress 1993: 6). Examples of ideologies are racism, sexism, classism, anthropocentrism and speciesism. 'Ideology' is frequently linked with 'power', as in the following definition by Giddens (1993: 722): 'values and beliefs which help secure the position of more powerful groups at the expense of less powerful ones'.

Impact: defined in the dictionaries as 'collision' and metaphorically as 'strong effect or influence'. The meaning used in this book follows one of the definitions in *Webster's Collegiate Dictionary* (New York: Random House 1996): 'the force exerted by a new idea, concept, technology, or ideology'.

Linguistic turn (of philosophy): a term coined by Richard Rorty (ed. 1967), an American philosopher who became sceptical about the future of philosophy. The solution to all philosophical problems was to be found in the analysis of language, asking questions such as the following: can there be an ideal language? Is language irrelevant for philosophy? Can language be improved so as to be useful for philosophy? Representatives of the linguistic turn are Carnap, the early Wittgenstein and Willard van Orman Quine. (See Leiss 2009: 151–172.)

Manipulation: a strategy is manipulatory, if it results in deception by means of a true statement (Utz Maas). 'Manipulation' is a strong term for 'deception through language' (see Chapter 17.4).

Metaphor: a figure of speech in which a comparison is contained. By calling a park 'the lungs of the town', the town is compared to a human being. Metaphor involves an 'image donor' (here the human body), an image receiver (here the town) and a common ground (here 'storing and providing oxygen').

Metonymy: a figure of speech in which a shift of meaning is involved. Most frequent type: *pars pro toto*. Example: 'Downing Street' for the British government.

Nominalism: '*nomina ante res*'. The view that the words were there first, the (ideas of the) things followed. Nominalism in its strongest form is a type of constructivism. Words construe our conception of the world for us. Opposite: realism (*res ante nomina*).

Phylogeny: the development of a species. The phylogeny of language is the development of language in the human species. Opposite: 'ontogeny' – development of individuals.

Pragmatics: branch of linguistics which was conceived as the study of the origins, the uses and effects of language (Charles Morris). Today, the study of the origins is excluded from Pragmatics. The philosophers Wittgenstein, Austin, Grice and Searle laid the foundation for modern Pragmatics (see Chapter 13). Wittgenstein's *Philosophical Investigations* (1953), in which meaning is defined as 'use', led to the **pragmatic turn** of philosophy and linguistics.

Prototype semantics: established by Eleanor Rosch in the 1970s, prototype semantics concerns categories: for each category (say, buildings or games), a prototype (i.e. the most typical example) is thought to be stored in the brain. All other members of the category are thought to be measured against the prototype. Related theory: Wittgenstein's family resemblances.

Realism: '*Res ante nomina*'. The view that things were there first; they were given names by humans. Opposite: Nominalism (*nomina ante res*).

SAE languages: a term used by B. L. Whorf for 'Standard Average European' languages. The world view based on these languages was contrasted by Whorf with that based on the Hopi language.

Sexism: giving preference to one of the sexes (usually the male). Discriminating against the other sex (usually women) or making them seem invisible; seeing males as the norm.

Speciesism: an attitude which takes the human species to be the most important. All other species are there to serve humans.

Strategy: a use of language with the aim of influencing or changing the views of others (or making others act in a certain way) – particularly in a manner which does not make this aim visible.

Appendix II

Commented List of Thinkers on Language Impact

Philosophers did not from the very beginning see in language a force which could shape ideas, determine behaviour and have an impact on the world (cf. Werlen 1989: 9). Nevertheless, it was the philosophers rather than the philologists and linguists who concerned themselves with the relation between language and the world. What follows below is a list of thinkers who expressed ideas related to language impact – together with short summaries of these ideas. The thinkers are listed in alphabetical order.

One may observe that **few philosophers** consider the possibility of having **more than one language** at one's disposal. The idea of a 'synergy of languages' to create ideas and represent the world in more than one way does not seem to have occurred to many philosophers. Rather, the thinking of some of them (e.g. Husserl and Heidegger) is strongly influenced by the language in which they philosophize. Heidegger even thought that philosophizing was only possible in German (and, perhaps, Latin). A notable exception to thinking in just one language is Hamann, who compares German with Latin, French and other languages (1967: 97–104) and talks about having to adapt one's thinking like a lover when writing in another language (1967: 94). Another example is Schopenhauer, who advises learning several languages: thought regains its flexibility when translated into another language and frees itself from linguistic bondage (*Die Welt als Wille und Vorstellung,* 1987, vol. 2: 77; see also Jaenecke 2002).

Agricola, Rudolph (1443–1485)
Humanist scholar, born near Groningen, died in Heidelberg. Following Aristotle's *Topica,* Agricola, in *De inventione dialectica* (1480), presents an introduction to 'dialectics', i.e. the art of arguing successfully. In the preface to this book he repeats the general opinion of his time that speech can teach, move and delight. Of these three functions, Agricola sees teaching as the superordinate one: speech cannot move and delight without teaching.

There are two forms of teaching: 'exposition', where only the thoughts of the speaker are represented, and 'argumentation', where someone tries to convince and persuade. Agricola enumerates 24 'topoi', which are useful for influencing others. A topos (*locus*) is for him a treasure-house which contains 'all means to achieve agreement' (a somewhat euphemistic way of saying: all persuasive devices). (Sources: Otto (ed.) 1984: 126–149; Agricola 1992: 9–11).

Apel, Karl Otto (*1922)
German philosopher. Together with Habermas, one of the founders of discourse ethics. Advocates a two stage model of discourse ethics: the first stage establishes the formal principle of argumentative consensus formation, the second delegates content-relevant theses for practical discussion in which the interests of all those concerned as well as the knowledge of experts (including philosophers) are integrated into the discourse (Apel 1988: 271; see also Störig 1987: 644 f).

Aristotle (384–322 BC)
Following Störig (1987: 176), Aristotle's writings can be categorized in the following way (according to topics):

> Logics (categories, syllogism; organon)
> Nature (physics, astronomy, etc.)
> Metaphysics (being and causes of being)
> Ethics (the famous *Nicomachian Ethic*, named after his son)
> Politics
> Literature and rhetoric.

The topic of 'language' occurs in several of his works, particularly in those on logics and on poetry. *De interpretatione – peri hermeneias* contains a discussion of the parts of speech, and thus in a way of grammar, and of language and logical conclusion, syllogism; in the *Poetics* and in his *Rhetoric* metaphor is discussed, particularly its conceptualizing and thus heuristic function. The volume *Classics in Linguistics* (Hayden *et al.* (eds) 1968: 1–17) contains Aristotle's section on metaphor from Book III of his *Rhetoric* (see also Formigari 2004: 23 f.).

Aristotle says little about the effect of language, except perhaps in the *Poetics*, where he establishes his well-known theory of 'catharsis', which states that drama can have a purifying effect on us: seeing cruel acts on stage prevents us from doing them in real life.

Austin, John L. (1917–1960)
The most typical representative of British 'Ordinary Language Philosophy'. Gave a series of lectures at Harvard University, which were printed after his death under the title *How to Do Things with Words* (1962). With his distinction between constative and performative utterances he laid the ground for the pragmatic view of language,

viz. the view of seeing uttering words as doing things and performing actions. His distinction between 'locution', 'illocution' and 'perlocution' was important for making philosophers and linguists aware that speaking is not just saying something, but also acting (illocution), and that this acting can have an effect (perlocution). Austin was influenced by Wittgenstein, whose 'language games' can be roughly equated with his illocutions of which there are (according to him) 10 to the power of four (i.e. 10,000; compare Wittgenstein's assertion that there are countless ways of using language, *PI* 23). John Searle's speech act theory is based on Austin's ideas. Both Austin and Searle give categories of things that can be done with words (called by Austin illocutions, by Searle speech acts).

Bacon, Francis (1561–1626)
Early Empiricist. In his *Advancement of Learning* (1605) and his later treatise *Novum Organum* (1620), Bacon speaks of four 'idols' or rather illusions which mislead humans and which through scholarly effort (empirical methods, e.g. induction) could be removed:

> Idola tribus (illusions simply due to being human)
> Idola specus (unconscious deceptions; cf. Plato's 'cave parable')
> Idola fori (human society, communication)
> Idola theatri (believing in tradition and authority).

Among the idola fori there are the deceptions through language, e.g. quarrels which arise through language, but particularly the confusion of words with the things they denote. In *The Advancement of Learning* (1605), Bacon writes about:

> the seducing incantation of names in numerous respects, their doing violence to the understanding. For words are generally given according to vulgar conception, and divide things by such differences as the common people are capable of: but when a more acute understanding, or a more careful observation would distinguish things better, words murmur against it. (Bacon 1900: 158)

Bacon is thus an early critic of language, whose ideas were later taken up by various thinkers, among others by Friedrich Kainz (see Chapter 6).

Bakhtin, Mihail (1895–1975) [German spelling Bachtin]
Russian literary theorist and semioticist. Distinguished between material, form and content. Became famous through his theory of the 'voices' in a work of literature. For Bakhtin, dialogicality is the basic principle of language. Monologue is single-voiced discourse, dialogue is double-voiced. He also wrote about the culture of laughter. Bakhtin's influence led Julia Kristeva to establish her theory of intertextuality.

Barthes, Roland (1915–1980)
French literary critic and philosopher. One of the first to study the relation between image and text. His distinction between 'anchorage' (image and text are anchored in each other) and 'relay' (image and text complement each other) is very often quoted.

Bateson, Gregory (1904–1980)
Anglo-American anthropologist and philosopher. His hierarchy of five types of learning (from learning 0 to learning 4) is frequently referred to. He also concerned himself with meta-communication and coined the term 'double bind' for a situation in which someone is confronted with contradictory messages.

Berkeley, George (1685–1753)
Irish philosopher, Anglican Bishop of Cloyne. As a 'Subjective Idealist', he believed that existence presupposes being perceived or perceiving: *esse est percipi (vel percipere)*. As an Empiricist, Berkeley acknowledged on the one hand the work language does for us (particularly storing knowledge and making it available for individuals), but on the other hand warned against the 'deception of words'. Berkeley suggested a radical method to get rid of the illusions words create: avoiding words altogether! 'We need only draw the curtain of words, to behold the fairest tree of knowledge, whose fruit is excellent and within the reach of our hand.' (See Chapter 6.1.)

Black, Max (1909–1988)
American philosopher of the analytic school. In his important work *Models and Metaphors*, he criticizes language – and is one of the few who consider specific languages other than their own. One of his points of criticism is grammatical gender (which, for instance, in German makes *das Kind* [child] a neuter noun). 'The indifference of the English language to the gender of nouns sufficiently demonstrates the superfluity of this particular grammatical feature. For the purpose of eventual metaphysical inference, gender is an accidental, a nonessential, grammatical category' (Black 1967: 332). Language is never a mirror of reality:

> To anybody who still feels that there must be an identity of logical form between Language and reality, I can only plead that the conception of language as a mirror of reality is radically mistaken. [...] Language must conform to the discovered regularities and irregularities of experience. But in order to do so, it is enough that it should be apt for the expression of everything that is or might be the case. (1967: 339)

More importantly, Black was a forerunner of modern metaphor theory and one of the founders of the 'conversion theory' of metaphor: the view that metaphor works both ways and does not just have an 'image receiver' which is compared with an 'image donor' (see Goatly 1997).

Boas, Franz (1858–1942)
German-born American anthropologist, who investigated Amerindian languages. Boas was the teacher of Edward Sapir, who taught Benjamin Lee Whorf. Whorfian relativism may well have had its roots in the ideas of Franz Boas.

Bourdieu, Pierre (1930–2002)
French sociologist, who introduced into Sociology, among others, the terms *capital* (social, cultural and symbolic) and *field* (economy, politics, art, science, education, etc. are fields). For impact linguistics, his view that language is not just a means of communication, but a mechanism of (symbolic) power is important – a view expressed in his collection of essays *Language and Symbolic Power* (1991).

Brentano, Franz (1878–1917)
German philosopher considered one of the forerunners of Phenomenology. Brentano suggested that the commonly perceived divide between speaking and acting was illusory. Speaking is itself a kind of acting (see Nerlich and Clarke 1996: 189). He introduced the notion of 'intentionality': every psychic phenomenon is directed towards some specific purpose. One of his pupils was Anton Marty (q.v.).

Butler, Judith (*1956)
American feminist philosopher. In her best-known book, *Gender Trouble* (1999/ 1990) – translated into German as *Das Unbehagen der Geschlechter* (1991) – she takes a constructivist attitude towards gender (gender is construed by action and language), but deconstructs the dichotomy female vs. male. In her chapter 'Language, Power, and the Strategies of Displacement' (1999: 33–44), she discusses various feminist attitudes concerning the role of language in the constitution of gender and sexuality. In her discussion of Julia Kristeva's work, Butler takes up the topic of poetic language. She writes:

> Consider that for Kristeva poetic language breaks the incest taboo and, as such, verges always on psychosis. As a return to the maternal body and a concomitant deindividuation of the ego, poetic language becomes especially threatening when uttered by women. The poetic then contests not only the incest taboo, but the taboo against homosexuality as well. Poetic language is thus, for women, both displaced maternal dependency and, because that dependency is libidinal, displaced homosexuality (1999: 110).

Carnap, Rudolf (1891–1970)
German philosopher of the Neo-Humboldtian school, who was for a time a member of the Vienna Circle of Philosophers. Emigrated to the USA in 1936. In his *Logische Syntax der Sprache* (1934/1936), Carnap distinguishes between object language and meta-language (i.e. the language in which theories about language are

formulated). For Carnap, the philosopher is a 'builder of languages' (*Konstrukteur von Sprachen*) (see Störig 1987: 662–664).

Cassirer, Ernst (1874–1945)

German philosopher. 'The last great representative of idealism, Ernst Cassirer, merged the lesson of Hegel [...] and that of Humboldt' (Formigari 2004: 151). In his *Philosophie der symbolischen Formen* (1923), language, together with science, myth, art, and religion, is studied as a specific articulation of experience. Cassirer's book *An Essay on Man*, written in 1944 while he was teaching at Yale, sums up his idea that it is the symbolic forms (which include language) that achieve the famous 'know then thyself' of Pope's 'Essay on Man'.

Chomsky, Noam (*1928)

American linguist. Founder of Generative-Transformational Linguistics. Based on Rationalist philosophy, his views on language acquisition include the assumption of a 'language acquisition device' (LAD) in the human brain. Concerning the phylogenetic development of language, Chomsky favours the view of the sudden emergence of language (for a critique of this, see Alexander 1973 and Sampson 2005). As a political activist Chomsky criticized US involvement in Asia, Africa and other parts of the world. In his book *Manufacturing Consent* (written together with Edward S. Herman in 2002), he also criticized the role of the media in politics (see Chapter 17.1).

Condillac, Étienne Bonnot (Abbé de Condillac, 1715–1780)

French philosopher, who took up some of Locke's suggestions concerning the critique of language (cf. Harris and Taylor 1997: 140). Condillac, particularly in his *Essai sur l'origine des connoissances humaines* (1746), criticizes Locke for not having enquired into the history and origins of language. For Condillac, language is never arbitrary (for how could people then understand each other?), but grounded in Nature. 'According to Condillac, languages were formed by groups of two children, one of either sex, lost in the desert after the deluge. These children, acting according to basic instincts, developed signs with which they could request and provide mutual help' (Juliard 1970: 31). The first signs were gestures, then words whose meaning developed from their first use via a series of analogies.

In his *logic* (1780), written just before his death, he expresses his ideas concerning the influence of language on our thoughts:

> Since languages, which take form in proportion as we analyse them, became so many analytical methods, it is understandable that we find it natural to think according to the habits that they caused us to acquire. We think with them. Rules of our judgment, they determine our knowledge, opinions, and prejudices. In short, they do in this domain everything good or bad. (Quoted from Harris and Taylor 1997: 153, translation by

Franklin Philip). (For more on Condillac see Harris and Taylor 1997: 139–154; Aarsleff 1982; Juliard 1970.)

Croce, Benedetto (1866–1952)

Italian Idealist philosopher and philologist. 'The rejection of any *science* of language was a common trait of philosophical idealism. It was shared by two philosophers active at the beginning of the twentieth century, Karl Vossler in Germany and Benedetto Croce in Italy. [...] This anti-scientific trend also brought about a final showdown with the Neogrammarian method' (Formigari 2004: 150).

Darwin, Charles (1809–1882)

In *The Origin of Species*, first published in 1859 (1996: 342), Darwin tries to apply his view of classification of species to languages, as follows:

> If we possessed a perfect pedigree of mankind, a genealogical arrangement of the races of man would afford the best classification of the various languages now spoken throughout the world. [...] Yet it might be that some very ancient language had altered little, and had given rise to few new languages, whilst others (owing to the spreading and subsequent isolation and states of civilization of the several races, descended from a common race) had altered much, and had given rise to many new languages and dialects.

This passage shows Darwin's view on the origin of language diversity, which he attributes to 'the spreading and subsequent isolation and states of civilization of the several races'.

In Chapter 3 of *The Descent of Man*, published in 1871, Darwin has a section about language, in which he argues against Max Müller that there is no insurmountable barrier between animals and humans because of language. He gives a number of examples of animal communication and argues that animals possess 'raw' and 'preliminary' forms of language. Darwin quotes Leslie Stephen who wrote that a dog forms a general concept of 'cat' or 'sheep' and knows the words for them just like a philosopher.

Davidson, Donald (1917–2003)

American philosopher, concerned primarily with truth conditions (see Lycan 2008: 109–133). Some of his ideas on metaphor (he denies the existence of metaphorical meaning) and first person authority, however, are interesting to think over. His most original contribution to the philosophy of language is his article 'A Nice Derangement of Epitaphs' (2006/1986), in which he solves the problem that no two people have the same language in the following way:

> I conclude that there is no such thing as a language, not if a language is anything like what many philosophers and linguists have supposed. There is therefore no such

> thing to be learned, mastered, or born with. We must give up the idea of a clearly defined shared structure which language-users acquire and then apply to cases. And we should try again to say how convention in any important sense is involved in language; or, as I think, we should give up the attempt to illuminate how we communicate by appeal to conventions. (2006: 265)

Davidson's denial of the existence of language is more than a witticism. It expresses the philosophical idea that 'language construes itself'. It is also in accordance with quantum physics in which the sharp distinction between things (material and immaterial) is called into question. (See Leiss 2009: 186–198 about Davidson's Nominalism and Skepticism.)

Descartes, René (1596–1650)

The Rationalist philosopher, whose ideas (concerning innateness) were taken up, among others, by Chomsky. Not content with natural languages, he conceived of the idea of creating an ideal language (see Heringer 1982: 6).

Foucault, Michel (1926–1984)

French philosopher and sociologist known for his critical studies of social institutions and his work on the history of human sexuality. Among his main interests was the relation between power, knowledge and discourse. Critical Discourse Analysts frequently refer to Foucault's understanding of Discourse as a force that creates truth for a society (see Chapter 18).

Gadamer, Hans Georg (1900–2002)

German philosopher of the Neo-Humboldtian school. 'Gadamer is the last true heir of Humboldt's philosophy, with which he shares (and takes to their ultimate consequence) certain crucial ideas: the belief that language cannot be transcended, that it exists prior to any other possible experience, and that the totality of a language and its associated world-view are contained in every word' (Formigari 2004: 150).

Habermas, Jürgen (*1929)

German philosopher and initiator of discourse ethics. The principles of discourse ethics are that no one is excluded or disadvantaged, only arguments are valid (not rhetorical tricks), and consensus should be reached without force. Discourse should be free from the exertion of power (*'herrschaftsfrei'*) and should follow a number of maxims (which are reminiscent of Grice's conversational maxims), e.g. arguments should be brought forth lucidly (cf. Grice's maxim of manner), and the speaker should believe in his/her own arguments (cf. Grice's maxim of quality). Habermas' distinction between communicative and strategic acting is the philosophical basis for the study of discourse strategies.

Hamann, Johann Georg (1730–1788)
German philosopher who called language 'die Gebährmutter der Begriffe' (*sic!*) [the womb of all concepts] (1967: 143). One of the earliest scholars in whose thinking the idea of a *reciprocal relationship* between language and culture is recognizable (cf. 1967: 90 f.). His comparison of a writer using his native language with a husband and a writer using a foreign language with a lover has become famous:

> Ich will mit ein paar Beispielen schließen, wo die Sprache in Meinungen und Meinungen in die Sprache einen Einfluss zu haben scheinen. Wer in einer fremden Sprache schreibt, der muss seine Denkungsart, wie ein Liebhaber, zu bequemen wissen – Wer in seiner Muttersprache schreibt, hat das Hausrecht eines Ehemanns, falls er dessen mächtig ist. (Hamann 1967: 94)

> *I would like to close with a few examples, where language seems to influence opinions and opinions influence language. Whoever writes in a foreign language must adapt his way of thinking like a lover – whoever writes in his native language has the domestic right of a husband, if he is potent to exercise it.*

Hamann was also one of the first writers in Germany to deal with the influence of language on thought. (For more about Hamann, see Miller 1968: 14–19.)

Heidegger, Martin (1889–1976)
German philosopher, together with Husserl one of the founders of Phenomenology. 'By defining language as "the house of being" […], Heidegger posits it as the unconditioned condition for any experience of the world' (Formigari 2004: 150). His philosophy of language is not always clear (see Kainz' critique of Heidegger discussed in Chapter 6.3).

Heraklitos (*ca. 540 BC)
Speaks of a 'logos' which governs everything in the world. It is unclear whether by *logos* he meant language, or rather 'principle', 'formula' or 'general law' (Störig 1987: 136). For Kirk *et al.* (cf. 1994: 204 ff.), Heraklitos' 'logos' is a formula shared by all things. Heraklitos' logos formula is reminiscent of the beginning of St John's Gospel (New Testament): 'In the beginning, there was the word'. Faust's struggle in translating this into German (*das Wort – der Sinn – die Kraft – die Tat*) is an often quoted passage from Goethe's play.

Herder, Johann Gottfried (1744–1803)
German philosopher, whose treatise *Abhandlung über den Usprung der Sprache* (1770) was his answer to the (Berlin) Academy's question 'En supposant les hommes abandonnés à leurs facultés naturelles, sont-ils en état d'inventer le langage? Et par quel moyens parviendront-ils à cette invention?' [*Would humans deprived of their natural faculties be able to invent language? By what means would they arrive*

at this invention?] In the first sentence of his treatise, ('Schon als Tier hat der Mensch Sprache' [*As animals humans already have language*] Herder turns against the idea expressed e.g. by Süßmilch that language was given by God, not invented by man.

Herder's main idea throughout his treatise is that language mirrors the culture and way of thinking ('*Denkungsart*') of a nation (not vice versa). As long as a people does not develop a certain idea, it will not create a word for it (cf. 2001: 70). Language follows the needs of the user: thus each language develops counting systems depending on its culture. The herdsman needs to count his flock, the Phoenicians, as traders, needed a more elaborate counting system than the herdsman (compare this with what Boas says about the development of numbers in different languages, see Chapter 5.3). However, in a few places Herder turns this reasoning round and concedes an influence of language on culture. (For more on Herder, see Werlen 1989: 30–42.)

Humboldt, Wilhelm von (1767–1835)
German philosopher, brother of the explorer and scientist Alexander von Humboldt. Humboldt's most often quoted pronouncement about language is that language is *energeia*, not *ergon* – an energy, not a fact. His study of the Basque language and of Amerindian languages led him to believe in the influence of language on culture and world-view. His ideas are often compared with those of Sapir and Whorf, and indeed there may have been an influence mediated by other thinkers (for more on Humboldt, see Werlen 1989: 43–90 and Trabant 1990; see also Chapter 4 this volume).

Hume, David (1711–1776)
Scottish philosopher, Empiricist. Like Locke and Berkeley, Hume complains that many philosophical controversies are merely about words (1902: 312). Using as examples the words *virtues* vs. *talents* and *vices* vs. *defects*, Hume observes that the boundaries between the meanings are not fixed and that a precise definition cannot be given (1902: 313). All in all, 'it is of greater consequence to attend to things than to verbal appellations' (1902: 322; 268) – a piece of advice which is less radical than Berkeley's 'drawing the curtain of words', but which nevertheless presupposes the possibility of thinking and reasoning without the use of language.

Jaspers, Karl (1883–1969)
German philosopher, who established a Philosophy of Communication. For him, existence can only be realized in communication; in accordance with this, he distinguishes three forms of communication which are linked to the forms of being:

- Communication connected with the struggle for existence: ambiguity, lying, and deception are part of this communication;

- Communication establishing truth or untruth, e.g. in a rational discussion;
- Communication in idea-determined spirituality of content (the content is determined by the idea of a whole: a state, a society, a family, a university, a profession, etc.).

Jaspers' Philosophy of Communication is discussed in some detail by Salamun (1985: 72–88).

Kainz, Friedrich (1897–1977)

Austrian psychologist and philosopher of language. Wrote a four volume psychology of language (1941–1956). His book *Über die Sprachverführung des Denkens* (1972) is the best summary of all the criticism of language that philosophers and other thinkers have expressed (see Chapter 6.3).

Kant, Immanuel (1724–1804)

German Idealist philosopher. His view that our reason does not discover the laws of Nature but prescribes them to Nature gave him the reputation of a destroyer and crasher of traditional views concerning reality and truth. Unfortunately, language is hardly taken into account by Kant, an omission which was already criticized by Hamann and Herder. However, Kant (with his thesis that reason – pure and practical – creates the world for us) is today seen as one of the forerunners of Constructivism (see Glasersfeld 1994: 17–19). (More about Kant and language in Mauthner 1921/ I: 331–345).

Korzybski, Alfred (1879–1950)

Polish count who in 1915 went to the USA to teach at various universities (e.g. Harvard). His work *Science and Sanity* (1933) marks the beginning of 'General Semantics', a critique of language in which abstract terms, generalization and illogical speech are chastised. Korzybski's most famous idea is the comparison of language with a map: 'the map is not the territory' – language is not reality, only provides guidance for it (see Chapter 7 and Appendix III).

Kristeva, Julia (*1941)

Bulgarian born literary scholar and philosopher, who in 1965 went to Paris. Rejects the idea (propagated by some feminist linguists) that language is responsible for perpetuating the patriarchal (male-dominated) system. Her distinction between the semiotic and the symbolic has become famous and is discussed at length by Judith Butler. Influenced by Bakhtin, she developed the concept of 'intertextuality'.

Langer, Susanne K. (1895–1985)

American cultural philosopher. Influenced by Neo-Humboldtian philosophy (particularly Ernst Cassirer), Langer (1957: 63) makes a distinction between sign and symbol: 'the sign is something to act upon, or a means to command action; the symbol is an instrument of thought'. About the origin of language, she writes (1957: 128 f.): '"Never a nomadic horde in the wilderness, but must already have had its songs," says Wilhelm von Humboldt, "for man as a species is a singing creature." Song, the formalization of voice-play, probably preceded speech.' Apart from Humboldt, Langer also refers to Jespersen and his idea that speech and song may well have sprung from the same source. (See also Chapter 2 above for Langer's story about Helen Keller.)

Leibniz, Gotthold Ephrahim (1646–1716)
German philosopher, contemporary of Goethe. In his *New Essays Concerning Human Understanding*, he discusses Locke's *Essay Concerning Human Understanding*, but disagrees with Locke's pessimism. We are not at the mercy of language. Language is a mirror of reason and also allows us to reason with ourselves (cf. Juliard 1970: 18 and Heringer 1982: 6). Leibniz was one of the originators of an aesthetic critique of language (with the ideals of purity, wealth, beauty and clarity – for the German language!) (see Heringer 1982: 9). Leibniz suggested creating an international written language which would 'aid man in his quest for truth by establishing absolute precision in reason' (Juliard 1970: 19; see also Werlen 1989: 16–20 and Formigari 2004: 112–113).

Lichtenberg, Georg Christoph (1742–1799)
German philosopher and one of the earliest German critics of language (cf. Heintel 1972: 102). For Lichtenberg, all philosophy is correction of language use (*Sudelbücher* II, 297; see Heringer 1982: 8).

Locke, John (1632–1704)
English Empiricist philosopher who took a critical view of language. Book III of Locke's *Essay Concerning Human Understanding* (first published 1690) is entitled 'Of Words'. Locke writes about words as signs for Ideas, but is aware of the arbitrariness of words. Chapter 9 of Book III is called 'Of the Imperfection of Words', Chapter 10 'Of the Abuse of Words'. Among the imperfections, Locke claims that words 'seldom in two men have the same signification' (1947: 237). Thus the word *gold* expresses, for different people, different qualities of 'the substance of gold' (1947: 239). Among the abuses of words Locke mentions particularly 'the taking them for things' (1947: 243). (See Chapter 6.1.)

Malinowski, Bronislaw (1884–1942)
Polish born anthropologist, who later taught at the London School of Economics. As 'Supplement I' of *The Meaning of Meaning*, Ogden and Richards in 1923 (1969: 296–336) printed an essay by Malinowski, 'The Problem of Meaning in Primitive

Languages', in which Malinowski writes: 'Language, in its primitive function, [is] to be regarded as a *mode of action,* rather than as a *countersign of thought'* (1969: 296; original emphasis). Later on in the article, Malinowski introduces the now famous term 'phatic communion' for 'a type of speech in which ties of union are created by a mere exchange of words' (1969: 315). In phatic communion, language is not used primarily to convey ideas and give messages, but 'has an essentially pragmatic [*sic!*] character'. 'It is a mode of behaviour, an indispensable element of concerted human action' (1969: 316). Malinowski also stresses that 'though the examples discussed were taken from savage life, we could find among ourselves exact parallels to every type of linguistic use so far discussed' (1969: 315).

Marty, Anton (1847–1914)
Swiss born philosopher who later taught in Prague. A volume of Marty's posthumously published works contains a section 'Vom Nutzen und Schaden der Sprache für das Denken' [*Of the usefulness and harmfulness of language for thought*] (1950: 79–85), in which Marty summarizes his ideas about language, thought and reality. Language, for Marty, helps us to remember thoughts, but should not be our 'guiding star' in logics. We should try to have power over language, not be dominated by it (see Chapter 6.2).

Mauthner, Fritz (1849–1923)
Austrian philosopher of language (born in Bohemia). His three volumes *Beiträge zu einer Kritik der Sprache* (1901–1902) contain the most radical critique of language imaginable. Even more drastic in his approach than the British empiricists, Mauthner list all the shortcomings of language and all the disadvantages language has in store for our thinking (see Chapter 6.2).

Occam, William of (also Ockham, 1270–1347)
English Franciscan priest, who studied at Oxford and Paris. His name is often mentioned in the phrase 'Occam's Razor', a kind of economic principle of philosophy: Occam admonishes us not to multiply things (and terms, ideas) beyond necessity (*entia non sunt multiplicanda praeter necessitatem*).

Ogden, Charles Kay (1889–1957)
British linguist who created 'Basic English', a simplified version of the English language. Together with I. A. Richards, he wrote *The Meaning of Meaning* (1923). (See Richards, I. A.)

Parmenides (*ca. 510 BC)
Pre-Socratic philosopher. In his philosophical poem 'peri physeos' (*On Nature*), Parmenides argues against Heraklitos' 'panta rhei' [*everything flows*] and denies

the existence of 'non-being'. Only 'being' exists, only what 'is' is. The philosophers who think that 'not being', 'becoming' and 'changing' are real are misled by language, which makes speaking of these possible. Using this argument, Parmenides can be said to be one of the first 'critics of language'.

Piaget, Jean (1896–1980)
Swiss child psychologist. One of the representatives of Constructivism. His debate with Chomsky about how much of language is innate (the 'nature nurture controversy') in the Abbey of Royaumont near Paris in October 1975 has become a legendary event in the history of psycholinguistics.

Plato (c. 427–348 BC)
Idealist philosopher, whose ideas are expressed chiefly in his *dialogues*, in which Socrates is the protagonist. In his *Kratylos*, the main topic is the origin of language, which in Kratylos' view is a natural one, in Hermogenes' however one of convention and agreement among humans. The topic of the effect of language on the world is addressed a few times. The word is called 'a tool', which names and distinguishes things for us just as the boxes of a weaver separate the different kinds of cloth.

Another of Plato's dialogues, in which language plays an important role, is the *Gorgias*. If the *Kratylos* is about language as a human faculty and as a system (*langage* and *langue* in Saussurean terms), the *Gorgias* is about *parole*, about 'discourse' and rhetoric. In this dialogue, Gorgias, a well-known rhetorician, agrees with Socrates that language in speeches is used to influence (persuade, convince) people. Upon Socrates' inquiry about the good of rhetoric, Gorgias answers (552d–e):

> What is there greater [...] than the word which persuades the judges in the courts, or the senators in the council, or the citizens in the assembly, or at any other political meeting? If you have the power of uttering this word, you will have the physician your slave, and the trainer your slave, and the money-maker of whom you talk will be found to gather treasures, not for himself, but for you who are able to speak and to persuade the multitude.

The 'power of words' could not be better expressed than in this passage from Plato's *Gorgias*. In a later part of the dialogue, however, Plato criticizes the Sophists who developed their rhetoric to such heights (and worked with the niceties of speech and the tricks of argumentation) that language (discourse!) became a device for manipulation and amusement (rather than a means to convince) (cf. Störig 1987: 145).

Apart from the *Kratylos* and the *Gorgias*, Plato wrote three Sophists' dialogues, among them the *Euthydemos*, in which two Sophists get even Socrates into a quandary by using their eristic tricks and linguistic strategies (see Chapters 3.2 and

17). For instance, a sophist proves that Socrates can give away or sell the goddess Athene ('she is *your* goddess'), that Kteisippos beats his father ('your dog has puppies, is thus a father, your father, and you sometimes beat him, so you beat your father' 298 e; 6.52), etc. Socrates' ironic conclusion is the advice to keep away from philosophy and trust one's own judgement of things only.

Port Royal Grammar

'The *Grammaire de Port-Royal* adopted a completely rational approach to the formation of language; it attempted to demonstrate that language could be explained rather than merely observed' (Juliard 1970: 14). The Grammar of Port Royal (1660) was written by Antoine Arnauld and Claude Lancelot and named after the monastery of *Port-Royal des Champs* in France. It is one of the first attempts to treat language not as God-given, but as an invention of humans. Grammar is universal because it mirrors universal mental processes. The influence of this view of grammar on Chomsky is evident.

Putnam, Hilary (*1926)

American philosopher, who believes in a universal linguistic division of labour. Not everyone in a linguistic community knows every part of the language. Putnam also speaks of semantic stereotypes: speakers know the stereotypical meaning of words, but not specialist meanings.

Quine, Willard Van Orman (1908–2000)

American Analytical philosopher who called himself a behaviourist (as a linguist). Interested in language acquisition, which he thought proceeded through trial and error, he criticized the 'indeterminacy' of translation. Most important for linguists is his book *Word and Object* (1960). Quine is quoted to have said the profound but cryptical sentence 'to learn is to have pleasure' (quoted from J.-J. Hodge 1983: 123). (More about Quine in Eden 1999: 258–275 and Sukale 1988: 122–138.)

Richards, Ivor Armstrong (1893–1979)

English literary scholar and philosopher. Together with C. K. Ogden, Richards wrote *The Meaning of Meaning*, an early (1923) treatise on Semantics. This book became famous for its representation of the linguistic sign in the form of a triangle (with the symbol at the left-hand corner, the thought at the top, and the referent on the right). The line between symbol and referent is dotted, because it stands only for an imputed relation (Ogden andRichards 1969: 11). By showing the 'indirectness of the relation between words and things' (1969: 10), Ogden and Richards turn against what later came to be called 'word realism' (e.g. by Kainz), a naïve view of language which according to Richards is at the core of much misunderstanding and conflict. *The Meaning of Meaning* also contains an interesting critique of Saussure (1969: 4–6), whose concept of *langue* (as opposed to *parole*) the authors call 'an elaborate construction' which is 'fantastic' as a 'guiding principle for a young science' (1969: 5). A discussion of 16 meanings of *meaning* (1969: 186–208) reveals the ambiguity of a term which both linguists and philosophers have used without questioning 'the reference'.

Ogden and Richards were among the forerunners of a pragmatic view of language. They talk about different uses of language (symbolic vs. evocative, 1969: 39) and criticize the linguists of their time because they do not deal with 'the ways in which speech, besides conveying ideas, also expresses attitudes, desires and intentions' (1969: 7). In their chapter 'the Power of Words' (1969: 24–47), they criticize all schools of thought which believe in 'verbal superstitions'. Ogden and Richards find such superstitions in all ages, but particularly in the twentieth century – some of them coming from Religion. The following is one of their examples:

> 'He telleth the number of the stars and calleth them all by their names.' Here we may note the delightful proverb which might appear on the title page of every work dealing with Symbolism: 'The Divine is rightly so called.' (1969: 28)

Rosch, Eleanor (*1938)

American psycholinguist. One of the initiators of 'Cognitive Linguistics'. Founded Prototype Semantics, in which categories are thought to have a 'best example' (prototype), against which all other members of the category are measured.

Rousseau, Jean-Jacques (1712–1778)

Swiss writer and philosopher, who also wrote about language. In his *Essai sur l'origine des langues*, necessity is at first rejected as the reason for the development of languages. Later he accepts that languages are formed 'sur les besoins des hommes' (*according to the needs of humans*). 'Rousseau provided three different answers to the question of the reasons for the existence of language: expression of the passions, discovery of the pleasures of companionship and the needs of man' (Juliard 1970: 24 f.).

Russell, Bertrand (1872–1970)

English philosopher, mathematician and educational reformer. In his treatise *The Principles of Mathematics*, Russell states that studying grammar – he does not say of which language – may throw light on philosophical questions (questions of logic and truth). This study, however, has to be a 'critical' one since distinctions of language may not correspond one to one with philosophical distinctions.

> Russell agreed [with Wittgenstein] that statements of ordinary language should be translated into another form. But for him the reason for such translation was not just that ordinary language, while it functions perfectly in ordinary life, misleads

philosophers, but also, and more important, that ordinary language really gives an incorrect portrayal of facts. And only by translating the statements of ordinary language into a form which *does* reflect facts accurately can philosophical progress be made. (Shapere 1967: 271)

In his book *My Philosophical Development* (1959), Russell has a chapter (13) entitled 'Language', in which he writes that the main task of words is to establish contact with general extralinguistic facts. It was mainly due to Russell that Wittgenstein's first book, *Tractatus Logico-philosophicus*, was published.

Sapir, Edward (1884–1939)
American anthropologist and linguist. Teacher of Benjamin Lee Whorf. The view that our native language determines our way of thinking is commonly called the Sapir-Whorf hypothesis. (See Chapter 5.3.)

Saussure, Ferdinand de (1857–1913)
Swiss linguist, considered by many to be the founder of Structuralism and of modern linguistics in general. Studied at Leipzig, Berlin and Paris. Taught in his native Geneva. His *Cours de linguistique générale*, published after his death (1913) in 1916, had a profound influence on linguistics and other disciplines.

Schopenhauer, Arthur (1788–1860)
German philosopher, who collected 38 linguistic strategies (devices / *Kunstgriffe*), with which it is possible to be 'in the right' *per fas et nefas* [whether you are right or wrong]. They were published in 1864, after his death, under the title *Eristische Dialektik: die Kunst, Recht zu behalten.* (Examples: using homonyms, argumentum ad hominem, speaking irrelevantly, relying on authorities instead of giving reasons etc.) (See Chapter 17.5.)

Searle, John (*1931)
American linguist and philosopher who introduced the term 'speech-act' for something one does with language. His classes of speech-acts – and thus things we do with language – are listed in the chapter on Pragmatics (13; cf. Mey 2001: 119–124).

According to Searle, we can do more than one 'thing' with an utterance. For this phenomenon, he introduced the notion of 'indirect speech-act' (1975). Speech acts can be used 'one on top of the other', and utterances can have more than one effect (on the same hearer or on different ones).

Socrates (ca. 469–399 BC)
Perhaps the best-known Greek philosopher; also important for linguistics, although his views about language and discourse are known to us only through Plato's dialogues (particularly the *Kratylos* and the *Gorgias*). The 'Socratic dialogue' is a method of

finding the truth by initiating a dialogue about a certain topic. This method, in which language (in its dialogic form) is used to make the participants in the dialogue come closer and closer to the truth, is also called 'meieutic' (thus compared to the midwife's art of bringing the baby to the light of the earth). (See also s.v. *Plato.*)

The Sophists (Greece, sixth and fifth century BC)
As practical philosophers, the Sophists believed in the power of words and taught rhetoric, taking money in exchange for this (Socrates jokes about this!). They were notorious for their word tricks and linguistic strategies. The best-known representatives of this 'school' are Protagoras (also famous for his phrase 'homo mensura' – man is measure of all things) and Gorgias, who provided the name for one of Plato's dialogues. In this dialogue, Plato makes Gorgias profess that rhetorics is the highest of all arts. Gorgias however has to admit that many rhetoricians exercise their art not for the sake of making people wiser. The power of a rhetorically trained speaker over others is shown (see under *Plato* above and Störig 1987: 144–148). Related school: Eristics – the use of language in conflict and debate.

Strawson, Peter (1919–2006)
One of the Oxford Ordinary Language Philosophers, or 'Analytical Philosophers' (as opposed to the 'Continental Philosophers'). In his essay 'On Referring' (1950) he criticized Bertrand Russell, arguing that Russell had confused referring and asserting. According to Strawson, a sentence can be meaningful or meaningless without being true or false. Influenced by Kant, Strawson later turned to 'descriptive metaphysics', with which he tried to introduce metaphysics into analytical Philosophy.

Vico, Giambattista (1668–1744)
Italian philosopher. '(Aristotle's) idea of the heuristic value of metaphor was taken up by Cicero, Quintilian, and 16th century commentators of the *Poetics*, such as Ludovico Castelvetro. Through them it passed on to Giambattista Vico, who called metaphor "a little definition" and posited it as a central mechanism for the linguistic understanding of the world' (Formigari 2004: 23 f.).

Goethe mentions Vico in the diary of his first journey to Italy (Naples, 5 March 1786), where he writes about Vico's *Principii di una scienza nuova* (1725): 'Bei einem flüchtigen Überblick des Buches, das [Freunde] mir als ein Heiligtum mitteilten, wollte mir scheinen, hier seien sibyllinische Vorahnungen des Guten und Rechten, das einst kommen soll oder sollte, gegründet auf ernste Betrachtungen des Überlieferten und des Lebens. Es ist gar schön, wenn ein Volk solch einen Ältervater besitzt; den Deutschen wird einst Hamann ein ähnlicher Codex werden.' [*After a cursory survey of the book, which friends presented to me as a sacrum, it seemed to me that here were sibyllinian presentiments of future good and right based on serious considerations of tradition and life. It is great for a people to have such an avatar; for us Germans, Hamann will some time be a similar authority.*] (Quoted from Mauthner, 1921: II, 479.) Some modern constructivists see in Vico one of their forefathers. (More on this view of Vico in Trabant 1990: 140–168 and König 2005.)

Vossler, Karl (1872–1949)
German philosopher in the tradition of Humboldt. The title of Vossler's most important book, *Geist und Kultur in der Sprache* (1960, written in 1925), shows Vossler's belief that a language expresses the spirit and culture of a people, though Vossler, at the very beginning of his book, calls the existence of 'language' itself into question:

> Die erste und offensichtliche Voraussetzung der Sprachwissenschaft will, daß es eine Sprache gibt. Und gerade das ist unsicher. So wenig wie aus dem Vorhandensein von Theologie folgt, dass es einen Gott gibt, [...] so wenig geht aus der gesamten Sprachwissenschaft die Gewähr hervor, dass es Sprache gibt. (Vossler 1960: 14)
>
> *The first and most obvious precondition for linguistics is that language exists. But this very existence is uncertain. In the same way as we can hardly conclude from the existence of theology that God exists, linguistics in its entirety does not guarantee that language exists.*

What certainly exists is speaking, e.g. in conversation, in which speaking, hearing, understanding and responding are involved. Vossler criticizes Saussure, Meillet, Bally and Sechehaye for only seeing the 'empirical reality of language within society' (1960: 146). All linguistic utterances are related to poetry, which can be found in all kinds of texts, just as spirit is in all living beings (cf. 1960: 176). Vossler, a Romance scholar, is one of the few thinkers who consider the interrelation between different languages.

Vygotsky, Lev Semyonovich (1896–1934)
Russian thinker and educationalist, renowned for his ideas on language and thought. In his book *Thought and Language* (originally in Russian, 1938, English edition 1962), Vygotsky first discusses Piaget's theory of child language acquisition and thought and reports on experiments about concept formation in children. Vygotsky's view concerning the relation between language and thought is that they have different roots (1962: 44). 'Initially thought is nonverbal and speech nonintellectual' (1962: 49). Proof of this comes from animals and from very young children. Later, however, 'thought development is determined by language, i.e. by the linguistic tools of thought and by the socio-cultural experience of the child' (1962: 51).

Vygotsky makes a distinction between thought and 'inner speech' (an autonomous speech function), so that in reality there are three phenomena: thought, inner speech and speech (1962: 130 ff.). For Vygotsky, thought is not divided into separate units. When thought is to be expressed in language, it has to be spread out temporally and made available in chunks. Most famous is Vygotsky's comparison of thought and speech with cloud and rain: 'In [a speaker's] mind the whole thought is present at once, but in speech it has to be developed successively. A thought may be compared to a cloud shedding a shower of words' (1962: 150).

Whorf, Benjamin Lee (1897–1941)
American chemical engineer and anthropologist, who studied under Edward Sapir. As a result of his work for an insurance company, where he had to assess the causes of fires (and from his interest in Amerindian languages, particularly Hopi), he came to see the importance of language in determining our view of the world. Linguistic Relativism and Linguistic Determinism are linked with his and Edward Sapir's name. (More about Whorf in Chapters 5.4 and 5.5.)

Wittgenstein, Ludwig (1889–1951)
Vienna born philosopher, who went to England and became Professor of Philosophy in Cambridge. The early Wittgenstein (of the *Tractatus Logico-philosophicus*, 1922) still saw in language only a medium for representing the world. In Wittgenstein's later book, the *Philosophical Investigations* (1953), meaning is defined as 'use' and language is called 'a toolbox'. His 19 'language games' are activities we perform with language. He is regarded as one of the thinkers who laid the ground for Pragmatics (see the Introduction and Chapter 3).

Appendix III

Language World Impact: Further Examples

Chapter 4: language as *energeia*

1. An example from Cassirer's *Philosophie der symbolischen Formen* (1923: 251 f.):

> 'Wenn der Mond im Griechischen als der "Messende" (μήν), im Lateinischen als der [die] "Leuchtende" (luna, luc-na) bezeichnet wird, so ist hier ein und dieselbe sinnliche Anschauung unter ganz verschiedene Bedeutungsbegriffe gerückt und durch sie bestimmt.'

> *In Greek, the moon is referred to as 'the measuring one' (μήν), in Latin as 'the luminous one' (luna < luc-na): one and the same phenomenon is placed in totally different semantic conceptual areas and is determined by them.*

2. Weisgerber gives the following example of the 'linguistic interworld' (*sprachliche Zwischenwelt*):

> 'Orion' is in reality approximately 20 stars which seen from Earth form a configuration resembling an archer. By naming this *orion*, language creates this constellation for us as a single entity. In reality the stars are light years apart (one is even a separate solar system). Language makes them exist as a constellation, at least in an interworld. Similarly with *weeds* and *fruit,* which do not exist as beings, but are the 'creations' of language. (Source: Werlen 1989: 112 f.)

Chapter 7: General Semantics

An Anecdote about Korzybski

During a lecture, Korzybski got out some biscuits and began to eat them. He asked the students in the front row whether they would also like some. A few students took a biscuit. Suddenly, Korzybski tore the white paper from the biscuits and revealed the original packaging. On it was a dog's head and the words 'DOG COOKIES'. The students were shocked, two of them wanted to throw up. 'You see, ladies and gentlemen', Korzybski remarked, 'I have just demonstrated that people don't just eat food, but also words, and that the taste of the former is often outdone by the taste of the latter.' With this he wanted to show that some human suffering originates from the confusion or conflation of linguistic representations of reality and reality itself. (Source: L. Derks & J. Hollander, *Essenties van NLP*, Utrecht: Servire 1996:58, quoted from Wikipedia, s.v. Alfred Korzybski)

Chapter 17: Discourse Strategies

Naming strategies: presenting issues in the media

Norman Fairclough (2000: vii) gives the following example of **media spin**:

> Media spin – constantly monitoring and manipulating how issues are presented in the media. This is largely a matter of making sure the right language is used – for instance, making sure that the approved expression 'public-private partnership' is used rather than the dreaded 'Tory' term 'privatisation'; and avoiding the even more dreaded 's'-word 'socialism'.

Naming in EU politics

At the Brussels summit of EU ministers (Council of the European Union) in June 2007, the question of an EU constitution was among the most important items on the agenda. Since such a constitution had been voted against in two referenda (France, The Netherlands) and since many other countries were against a constitution, the following 'elegant' solution was found: instead of *constitution* the term ***Reform Treaty*** was used, and, suddenly, the summit became active again and reached an agreement. (The Reform Treaty was signed on 13 December 2007, and came into force on 1 December 2009.)

Naming may influence the history of science

When Rudolf Virchow, in the nineteeth century, discovered a certain type of cells in the brain, he named them '**Gliacells**' (*glia* = Greek 'glue'), because he thought their main function was to provide the 'glue' for holding together the brain cells. This name prevented researchers from attaching higher importance to these cells, until after an investigation of Einstein's brain their significance for storing information and for creativity was discovered. (Source: *Bild der Wissenschaft*, Sept. 2008.)

Giving something a name makes it real

Burn-out syndrome, sexual harassment and other situations and processes became real by having a name (cf. Spender 1985: 184 f. about 'sexual harassment'). What has a name can be cured, criticized, antagonized, made the object of accusation, discussed in TV shows, etc. It thus becomes part of what a society holds to be true.

Chapter 18.4 Misunderstanding and Mistranslation

Translation with serious or humorous consequences

Translation may introduce different connotations and thus change the effect of the message.

Weisgerber (1961: 8 ff.) gives the following example of this:

> The document about the province of Bolzano (in the armistice treaty after the 2nd World War) was written in English, German and Italian. The English version contained the following passage:
>
> > German-speaking inhabitants of the Bolzano Province [...] will be assured complete equality of rights with the Italian-speaking inhabitants, *within the framework of special provisions* to safeguard the ethnical character and the cultural and economic development of the German-speaking element.

'Within the framework of special provisions' was translated into German as 'im Rahmen besonderer Maßnahmen' and into Italian as 'nel quadro delle disposizioni speciali'. Differences in denotative and connotative meaning between *framework, Rahmen* and *quadro* led to an understanding in German and Italian that the safety of the German language and culture was by no means assured, but still had to be fought for. Protests and even terrorist acts were the consequence.

Mistranslations may have serious consequences in politics, but they may also give rise to laughter and thus create a relaxed atmosphere. Charles Berlitz, in his book *Native Tongues* (1982) has a chapter (22) entitled 'undiplomatic translations'. In this chapter, the following examples of mistranslation creating humorous effects can be found:

1. A French speaking African delegate said at a committee meeting 'l'Afrique n'érige plus des autels aux dieux' (*Africa does not erect any altars to the gods any more*). This was misunderstood by the interpreter as 'L'Afrique n'érige plus des hotels odieux' and thus translated as 'Africa does not erect any odious hotels any more' (Berlitz 1982: 178).

2. Before achieving independence, Tanganjika introduced an 'Organic Act'. The interpreter translated this into Russian as 'organitscheski Akt', an expression which in modern Russian also has the meaning of sexual intercourse. When the details of this act were being discussed, the Russian delegates and finally all delegates with Slavonic languages broke into storms of laughter (Berlitz 1982: 179 f.).

3. A UN representative from India criticized the slowness of decolonialization. He said: 'The colonial powers remain unchanged, still holding in their hands their long-standing fallacies.' Unfortunately he pronounced the word *fallacies* so that it sounded like 'phalluses', so that the English speaking delegations

broke into laughter which spread to the other delegations and 'changed a sleepy afternoon session of the plenum to a hilarious interlude enjoyed by all three worlds' (Berlitz 1982: 181).

Chapter 20.6 The Functions of Linguistic diversity

There is a close relation between linguistic diversity and biological diversity. A name may exterminate – or save – a whole species. Peter Mühlhäusler (1996: 107) found the following story which illustrates this (text from the *Advertiser,* Adelaide, 15 September 1995):

> Australian rat-like animals may soon be given new names to help save them from extinction. Their image problems stem from being called rats and mice when they actually are not related to the varieties which Europeans introduced with settlement more than 200 years ago. Scientists are worried that names like 'black-footed tree rat' have little or no appeal for the average Australian. They say this attitude has resulted in many of the animals being exterminated as pests.

In response, CSIRO [Commonwealth Scientific and Industrial Research Organization] wildlife and ecology division researchers have suggested replacement names drawn from a list of 2000 Aboriginal words. The names, to be displayed in a paper to be presented by the Australian Nature Conservation Agency, include *rakali* for the water rat and *dkintamoonga* for the black-footed tree rat. [...]

'Who is going to join an effort to save animals with dreadful names like the plains rat, the false water rat or the greater stick-nest rat?' CSIRO researcher Mr Steven Morton asks in an article published in the *New Scientist.* 'These animals are unique but the public associates the words rat and mouse with vermin, filth and disease.'

The latest studies by the CSIRO show seven of 62 native species have already disappeared, and another 12 are considered endangered or vulnerable.

The use of Aboriginal names for endangered species (instead of derogative ones such as *water rat*) may contribute to keeping these species from extinction. More examples of how words may have an impact on our treatment of Nature are given in Mühlhäusler (2003: 51 f.).

To the reader: further examples of language impact at all levels are welcome. Please view www.alwinfill.at and send your examples and comments to the e-mail address given there.

Index

CPSIA information can be obtained at www.ICGtesting.com
Printed in the USA
BVOW051211040312

284320BV00002B/3/P

9 781845 537784